Every 90 Seconds

*Our Common Cause Ending Violence
Against Women*

ANNE P. DEPRINCE

OXFORD
UNIVERSITY PRESS

OXFORD
UNIVERSITY PRESS

Oxford University Press is a department of the University of Oxford. It furthers
the University's objective of excellence in research, scholarship, and education
by publishing worldwide. Oxford is a registered trade mark of Oxford University
Press in the UK and certain other countries.

Published in the United States of America by Oxford University Press
198 Madison Avenue, New York, NY 10016, United States of America.

Library of Congress Cataloging-in-Publication Data
Names: DePrince, Anne P., author.
Title: Every 90 seconds : our common cause ending violence against women /
Anne P. DePrince, Ph.D.
Other titles: Every ninety seconds
Description: New York, NY : Oxford University Press, [2022] |
Includes bibliographical references and index.
Identifiers: LCCN 2021046074 (print) | LCCN 2021046075 (ebook) |
ISBN 9780197545744 (hardback) | ISBN 9780197545768 (epub) |
ISBN 9780197545775
Subjects: LCSH: Women—Violence against. | MeToo movement. |
Intimate partner violence.
Classification: LCC HV6250.4.W65 D475 2022 (print) |
LCC HV6250.4.W65 (ebook) | DDC 362.88082—dc23
LC record available at https://lccn.loc.gov/2021046074
LC ebook record available at https://lccn.loc.gov/2021046075

DOI: 10.1093/oso/9780197545744.001.0001

1 3 5 7 9 8 6 4 2

Printed by LSC communications, United States of America

To Susan, with love and gratitude.

Contents

Acknowledgments

My heart is full of gratitude for the many people who made this book possible. First and foremost, I'm forever grateful to the girls and women who participated in the research described throughout this book. Simply put: This book exists because of their willingness to share their stories, experiences, and insights. Thank you, too, to the community partners whose generosity and wisdom made our research collaborations and, ultimately, this book, possible especially Margaret Abrams, Karmen Carter, Maro Casparian, Jennifer Eyl, Kazi Houston, Linda Loflin Pettit, Emily Tofte Nestaval, Steve Siegel, Scott Snow, and Reenie Terjak. They inspire me daily in their stalwart commitment to make our world a more just place.

The graduate students with whom I've had the honor to work over the years are everywhere in these pages—from the research described to the inspiration to make psychology matter for creating a new way forward. Traumatic Stress Studies Group alums have left their mark on our team and this book in particular, especially Drs. Ann T. Chu, Melody Combs, Rebecca Babcock Fenerci, Kerry L. Gagnon, Claire Hebenstreit, Michelle Lee, Ryan Matlow, Julie Olomi, Rheena Pineda, Aimee Reichmann-Decker, Tejaswinhi Srinivas, and Courtney Welton-Mitchell. I'm particularly grateful to current graduate student team members who have moved our work forward while providing invaluable feedback (and cheerleading) on early drafts of the book manuscript, including Maria-Ernestina Christl, Kim-Chi Pham, Adi Rosenthal, Rebecca Suzuki, and Naomi Wright. Thank you to Francesca Dino for her work as a research assistant early on in the development of this project.

I am deeply grateful to colleagues who gave detailed feedback on full versions of this manuscript, including Drs. Apryl Alexander, Joanne Belknap, Ann T. Chu, Heather McCauley, and an anonymous reviewer. Their observations and insights are woven into each chapter. I am also incredibly thankful to colleagues whose feedback on the proposal and chapter drafts was essential, including Maro Casparian, Katie Kleinhesselink, and Linda

Loflin Pettit as well as Drs. Kathryn Becker-Blease, Joan Cook, Cara DiEnno, Lynn Schofield Clark, and Courtney Welton-Mitchell.

I've been fortunate to work with many incredible collaborators, colleagues, and friends whose influence runs deep throughout my work and this book, especially Drs. Joanne Belknap, Kim Bender, Ann Chu, Joan Cook, Martin Dorahy, Julia Dmitrieva, Jennifer Freyd, Kim Gorgens, Jennifer Karas, Stephen Shirk, and Sarah Watamura. I'm also grateful to be part of a network of scholars working across disciplines around the world to understand trauma—particularly violence against women—and its consequences. While I've cited many of those scholars in this book, there wasn't space to discuss so much important and exciting research that will be essential to our collective efforts to end violence against women going forward.

I acknowledge and honor the Indigenous peoples of the land on which I have had the privilege to live and work. I recognize the long history and current reality of intimate violence perpetrated against Indigenous girls and women and hope this book can contribute to the work of healing and justice.

Research studies involving my team that are described in this book were made possible by funding from several sources, including the National Institute of Justice (2012-W9-BX-0049, NIJ-2009-MU-MU-0025, 2007-WG-BX-0002), Office for Victims of Crimes (2012-VF-GX-K018) (US Department of Justice), National Institute of Mental Health (1 R03 MH068624-01A1), MINDSOURCE Brain Injury Network and Office for Victim Programs (State of Colorado), Rocky Mountain Victim Law Center, Campus Compact of the Mountain West, and the University of Denver. The opinions, findings, and conclusions or recommendations expressed in this book are mine and do not necessarily reflect those of the Department of Justice or any other funding agency.

Thank you to my agent Deirdre Mullane for seeing the potential in the project, making the foundation as strong as possible, and guiding me through the process with grace and humor. Thank you to Sarah Harrington at Oxford University Press for the perfect combination of feedback, collaboration, and room to realize the vision I had for the book.

It's hard to put into words the impact of a handful of people (and dogs) who have brought me joy and inspiration in life generally and during this book's journey specifically. I'm forever grateful to Elizabeth, who encouraged me at every turn in this writing adventure; Margaret and Francine, who amaze me in a million ways; Jenny, my constant BFF; and the dogs who spent many very early mornings and long walks with me and this book.

Finally, thank you to my partner, Susan. Years ago, she told me that she heard a book idea in a lecture I gave. Her belief in that idea and in me has been everything.

Introduction

Our Common Cause

I arrived to a high-ceilinged hotel mezzanine as the lights of downtown Denver flickered through enormous glass windows in 2017. In terribly uncomfortable shoes, I made my way over to a group of women I had known over many years of collaborating with agencies in Colorado to do research on violence against women. Gathered for a fundraiser and dressed in far different clothes than we usually wore when we met across conference rooms, our conversations differed, too. Earlier that week, the movement that Tarana Burke started in 2006 had exploded onto social media as #MeToo in the wake of reporting about media mogul Harvey Weinstein.

"Would things be different this time?" wondered this group of women who had spent decades working with victims and survivors of intimate violence.[i]

After all, women have endured sexual and physical violence at the hands of romantic partners, invading armies, and powerful men over millennia. Across that history, women's stories of violence have occasionally bubbled up to capture public attention only to fade away.

Something *felt* different though. Then and now.

Awareness of violence against women in its many forms—sexual assault, domestic violence, intimate partner abuse, stalking, and sex trafficking—has never been greater. Since 2017, social media feeds have continued to share #MeToo posts and stories of sexual assault. News outlets tell us about the rise in murders of women by their lovers along with the toll that physical violence, stalking, and sex trafficking take on women around the globe. Award-winning films and television series, from prestige cable dramas to hard-hitting independent documentaries, bring the sights and sounds of relationship violence into our homes. Nonprofits across the country continue

---

[i] I use "victim" and "survivor" interchangeably throughout the book and recognize that people vary in the terms they prefer be used. I also recognize that while I refer to people using the terms "victim" and "survivor", intimate violence is but one part of women's stories.

the unending work of providing victim services and advocacy. The federal government invests billions in victim services.

Yet rates of violence against women persist in the United States (US) at jaw-dropping levels, measured in lost dignity and potential across moments and lives. Every ninety seconds, a woman is sexually assaulted. In that same minute and a half, a current or former intimate partner victimizes a woman. Every sixteen hours, one of those current or former intimate partners shoots and kills a woman. Nearly one out of every six women is stalked. One woman in sixteen is raped during her first sexual experience. One in five women is sexually assaulted while in college.[1]

For generations, violence against women has been wielded to control and marginalize Women of Color and their communities. The sexual assault of Black and Indigenous women by White men across US history has brutally reinforced racial hierarchies and white supremacy, tearing at the social fabric of families and communities. That history lives on today, reinforcing the supremacy of White, cisgender, able bodies. Indigenous women are murdered at a rate that is up to ten times the national average, while Black and Brown transgender women are murdered more often than their cisgender peers. Bisexual women and women with disabilities face higher rates of sexual assault than other women. Latina women are trafficked and abused at the US's southern border.[2]

The violence perpetrated against women has gone by many names. Sometimes the names have meaning in particular systems, such as the use of the term "domestic violence" in the legal system. What lawyers call "domestic violence" researchers might call "intimate partner violence"—both terms signal that the abuse happened in the context of a current or former romantic relationship. Still others might use the term "intimate partner abuse" to reflect that psychological coercion and control are common, in addition to physical violence. The phrase "sexual assault" gets applied to acts ranging from molestation to rape. Sometimes sexual assault is also part of domestic violence and intimate partner abuse, sometimes it is perpetrated by bosses and friends.

Regardless of the particular terms used, different forms of violence against women have in common that they are *intimate*. *Intimate* violations of women's physical, emotional, and spiritual worlds, whether perpetrated by a spouse or acquaintance, a boss or stranger.[ii]

[ii] Throughout the book, I frequently use of the terms "violence against women" and "intimate violence" to reflect that different forms of violence against women share much in common. I also use

In the aftermath of intimate violence, women face psychological and physical health consequences that can go on for years. Violence curtails their educations, careers, and lives. Survivors who look for services face waitlists and staggering barriers to getting their basic health and legal needs met. The impacts of violence wielded against Women of Color to enforce racial hierarchies stretch across generations.[3]

Policies miss their targets, failing to ensure even basic safety. After decades of attention to prosecuting domestic violence and sexual assault, women are still victimized in their homes, schools, and workplaces.[4] Active shooter drills instill fear in the hearts of schoolchildren, though bulletproofing doors will never prevent the misogyny that drives boys and men to perpetrate mass shootings. Arrests for domestic violence charges do not deter recidivism.[5]

The people who abuse women—who are mostly but not always men—rarely face consequences for their actions. When Congresswoman Alexandra Ocasio-Cortez took to the House floor in June 2020 and repeated violent language used against her surrounded by other women legislators who told stories of their own sexual harassment, news coverage dismissed her speech as media-savvy brand management. A Republican colleague bemoaned that Congresswoman Ocasio-Cortez and others had not forgiven Representative Yoho for calling her a "fucking bitch."[6] And then the news cycle moved on.

Even when people face consequences for violence against women, justice still seems out of reach. That's how it felt for many when 2018 headlines about Bill Cosby's conviction for sexual assault in the wake of accusations by more than fifty women gave way to 2021 reports that the Pennsylvania Supreme Court overturned his conviction on a legal technicality.[7]

Through all the news headlines and personal stories, in one way or another, we keep turning back to the promise that once enough people become *aware* that violence against women happens to our sisters, daughters, wives, friends—with potential for lifelong consequences—then violence will ebb. Public service announcements and social media memes tell us that real men don't abuse. Women are strong. Not one more. It's on us. It's not ok. There's no excuse.

terms such as "domestic violence," "intimate partner violence," "sexual assault," and "gender-based violence," particularly when describing systems or research that distinguishes between those forms of violence (e.g., the criminal legal system's treatment of domestic violence versus sexual assault; research on the impact of sexual assault specifically; or gender-based violence perpetrated against girls, women, and gender non-conforming groups).

Of course, we already know that violence against women happens. People of all genders understand that girls and women are at risk of violence in dating relationships and marriages, on the streets and in workplaces. The threat of violence against women is so clear, in fact, that people tend to blame women for *not avoiding* victimization.[8] People assume she should have known she was at risk and done something different to avoid getting raped, beaten, or harassed. She shouldn't have taken that job, gone on that run after dark, worn that outfit, or married that guy.

Focused on what any woman did or didn't do, we miss the bigger picture: that the causes and consequences of violence against women are interconnected with the great public issues of our time—healthcare and gun violence, education access and immigration policies, economic security and legal reforms. Violence against women ripples out to affect each of us, regardless of our own genders or life histories. This means we each share a common cause in ending violence against women and restoring the dignity, fairness, opportunity, and safety that violence takes from girls, women, and our communities. No matter what form that violence takes.

This book is about how we can work together across the things we're each passionate about to imagine into existence a future that none of us has known: one in which girls, women, and communities thrive free from intimate violence.

Building that world will require letting go of the idea that violence against women is an isolated issue or a problem for just those who are victimized, and the promise that awareness is enough. We'll also have to set aside some of the things we tell ourselves—that the problem is too big or is someone else's—to discover that we each have the potential to act in ways that connect to our intersecting self-interests and talents. In acting together in those spaces where problems overlap and can seem the most overwhelming, we actually have a chance to build a new approach to change: one in which we work together to ensure that ending and responding to violence against women also affects critical reforms to healthcare (Chapter 1), immigration (Chapter 4), and education (Chapter 3) systems. A future where restoring opportunity and dignity for girls and women also means stopping gun violence (Chapter 2), promoting economic justice (Chapter 5), and addressing inequities in legal systems (Chapter 6).

Where our passions and interests intersect, we have the potential to act together. But shared action will require first looking at our desire to do something against the backdrop of history to build a new way forward.

A Desire to Do Something

In the past few years alone, a sexual assault allegation shadowed Supreme Court Justice Brett Kavanaugh's confirmation, and Jeffrey Epstein died in a jail cell while held on charges related to sex trafficking of girls and women. Silence breakers revealed long-standing patterns of abuse by high-profile media figures, from Roger Ailes and Matt Lauer to R. Kelly and Harvey Weinstein. A jury convicted Weinstein on two counts of sexual assault as he faces an array of other lawsuits, while R. Kelly awaited a criminal trial, giving the public a window into how slow and complicated legal responses to violence can be.

Awareness of the indignity and unfairness of these high-profile cases along with too many #MeToo stories has culminated in a national desire to make sense of recent events and *do something*.

I recall when my awareness of violence against women changed and I felt that urge to *do something* as a college student in the 1990s. I noticed threads that connected across my classes. In a nineteenth-century literature class, Emily Brontë's protagonists faced abuse and violence that seemed to share much in common with contemporary women's accounts of violence in my women's studies class. A class on the history of science showed me that places like the Salpêtrière Hospital in Paris, which played a central role in the founding of the modern fields of psychiatry and psychology, were little more than warehouses for abused and sexualized women who were written off as hysterical (Chapter 1). A German history course had me reading Freud's accounts of psychoanalysis and sexual abuse as a new field of trauma psychology was taking shape.

My academic learning about violence against women through majors in psychology and history collided with powerful lessons outside the classroom. Late-night dorm conversations over Ben and Jerry's ice cream turned to rumors about which groups on campus closed ranks around men accused of rape. Friends shared advice and tried to keep each other safe. Don't exercise on this path after dark. Don't drink with him or go to parties in that frat. Here's how to get emergency contraception. This counselor at the health center gets it, so ask for her if you need to talk to someone.

Awareness and conversation eventually paved the way to action. I went to my first Take Back the Night march in North Carolina around the time that the state became one of the last to end a so-called marital rape exemption to existing statutes. The exception was a vestige of long-standing beliefs that women were the property of husbands and the view that consent given once was consent given always. With classmates and campus staff, I bore witness to ribbons hung on the main campus quad by survivors and their loved ones, each color representing a different kind of intimate victimization. We wrote letters advocating for sexual assault support services on campus and coordinated with student activists from across the country.

Translating my evolving academic awareness of violence against women into action felt powerful. Each conversation or letter felt like breaking millennia of silence, shattering taboos; as if we were on the cusp of a cure for epidemic-levels of violence against women. We were sure that if the world *knew* just how common intimate violence was, people would take action to stop it. We just had to let the world know.

Around that same time, the public heard about violence against women as Congress began hearings on the Violence Against Women Act (VAWA). That sweeping legislation passed in 1994, the same year that I made my way to Washington DC, where I had a window seat view of some of the seismic shifts taking place. I worked for a nonprofit doing public education about child abuse. For part of my day, my job was to hunt down new research on violence to build education campaigns. As trauma science exploded, new discoveries seemed to pile up each month about the frequency of violence and abuse suffered by girls and women in the US, and their far-reaching health consequences.

As much as this fast-growing body of research documented girls' and women's experiences of violence and abuse, other voices emerged to argue that violence was overestimated; that girls and women made things up or misremembered. Cultural critics gained prominence for their comforting folk psychology: *Feminists say rape happens to one in four college students. I don't know one in four friends who were raped; so their numbers are wrong.*[9] The call to doubt women was reinforced by a small but earnest group of advocates and researchers who said that women's memories of abuse were often false.[10]

In that mix of optimism and backlash, I would walk across the city to work each day. When I arrived, one of my jobs was to answer calls on a resource line. These were early Internet days, when search engines didn't get you very far. Finding information about and resources for violence was a technological challenge as much as an emotional one. Calls rolled in steadily each day, primarily from women who needed referrals to counseling, shelters, or lawyers—and sometimes all three. They were worried about the impact of witnessing domestic violence on their kids' mental health and school perfor-mance. They were thinking about leaving, but didn't know where the nearest shelter was. They needed lawyers because the court had ignored evidence of abuse in finalizing child custody arrangements.

One afternoon, my youthful enthusiasm ran dry. I was tired of answering the phone. I didn't want to tell one more woman that I didn't know of any lawyers in her state or shelters near her; that I understood why she feared that disclosing domestic violence during divorce proceedings would get used against her; that I was sorry that she feared for her child and her life. Had she considered calling the police if the situation was life-threatening? *Oh, he works for the police?* Scratch that, then.

Instead of heading home after work, I wandered down to the Mall, a place I loved for its changing character of light and sound. Sometimes bright and riveting during daylight marches. Other times somber and reflective as people made pilgrimages to war memorials.

That evening, I made my way to the Lincoln Monument and turned to-ward the Vietnam Veterans Memorial Wall. The Mall was quiet, almost rev-erent, with only a handful of late-day tourists. I descended down along the Wall, my only company the etched names of those who died in war. I was eager for the feeling that comes at the moment of transition from the shadow of the Wall up into the light and then to continue a bit further to the Vietnam Women's Memorial, which beckons from beneath a canopy of trees. There bronze nurses memorialized the many faces of women's strength, anguish, and vulnerability in my favorite monument. Even today, I take that same walk whenever I get the chance to visit the nation's capital.

That evening, however, the Wall and the nurses offered no solace. Instead, I just felt angry. Angry that the women I talked to each day didn't have a monument. The most they got were one-off awareness-raising events— a Clotheslines Project display on college campuses, a Take Back the Night march, their empty shoes left on the steps of a state capital to show how many of them died last year. Somewhere under my anger, I understood those were important events. Important for awareness and the promise of change. I was coming to learn, though, that awareness could get packed up and put away. Shoes and painted t-shirts could get boxed to make way for the next vigil for some other cause.[11]

I took that memory with me when I left DC and the east coast for Oregon, where I spent five years in graduate school training to become a clinical psychologist. From a lab room on the third floor of an old dorm that was the then-home of the psychology department at the University of Oregon, I started my career of measuring—in milliseconds and memories—the impact of gender-based violence. Across a year of clinical work at the University of Washington Medical Center, I saw violence against women show up in every rotation, whether I was working on inpatient or rehabilitation units.

Having finished my graduate training, I made my way to Colorado in 2002 to start my life as a psychology professor at the University of Denver. Across all those miles and years of training, the feelings from that evening on the Mall never went away. I never shook my misgiving and frustration that the women who survived or died from violence had no monuments to their private strength and vulnerability; their lives and deaths. Something permanent. I held out hope that research was the way that I could be part of building monuments for them. Not physical, of course, but using writing and speaking as a testament of sorts to their stories. A recognition that their suffering and strength mattered.

I had put a lot of stock in that monument memory, certain for so many years that monuments mattered—would matter, if women had one to their private wars. Eventually my aspirations for monument-building ebbed, too. I came to see that monuments were about building awareness, and the promise of awareness had tarnished. Study after study, interview after interview, intervention after intervention—women were still being victimized. I had a growing catalogue of the price they paid for violence, but that wasn't change. What would *change* take?

As that question became more pressing for me, I first heard the parable of the babies and the river from Jesús Torres, a Minnesota-based community organizer.[12] The story, which gets told and retold at organizing trainings across the country, went something like this when Torres shared it:

> Imagine a village by a river. The villagers hear babies wailing from the river. They run to the river to find babies in baskets. Someone upstream must be throwing the babies into the river.
>
> At first, the villagers rally to save the babies. The village's strong swimmers pull them from the water while others set up a network of volunteers to care for the babies. Someone starts a charity program to feed and clothe the babies. Someone else establishes a school for the babies. A group of neighbors organize a day of action to collect donations for the babies. And still, the babies keep coming down the river.

Over time, some villagers start to get angry about the resources being used up by the babies. What about the people who already live in the village? What about their needs? Realizing that these babies are costing the village a lot, several groups start initiatives to criminalize babies in the river. We have to take care of our own, their thinking goes. If we outlaw babies, then they won't come here and take our resources.

Once word gets out about the criminalization initiatives, other neighbors are positively outraged that anyone would try to criminalize babies. This whole situation isn't the babies' fault, they cry! They hire lawyers to represent the babies and hold rallies to protest the criminalization initiatives.

Soon activists occupy the river because they believe in a world without exploited babies.

Months into this mess, the village has tried awareness, charity, services, advocacy, activism, and legal intervention. At the end of the day, babies are still coming down the river in baskets, at the exact same rate.

The relevance of this parable to the arc of awareness and action over the past fifty years startled me. The problem of violence against women in homes, workplaces, and on the streets was the metaphorical babies-in-the-river. Over fifty years, people have marched and made laws, created services and studied their impact, and fought over the legitimacy of violence against women as a problem. And still a woman is a victim of intimate violence every ninety seconds.

A Decades-Long Promise

The promise that awareness can end violence against women goes back at least to the popularization of consciousness-raising in the Women's Movement of the 1960s and 1970s. At the time, the only available research on violence against women portrayed rape as rare, the fault of the victim, and perpetrated by strangers.[13] Yet when women told the stories of their lives to each other, a different picture emerged—one in which intimate violence as well as other forms of gender discrimination and oppression were commonplace and interconnected. Consciousness raising promised to reveal the "most radical truths about the situation of women in order to take radical action."[14] The key was awareness: as women became aware of the ways that oppression constrained and contorted their lives, they would take actions to dismantle the very systems that perpetuated violence and discrimination.

By the mid-1970s, radical ideals about dismantling systems of gender oppression gave way to a focus on individual well-being. White women's consciousness-raising efforts got largely co-opted for nonpolitical purposes focused on personal growth.[15] Nonetheless, the Women's Movement continued to draw attention to intimate violence, including from researchers. For example, Professors Ann Burgess and Lynda Holmstrom broke new ground when they interviewed more than 100 women who sought emergency care after rape. Based on those interviews, Burgess and Homstrom identified a constellation of reactions to rape, which they called *rape trauma syndrome*, in a 1974 paper. Their proposed syndrome recognized that women varied considerably in their initial reactions to rape. Some expressed fear and anger through sobs and restlessness; other displayed a masked sort of composure. In the weeks after sexual assault, women described stomach problems, physical tension, nightmares, intense emotions, and many fears—fears of being alone and in crowds, of being indoors and outside, of sex. Rape trauma syndrome, Burgess and Holmstrom advocated, "is not a private syndrome. It should be a societal concern, and its treatment should be a public charge."[16]

Meanwhile, veterans of the Vietnam War took up their own consciousness-raising mantle in "rap" groups across the country. Vietnam vets had returned to the US from an unpopular war at a time when the country knew little about the long-term consequences of combat and other traumatic stress. They suffered from flashbacks, sleeplessness, and guilt that oscillated with feeling numbed out, alienated, and empty. Yet many were denied services at the Veteran's Administration (VA) while others were misdiagnosed by a medical system that failed to realize their symptoms were tied to combat.[17] Vets turned to each other, creating rap groups to talk about the impact of the War and the symptoms that wreaked havoc on their lives. A handful of psychiatrists attended the groups and bore witness to the psychological harm of war. One of those psychiatrists, Chaim F. Shatan, took to the pages of the *New York Times*, in 1972, to describe what he had learned from vets in rap groups about patterns of guilt, rage, and alienation. He urged recognition of a post-Vietnam syndrome in which a "never-ending past deprives the present of meaning."[18]

The harm disclosed by women to researchers and veterans in rap groups was not new. Over the centuries, these reactions have gone by different names: hysteria, soldier's heart, railway spine, battered women's syndrome. At that moment in history, though, the similarities between women survivors' and veterans' stories came into view for those willing to see: women victimized in their homes, schools, and workplaces suffered consequences strikingly similar to those of veterans of wars and other traumas.

As research expanded on trauma and violence, so did services. Feminists founded the first rape crisis centers in the 1970s, as the number of battered women's shelters grew across the country. These centers played a central role in services as well as in state and national advocacy throughout the decade. For example, the Washington DC Rape Crisis Center brought Black and White women together to join a growing coalition to Free Joan Little. Imprisoned in North Carolina, Little killed a jailer when he entered her cell naked from the waist down. Little faced prosecution for murdering her would-be rapist, accused of seducing him into her cell. Her case became one of a handful that rose to national attention to stop the prosecution and incarceration of Black and Brown women for killing their assailants.[19]

The broad coalition that advocated for Little and against the incarceration of women who fought back against their abusers was at the fore of the modern prison abolition movement. Even as the abolition movement gained traction in the 1970s, so did work to *expand* criminal legal responses to violence against women in state laws. Though laws against sexual assault dated back hundreds of years, they varied considerably by state. Some state statutes had rape exemptions for husbands, required corroboration, or distinguished between stranger and acquaintance assault.[20] Other states varied considerably in the protections available to women abused by intimate partners. A woman living in one state might have the benefit of a protection order that restricted an abuser's contact with her *there*. However, another state might not recognize or enforce that order. This meant that she might have some degree of protection while making dinner at home, but not once she stepped off the train to make her way to a nondescript office building the next state over.

The lack of equal protection across state lines would eventually become an impetus for addressing violence against women through federal legislation—one in a string of different reasons used to motivate federal action.[21] Regardless, having laws on the books didn't mean that police and prosecutors took intimate violence seriously. Even when they did, forensic evidence was poorly collected or lost entirely.[22] If sexual assault cases went to trial, victims' own sexual histories often became the focus.[23]

And so the 1970s marked the start of periodic Congressional hearings on violence against women. Early hearings and growing awareness of the problem of rape in the US played a role in the founding of the National Center for the Prevention and Control of Rape. This center funded some of the earliest contemporary research on rape and sexual assault that guided policy until it was closed in the 1980s. At the same time, conflicts that would unfold over the decades ahead began to emerge. For example, Congress was reticent to take up domestic violence because of concerns that shelters might contribute to the disintegration of the family.[24]

Against this backdrop in the 1970s, a group of Black feminist women came together to forge a new political home for themselves. Marginalized by the prioritization of White women's concerns in the second wave of feminism and the lack of anti-sexist work in Black liberation and White liberal male politics at the time, they founded the Combahee River Collective. The group penned the *Combahee River Collective Statement* in 1977. Their treatise made the case that gender oppression included harassment and violence; and that gender could not be separated from other identities, such as ethnicity, sexual identity, and socioeconomic status. They laid out a roadmap for recognizing where gender and violence intersected with other injustices and inequities. Change, they argued, would have to come from a politics that centered Black women while recognizing and responding to situations that impinged on the lives of all who were marginalized.[25]

From Awareness to Criminalization and Medicalization

Consciousness-raising and marches brought much-needed attention to the problem of violence against women. Feminist advocates and organizers radically changed the landscape of services available after intimate violence. New professional organizations and coalitions emerged to address the problems caused by violence against women as researchers and medical providers paid more attention to survivors. By 1985, the growing interest in studying trauma, including violence, and its consequences led to the founding of the International Society for Traumatic Stress Studies (ISTSS).

Violence against women also attracted the attention of legislators. In 1990, Congress began the first of several years' worth of public hearings on what would eventually become VAWA, championed by then-Senator Joe Biden. In 1993, Biden wrote that the hearings revealed the costs of violence against women to public health, education, and the criminal legal system.[26]

He pointed to injuries suffered by women and the frequency of rape among adolescents, as well as the failure of prosecutors to take cases perpetrated by acquaintances, leaving offenders free to assault again. Largely ignored by the criminal legal system, women had few options in the civil legal system either. States varied widely in how cases were treated if women sought damages for the harms caused by violence. Unlike other forms of racial and religious discrimination, violence against women was not yet seen as a violation of civil rights. Biden argued, then, that VAWA would play a critical symbolic role in sending the message that violence against women was a civil rights violation that had to end.[27]

As chronicled by social movement scholar Nancy Whittier, Biden's staff pulled together an unlikely group of allies to pursue federal action on violence against women. The coalition-building effort brought together organizations as diverse as the National Organization of Women (NOW), the Girl Scouts, and conservative lawmakers. However, the motivations and priorities varied considerably across the groups under this big tent.[28]

According to Whittier, conservative groups came to the coalition motivated to protect women and the country from violent crime. They saw violence against women as a part of a larger epidemic of violent crime across the US that required bold federal action to expand the criminal legal system to protect Americans. Feminists, however, saw violence against women as contributing to the social control and oppression of women. To end women's oppression would require stopping violence against women and recognizing the ways that violence interconnected with women's multiple identities—such as their ethnicity and abilities—and other forms of discrimination. While an intersectional approach, such as that advocated for by the Combahee River Collective, was important to feminist arguments, what to do about the problem of violence against women was (and still is) a matter of debate among feminists. Some feminists advocated for expanding criminal legal responses as a central solution; others, particularly Women of Color, warned that expanding criminal responses would harm Communities of Color.[29]

Regardless, the feminist intersectional approach rarely got center stage at hearings. Instead, Whittier observed that hearings tended to focus on arguments that fell somewhere between the feminist and conservative positions. Witnesses and legislators recognized the gendered nature of intimate violence but did not take up the mantel of women's rights nor solely adopt the language of violent crime. This approach held the big tent together, which was key to pushing VAWA through to passage in 1994 as part of the Crime Bill.[30]

The final version of VAWA had a mix of components, including a historic provision that recognized violence against women as a violation of women's civil rights. With that provision, VAWA created a means for women to take civil legal action in federal court, expanding options outside the criminal legal system. That provision, though, was struck down by the courts in 2000. The remaining components of VAWA emphasized criminal responses to violence, such as mandatory arrest policies, and made funding available for a range of services. Some saw VAWA as a win for addressing the problem of police and prosecutors not taking violence against women seriously. Others saw the law as part of the rapid expansion of criminal legal approaches to violence against women, one that would inevitably have disproportionate impacts on Communities of Color.[31]

Today, communities across the country rely on VAWA-related and other federal funding to provide services to women and their children after violence. Rooted in augmenting criminal legal responses, VAWA funding has driven practice and policy nationwide to emphasize collaborations between community-based organizations, law enforcement, and prosecutors to respond to violence against women. As Women of Color warned when VAWA was being drafted, the larger Crime Bill drove the exponential growth in mass incarceration, particularly of Black and Brown people. For VAWA's part, the introduction of mandatory arrest policies, which required police officers to make an arrest in domestic violence cases when they discovered probable cause, corresponded with rapid growth in the incarceration of women.[32]

Since 1994, advocates and lawmakers have tried to leverage periodic reauthorizations of the law to chip away at a slew of important and complicated issues unaddressed by the original bill. For example, a patchwork of laws across Indian Country meant that non-Native people escaped consequences when they victimized Native American women who lived on reservations. Lesbian, bisexual, and transgender as well as immigrant women nationwide faced unique threats and barriers to safety, from discrimination to not qualifying for services.[33] However, each reauthorization became more difficult because addressing the specific needs among lesbian, bisexual, transgender, Native, and immigrant women ran afoul of conservative officials' narrow focus on violent crime.[34]

The policy fights over VAWA reauthorizations have reinforced that some victims in the US are seen as deserving of help while others are not and that many interests are put ahead of women's lives. As of this writing, the Senate has failed to reauthorize VAWA in the wake of gun lobby pressure to block efforts to close a so-called *boyfriend loophole*. Where current and former spouses as well as partners who lived with or had children with victims are not allowed to possess guns after domestic violence convictions, the federal law does not apply to other intimate partners—such as dating partners who do not live with the people they victimize.[35]

As criminalization expanded in the 1990s, so did the medicalization of responses to intimate violence. The introduction of *posttraumatic stress disorder* (PTSD) into medical nomenclature in 1994 was revolutionary for marking that trauma has identifiable and serious consequences for victims and survivors. Research on PTSD and its prevalence has played an essential role in understanding women's experiences after violence and in expanding care. Such work was also critical to showing that violence against women can have the same impacts as other sources of traumatic stress, such as war and natural disasters. And yet medicalization also focused attention on what is wrong with victims, often to the exclusion of asking what's wrong with the people who perpetrate or communities that tolerate intimate violence.

Indeed, focusing on what is wrong with victims has been built into our medical approach and public discourse for centuries, as we'll trace in Chapter 1. Today, this focus shows up in headlines, such as the 2019 one that declared "Women Are More Than Twice as Likely as Men to Suffer from PTSD: Studies Are Underway to Find Out Why."[36] The subsequent article explained that girls and women are more likely to be sexually assaulted and to experience violence earlier in life than are boys and men, factors that likely play a role in gender differences in PTSD. After giving that context, though, the article turned to cataloguing other differences between men and women that might explain why women have higher rates of PTSD than men. For example, experts explained that men and women vary on sex hormones and genetics, and men seem better able to "unlearn" fear than women. Focusing on what's unique about women's genes, learning, stress hormones, and so forth might lead to improvements in treatments for women.

As a clinical psychologist, I can attest that developing and disseminating effective treatments for PTSD is incredibly important. However, the article illustrated a slippery slope. When we focus too narrowly on *women's* biology, emotions, or learning, we risk getting lulled into thinking that PTSD can be reduced down to something about *women's* bodies and minds. When we do that, we miss how the *contexts* in which girls and women live affect their chances of being victimized, their responses to violence, and *our* responses. Focused on what's wrong with women rather than what happened to them, we lose sight of the systemic problem: that intimate violence is commonplace and our society responds poorly when it happens.

Two-plus decades ago, Dr. Judith Herman wrote in a landmark book, *Trauma and Recovery*, that traumatic stress had gained legitimacy as an area of study. This was a huge achievement, given the tendency across history to ignore violence against girls and women. She cautioned, though, that "The very strength of recent biological findings in PTSD may foster a narrowed, predominantly biological focus of research. As the field of traumatic stress matures, a new generation of researchers will need to rediscover the essential interconnection of biological, psychological, social, and political dimensions of trauma." In short, she foretold the risk that we would ultimately drift to focus on what was wrong with victims rather than the societies that allow violence to continue relatively unabated.[37]

It's tempting to look around and say that Herman's worry was for naught. After all, everywhere we turn programs, schools, and agencies declare themselves *trauma-informed*. Trauma-informed schools, for example, promote the importance of adapting policies, practices, and playgrounds to meet the needs of individuals who were victimized, as we'll explore in Chapter 3. Adapting institutions because victimization happened is great, but not enough without also interrupting the larger culture and context in which violence happens in the first place, as my colleague Dr. Kathryn Becker-Blease has warned.[38]

Even as communities seek to respond to violence against women through coordinated services and courts, a vocal minority make the case that our reaction to violence against women is misplaced. *What about men's rights?* they ask. Periodic backlashes have punctuated the past fifty years of awareness building and action. Consider what happened when the Obama administration took action on campus sexual assault, arguing that gender-based violence interrupted girls' and women's equal access to education. Before long, pundits and parents claimed that survivor-centered policies were inherently anti-male.[39] By 2020, evidence mounted that small advocacy groups for men's rights had dramatically turned the tide against campus sexual assault survivors with implications for women's access to opportunity and safety.[40]

The Movement We Need Now

Survivors, activists, and researchers who shed light on violence against women in the 1960s and 1970s changed the world in many ways. Their consciousness raising and direct action had impacts large and small. They worked within and around the structures of their time—printing leaflets to free Joan Little, showing up in the halls of state houses to get the police to pay attention to sexual assault, staging sit-ins for justice. They built rape crisis centers and domestic violence shelters and revolutionized medicine's view of the trauma of violence against women. Like all movements, though, these approaches had successes and setbacks, getting co-opted to varying degrees. White women's consciousness raising gave way to more apolitical self-help; grassroots activism got professionalized; coalition building emphasized criminal legal solutions. Women of Color scholars and activists spoke out about the failings of antiviolence organizations to address the intersectional nature of violence against women and their focus on social services instead of structural change.[41]

As the decades wore on, so did a sense that violence against women was someone else's problem. Instead of talking to each other about violence—across clotheslines and at marches—to design and drive actions that make sense in our communities, lots of us learned to rely on nonprofits to handle the messiness of violence against women in our communities for us.

Public awareness of the 1970s gave rise to a triumvirate of services, legislation, and research over the next fifty years. Yet violence against women continues relatively unabated today. To be sure, some forms of violence have declined a few percentage points over the decades, but others are on the rise, such as murders by intimate partners and rapes where the assailant uses physical force.[42]

Today, we have a new mix of awareness and activism alongside some of the same essential dynamics. Research on violence against women has exploded through disciplines as varied as social work, medicine, psychology, criminology, economics, and public health. Those research investments have amassed evidence that violence against women damages physical and mental health, diminishes educational achievement, and paves the way to poverty and prison.

A new generation of leaders has emerged, fighting battles for equity on college campuses where stopping violence against women is one thread connected to others. #MeToo reignited a sense that awareness had the potential to move the needle as the media paid attention to the persistent dangers women and girls confront for simply being women and girls.

The media turned a spotlight on domestic violence in the early days of the pandemic with reports of women locked down with their abusers. I watched these new stories pick up on my social media feeds, but the spike in tweets about coronavirus and domestic violence gave way to other issues. Reading tweets linked to stories about women trapped may have *felt* like a change, but change did not come from that collective moment of social media awareness.

Echoes of the same overpromise of awareness play out in interconnected movements today. In response to George Floyd's murder by police in 2020 and the killings of Black people of all genders, many White people wanted to take action. Antiracist books sold out as White readers flocked to book groups with antiracist reading lists. People of Color cautioned White readers that learning things can *feel* like action, but knowledge does not correct injustice in and of itself. Awareness is not the same as action to correct systemic, institutionalized injustices.[43]

We need a different approach to change. We must find a way to imagine and then make real a world none of us has ever known: One in which women and girls aren't victimized for being women and girls, and the harm of violence is met with the restoration of dignity, fairness, opportunity, and safety.

The audacious goal to end millennia of violence against women and heal its harms will require a fundamental shift in how we think about that intimate violence, particularly whose problem it is and who has the capacity to do something about it. For most of the modern era, ordinary people have largely seen violence as a problem for victims. Even violence prevention efforts historically reinforced the idea that violence is about potential victims and offenders, not all of us. When violence happened, people have been quick to see the problem as one of victims who didn't fight back hard enough, not as a problem that is yours and mine. Public discourse and popular media have amplified these views with repeated messages about what women wore or drank before an assault. Such narratives have told us time and again, in subtle and not-so-subtle ways, that violence is the purview of women and dependent on the decisions they make.

In recent years, youth prevention approaches have changed dramatically, which bodes well for the rest of us changing, too. Today, prevention programs emphasize that *all youth* have a role to play in stopping violence.[44] Youth learn that they have a responsibility to take actions to stop violence in their high schools and college dorms because they have a stake in the well-being of their communities. This evolution in programming capitalizes on a sense of shared community to ask youth to do what is sometimes hard in situations where saying "not my problem" would be easier than confronting a bully or a drunken friend.

Going back to the babies in the river, this is akin to helping people find a good enough reason to climb upstream, figure out who is throwing babies in the water, and stop them. You might convince me to haul myself over boulders to get upstream because you know I care about the damage caused to babies' developing brains when they get thrown in rivers. I might convince you to leave your family to head into the unknown because by stopping this baby problem, you will have more resources to put toward ending food insecurity in our village. To do difficult things, we need a reason, a stake. We need what community organizers call a *self-interest*.

Reality is, of course, more complicated than hiking upstream. And even more complicated because we're talking about violence against women. After all, our own defenses work against collaboration by telling us to keep thinking that victims are different from us. We tell ourselves stories all the time about how *we* (or our sisters, daughters, wives, friends) wouldn't have let that happen. *We* would have handled the situation differently. *We* would have divorced the bum. *We* wouldn't have ended up with drug addictions or unplanned pregnancies.

We tell ourselves these kinds of stories—that violence isn't our problem and won't affect us—so that we have the courage to step out the door each morning into an uncertain world.[45] That's great for getting out the door but a problem for discovering ways to work together to create change.

To be sure, successful change movements have long relied on building solidarities among people to inspire cooperative action. Across labor and civil rights movements, for example, change has come about with the mass participation of ordinary people—including those who didn't initially see themselves as directly affected by discrimination in housing, unfair wages, or unsafe conditions in a production plant. Movement successes have hinged on getting ordinary people to see their self-interest in fair workers' wages and ending White-only lunch counters regardless of whether they worked in factories or the color of their skin. Those movements inspired people to do difficult things, often arising out of a deep sense of community built through the places they had in common—shared churches, neighborhoods, schools, shop floors, and breakrooms.[46]

Spaces and places continue to connect people in contemporary movements. For example, teachers who called West Virginia home collectively walked out in 2018, shuttering schools until they won concessions in wages and benefits. Their fight for wages got national media attention, though their strike was about much more than their own financial compensation. They also demanded the governor veto a bill that was making its way through the legislature, which they believed would be harmful to children's education across the state.[47]

By 2019, Los Angeles teachers were bargaining for the "common good." Strong relationships with community organizations meant that the United Teachers Los Angeles brought immigrant and housing rights issues to the bargaining table as community members backed the 30,000 teachers whose strike dragged on for six days.[48]

That same year, hospitality workers in Sacramento took action against Marriott in response to the chronic sexual harassment of hotel cleaning staff, who were mostly Women of Color and immigrant women with little political power. Workers demanded a new contract that would provide cleaning staff with a panic button to use in emergencies. Eventually, their influence went far beyond Marriott when they persuaded Oakland voters to pass a hotel worker safety law by a margin of more than fifty points.[49]

You and I don't share a city or a breakroom, a school, or even a state. But we do have this in common: violence against women costs both of us in terms of the progress we urgently want to see on the issues we each care most about. For you, maybe it's your passion for improving the state of our nation's schools. Or addressing the racial inequities laid bare in the urgent need for criminal justice reform. Perhaps you want to make progress on the staggering costs of healthcare. Or you want schools to be free of the fear of mass shooting. Maybe you feel a palpable urgency to see immigration policies reformed. Maybe you've survived violence yourself, and maybe you haven't. Regardless, you and I share what community organizers call a collective self-interest in stopping and ameliorating the effects of violence against women, even if violence never affects us directly.

As the Black feminists of the Combahee River Collective told us fifty years ago, there's no separating violence against women from the intersecting problems and possibilities in the world. Today, their intersectional approach remains essential to finding a way from awareness to the action we need now. Indeed, history shows that change happens when we see our fates tangled up with someone else's in order to take action.

That's what this book is about: finding where you and I share self-interests to end violence against women and heal its effects because violence costs us all—individuals and whole communities—from healthcare, education, and immigration policy to basic safety from guns, economic wellbeing, and justice.

But that's not all this book is about. Uncovering our shared self-interests could be just another exercise in awareness-building—identifying one more way that we know violence against women happens and is bad. Instead, we have to figure out how the threads that connect our self-interests prepare us to build a vision for a new world that inspires us and others to action. In recognizing our enlightened self-interest, we can imagine a new future together.

As we'll see, our current world is one in which the short-term and life-long health consequences diminish women's opportunities and cut short their potential. Gun violence has roots in violence against women, making gendered violence a threat to all of us in our synagogues, shopping malls, and workplaces. Witnessing domestic violence primes school-to-prison pipelines long before intimate violence disrupts women's access to and success in college. Women flee intimate violence across international borders, risking revictimziation even as they seek safety.

This picture could stop us in our tracks, too overwhelming to act. But here's the secret: the answers and inspiration are right there in the interconnected problems themselves. Violence against women strips away dignity, fairness, opportunity, and safety from girls, women, *and* communities. You and I have a common cause to work together to reimagine and create a world that restores and ensures dignity, fairness, opportunity, and safety for women and communities. Doing so is good for you, for me, and for the issues and people we each care about.

We've been slow to see our shared self-interest in ending violence against women, in part because we've been asking the wrong question for centuries. From courtrooms to medical offices, we keep asking what's *wrong with victims* instead of asking how violence against women diminishes all of us and what we're going to do about it together. Shifting that legacy promises to open new doors to making progress on the great public problems of our time—starting with health and healthcare.

1

Of Hysteria and Health

For many people, healthcare is a defining issue of our time. Coworkers and neighbors worry about the costs of premiums and medical care, knowing that they might be one health crisis away from financial ruin. Healthcare advocates denounce an unfair system in which poor people and People of Color face extraordinary barriers to getting care. Public health experts warn that health systems are consumed by treating illness rather than promoting wellness. A child's zip code defines their health—and even mortality—for decades by affecting access to healthy food, clean water, and breathable air.

Violence against women also defines health. Immediate injuries cause pain and suffering while driving up preventable healthcare costs in emergency rooms. Years after abuse, physical and psychological health problems diminish school, work, and other opportunities. The impacts of violence continue to ripple out across the decades, affecting the next generation's health, too.

The widespread, long-lasting health impacts of violence against women should be a clarion call: Health and healthcare reform require also addressing the entirely preventable problem of violence against women. Yet conversations about health and healthcare reform in the US have been slow to include discussions of violence against women, even after fifty years of awareness building. Perhaps because an even longer history drowns out the clarion call.

More than two centuries ago in Paris, seeds were planted that feed our collective tendency to see the health impacts of intimate violence as a *woman's* problem. *Her* depression or pelvic pain. *Her* heart disease and binge drinking. *Her* hysteria. Yet improving health and healthcare in the US will require that we break that long-standing habit to recognize that the health consequences of intimate violence are *our* issue. With a bit of history, we can trace the roots of our habit and build a new way forward.

A Lot of Noise Over Nothing

On Paris's Left Bank, the dramatic entrance of the Salpêtrière Hospital would have loomed large as fourteen-year-old Louise approached, her path to the hospital marked by abuse and violence. She had survived molestations as a girl only to witness brutal domestic violence perpetrated against an important mother figure. She evaded several attempts by her mother's sometimes-lover to force her into sex until the day her luck ran out. He threatened to cut her with a razor, plied her with alcohol, and raped her. The next day, she couldn't walk. She complained of tremendous pain in her abdomen, which a doctor wrote off as something to do with menstruation. Soon one side of her body became paralyzed. Emotions overwhelmed her.

The year was 1865. Her diagnosis was hysteria.[1]

Louise joined other adolescent girls and women diagnosed with hysteria at the Salpêtrière Hospital, where they were known for displaying all manner of bizarre symptoms. They fainted, forgot who they were, convulsed, became agitated, went catatonic, suffered paralysis of various body parts, and struck sexual poses. Early medical photographs and drawings illustrated the throes of hysteria in a truly haunting catalogue of nearly inhuman poses.[2]

When Louise arrived at the hospital on Paris's Left Bank, women were being diagnosed with hysteria at a dizzying rate. The hospital itself had long been a place where poor and problematic women were tucked away, out of sight. A minority of those women would eventually be cured, though many would perish within the hospital walls. In 1862 alone, more than 250 women died from causes that ranged from blows and wounds, cholera, alcoholism, love and joy to misery, bad reading habits, masturbation, debauchery, and licentiousness, according to medical records from the time.[3]

Before entering the hospital, women's lives had been punctuated by chronic sexual abuse and rape, physical violence, extreme poverty, and the tragic deaths of family members. Hysterical patients told their doctors about flashbacks and memories of witnessing abuse, being raped and attacked, all documented in medical notes.[4]

At the time, doctors did not connect lifelong intimate violence and trauma to women's hysterical symptoms. Instead, hysteria was the medical mystery of the day at a time when the public imagination was captivated by mesmerism, suggestibility, and hypnosis. Hysteria was so captivating that elites from across Europe flocked to salons at the Salpêtrière where Jean Charcot, who would later be credited as the father of modern neurology, gave lectures on hysteria. During his lectures, women patients appeared with Charcot to demonstrate their bizarre symptoms. Louise was a frequent patient-performer for Charcot's rapt audiences.[5]

Charcot's lectures and the times were memorialized in the painting, *A Clinical Lesson at the Salpêtrière*. The canvas shows Charcot standing at the center of the image lecturing to an all-male audience, which included many of his famous protégés. The men stare attentively at a woman who is draped across an assistant's arms, her blouse slipping from her shoulders as she appears to faint.[6]

The image always reminds me of an oft-quoted excerpt from one of Charcot's lectures. In the transcript, an assistant has just pressed on the pelvic area of a patient as Charcot explained, "Let us press again on the hysterogenic point. Here we go again. Occasionally subjects even bite their tongues, but this would be rare. Look at the arched back." When the woman said she's frightened, Charcot responded, "Note the emotional outburst." She called out again and he said, "Again, note these screams. You could say it is a lot of noise over nothing." Charcot then turned attention to the use compression belts, which tightly bound the abdominal region with a vice-like tool, sometimes for hours on end, to stop patients from screaming, carrying on, and otherwise being hysterical.[7]

Looking back, we're left to wonder why Charcot and his colleagues didn't connect women's "outbursts" and hysterical symptoms to the intimate violence and other adversity documented in their medical records.[8] The answer, argued psychiatrist Judith Herman in her landmark book, *Trauma and Recovery*, lies in looking at the context. At the time, women didn't have the vote or property rights. In France, they weren't in the workforce and were banned from wearing pants or printing feminist materials. In short, they lacked any structural or institutional power. In such an environment, listening to and really trying to understand the impact of intimate violence in women's lives were terribly unlikely, especially when men—who did have structural and institutional power—stood to be the ones accused of doing the harm.[9]

Soon, though, a brief window of time would open up when listening to women became politically useful, Herman argued. By the 1880s, France was engaged in a full-blown struggle for power, with the monarchy and religion on one side and a republican, secular government on the other. In this context, understanding the psychology of women began to matter. Jules Ferry, a prominent French republican, put it this way: "Women must belong to science or they will belong to the church."[10]

Ferry and others recognized that leaving medical mysteries, such as hysteria, to the church to explain—say, as the result of women's inherent immorality—would reinforce the influence of the church and monarchy in society. If science could better explain the ailments, then there would be an opportunity to demonstrate the importance of scientific ways of knowing, championed by the secular republic. Medicalizing women's experiences, then, became useful for showing the public that physicians were more important than priests. Women and their stories became politically relevant, though they had little political power. In this socio-political context, where understanding women's experiences mattered, Charcot's protégés started listening closely to women. One of those men was Sigmund Freud.[11]

To understand Freud's role in this tale, we have to heed Herman's caution to keep returning to the socio-political context. At the Salpêtrière, Charcot and his protégés worked with women on the margins of society—poor women, beggars, and prostitutes. One of those protégés, Pierre Janet, theorized that unbearable emotions from abuse led to altered states of consciousness. According to Janet, those altered states drove the physical manifestations of hysterical symptoms: fainting and forgetting, paralysis and convulsing. Meanwhile, Freud—a rival of Janet's—traveled to Paris to train with Charcot from his home in Vienna where he treated well-to-do patients who were the daughters and wives of rich and powerful men.[12]

Back in Vienna, Freud raced his rivals to uncover the origins of hysteria. He listened closely to his women patients, many of whom recounted stories of sexual violence. From their stories, Freud believed he had discovered the roots of hysteria, which he shared in an 1896 paper titled, "The Aetiology of Hysteria." In that paper, Freud made the case that the ultimate cause of hysteria was sexual abuse. Unfortunately for Freud, his theory implicated in abuse the very rich and powerful fathers, uncles, and husbands of his women patients at a time when the socio-political sands were shifting under his feet.[13]

By the 1896 publication of his treatise, secular governments were firmly established in France and across Europe. This meant that understanding women had far less political value, particularly when the truth of their lives was painful and threatening to powerful people. Indeed, Freud described his colleagues' reception of a lecture on the etiology of hysteria as "icy," with one colleague calling it a "scientific fairy tale."[14]

A few years after the publication of "The Aetiology of Hysteria," Freud's correspondence spoke volumes: "I am as isolated as you could wish me to be: the word has been given out to abandon me, and a void is forming around me."[15] A century later, Herman would aptly describe the dilemma in which Freud found himself: "Those who bear witness are caught in the conflict between victim and perpetrator. It is morally impossible to remain neutral. . . . The bystander is forced to take sides. All the perpetrator asks is that the bystander do nothing. The victim, on the contrary, asks the bystander to share the burden of pain."[16]

In the face of professional scorn and isolation, Freud started wondering if he'd gotten it wrong. Reversing course, he introduced the concept of repression, which blamed women's symptoms on guilt about sexual fantasies and desires. Freud reasoned that women believed their fantasies of being abused so deeply that they had duped even him with their tales.[17]

Meanwhile, back at the Salpêtrière, the neurologist Joseph Babinski took the helm when Charcot died. Building on growing interest in hypnotism, Babinski championed the role that suggestibility—rather than violence— played in hysteria.[18] Like Freud's repression concept, the thinking went that women made up their symptoms, imagining or responding to suggestions from doctors that they were ill.

Over those few short years, the seeds of our modern tendency to assume women invent stories of rape, abuse, and violence were planted. Freud and Janet, a pair of rivals, had both discovered that hysteria was due to violence perpetrated *against* women and girls. With the shifting political sands, however, Freud and others relocated the problem *inside* women and girls. The illness was *her* fault, caused by *her* own instincts, urges, fantasies, and suggestibility.

Unfortunately, this is more than an interesting story from a history book. This history is very much alive today in a medical system that tends to ignore and minimize women's pain and a worldview that paints the health consequences of intimate violence as a *woman's* issue instead of *our* issue.

Violence Against Women Is Bad for Health

Women are unlikely to walk out of a doctor's office today with a diagnosis of hysteria, though women's pain still gets ignored, minimized, and labeled as hysterical. Indeed, a review of seventy-seven studies found that women who reported pain were characterized as hysterical, emotional, and malingering while men tended to be described as stoic.[19] Those pervasive gender biases, along with racial biases, have real impacts on healthcare.[20] The confluence and deadly consequences of these biases come into sharp relief when looking at rates of maternal mortality, for example, where Black women are three to four times more likely to die than White women in childbirth.[21]

Against this backdrop of modern gender and racial biases, women face a staggering number of ailments after intimate violence, just like their historical counterparts at the Salpêtrière. Some of those health problems are immediate, while others unfold and require treatment in the months and years after the violence occurs—from acute physical injuries to smoking, alcohol abuse, and drug abuse as well as sexually transmitted infections, gastrointestinal diseases, depression, anxiety, and suicide, among others.

The range of health problems linked to intimate violence has been obvious and available to policy-makers for years: one of the earliest and largest studies available was conducted in 2005 by the US Centers for Disease Control and Prevention (CDC), which surveyed 40,000 women.[22] Ten thousand of those women had survived intimate violence and were more likely than the other 30,000 women to have a long list of health problems: arthritis, asthma, activity limitations, stroke, smoking, binge drinking, high blood cholesterol, heart attack, heart disease, risk factors for HIV or sexually transmitted infections, and disabilities that require assistive equipment.

That early CDC research is echoed by dozens of studies since then that have linked intimate partner violence and sexual assault to poorer overall health, chronic diseases, and somatic problems long past the initial assault.[23] Sexual assault in particular can result in some obvious and immediate consequences, such as unwanted pregnancies, sexually transmitted infections, and injuries. Other impacts unfold over time, like excessive menstrual bleeding, genital burning, painful intercourse, dysmenorrhea, menstrual irregularity, and lack of sexual pleasure.[24]

The health impacts of violence against women continue even much later in life, illustrated by a recent study of more than 70,000 women veterans, now in their mid-fifties to eighties. Those who were sexually assaulted while serving in the military had more health problems than other women, especially sleep disorders and pain.[25] A 2020 study of primary care patients in the United Kingdom reported that domestic abuse was linked with cardiovascular disease, type 2 diabetes, and mortality.[26]

Several years ago on my own research team, we began routinely asking women to look at a list of about sixty different medical issues. That list included problems that ranged from gastrointestinal symptoms to liver disease, infections, and gall bladder problems. In studies focused on the months after sexual assault and domestic violence, women told us about an average of nearly ten different health issues. The picture was even bleaker for women after sex trafficking. They had to manage long lists of health issues while also trying to avoid the (mostly) men who had trafficked them and find new ways to meet their basic needs—from housing to food—in jobs that did not involve sex work.[27]

Like survivors nationally, some of the women we have interviewed over the years had access to healthcare, others did not. Some relied heavily on emergency rooms for routine care, which meant expensive care without the benefits of an ongoing relationship with a doctor. Others avoided doctors at all costs for reasons that ranged from fear to finances. The same reality bears out nationally: women who have been abused show up at the extremes of healthcare utilization as both high- and non- or low-users.[28] Both extremes put stresses on women's individual health and the healthcare system. Women who rarely or never go to the doctor or dentist may miss critically important preventative care that can save money and lives later by supporting health, including reproductive health.

Reproductive Health

During hysteria's heyday at the Salpêtrière, women's moral character was impugned and their deaths blamed on masturbation and debauchery even as medical records documented physicians having sex with patients and lifetimes of intimate victimization.[29] Even the word "hysteria" itself was a sort of impugnation, reflecting a millennia-long habit of blaming women's bodies for maladies and madness. The term comes from Latin, roughly translated as a "wandering uterus." As early as the fourth century BCE, Hippocrates and his contemporaries imagined that a woman's uterus behaved much like a restless animal, prone to following its own wayward course. The wandering, then, caused visions, unexplained pain, and even madness.[30]

Today, we don't have to worry that the uterus will get to wandering about. However, we do have to contend with the ways that intimate violence is tangled up with reproductive health, causing problems for individual women, their children, and our healthcare system.

As early as the 1990s, researchers started sharing what they heard from some women whose abusive partners pressured them to get pregnant or controlled their access to birth control.[31] Partners threw out women's birth control, controlled their money so they could not purchase birth control themselves, and refused to use condoms. Some partners coerced women into getting (or not getting) pregnant and having (or not having) abortions.

Despite that early research, Dr. Heather McCauley, an expert in reproductive coercion, has observed a collective tendency, even among healthcare providers, to assume that lack of condom or contraception use is an awareness issue—that people don't *know how* to use condoms or contraception. "When I train clinicians around the country, I ask them to challenge their thoughts about 'ambivalence' around pregnancy intention and consider whether their patients were able to safely negotiate their sexuality and contraceptive/condom use. In other words, it's not a knowledge problem."[32] It's a coercion problem.

More recently, research has revealed just how common reproductive coercion is, especially among adolescent girls and young women as well as Women of Color. For example, across adolescent health clinics, more than 40% of adolescent girls reported being physically or sexually abused by a partner. Intimate partner violence was linked, in turn, with significantly higher odds of reproductive coercion and deception, such as partners refusing to use condoms or having sex with others.[33] Meanwhile, more than one in ten sexually active adolescent girls seeking care at their high schools reported reproductive coercion in the previous three months.[34] Among women seeking family planning care, Black and multiracial women were more likely than other women to report reproductive coercion, even though overall rates of intimate partner violence did not differ by ethnic group.[35]

While researchers initially noticed and studied reproductive coercion in already physically violent relationships, a 2018 review suggested that reproductive coercion might also be a warning sign for future physical violence.[36] This makes sense given what is being discovered about men who engage in *stealthing*. Stealthing refers to intentionally removing a condom during sex without the sex partner's knowledge or consent.[37] When lawyer Alexandra Bodsky addressed questions about the legality of stealthing, she identified online communities that promoted the nonconsensual removal of condoms and justified the practice based on men's sexual supremacy.[38] Psychologist

Kelly Cue Davis discovered similar patterns when she surveyed more than 600 males who used condoms inconsistently. About 10% of those men indicated that they had removed condoms without their partners' consent. Men who engaged in nonconsensual condom removal also had more severe histories of sexual aggression as well as greater hostility toward women.[39] Hostility toward women has long been linked with violence against them.[40]

In addition to portending future violence, reproductive coercion can have immediate and long-term effects, from poorly timed and unintended pregnancies to potentially serious consequences if women can't access preventative care and even mental health consequences.[41] The emerging research evidence on reproductive coercion should worry us very much in today's current political climate, which has made it easier for abusers to limit access to reproductive healthcare and contraception, especially for poor girls and women. If a woman has to drive hours to get to a provider she can afford or who will give her a prescription for birth control, it's that much easier for an abuser to disrupt her plans. Unintended pregnancies and subsequent single parenting can affect women's lives in significant ways for years to come, even putting them at risk for lifelong poverty. Such risks are compounded for adolescents. Pregnancy and birth in the teen years can lead to serious consequences for mothers and their babies—from their health to their economic well-being. Babies born to teen mothers are at risk of being preterm, low birthweight, small for gestational age, and to have malformations.[42] Premature babies go on to face a host of health challenges that are difficult for the baby and mother as well as the health system.

Pregnancy itself can usher in new or increased violence.[43] Violence that occurs around the time that women get pregnant tends to continue during pregnancy, and risks are highest for women with unintended pregnancies.[44] In fact, women who had unintended pregnancies were 2.5 times more likely to have been abused than were women who had planned pregnancies.[45] Women experiencing physical violence from their partners were more likely than other women to be hospitalized during pregnancy, including for their own substance use and mental health diagnoses.[46] In my community, victim service providers pay particular attention when women are pregnant, given their experiences of seeing violence escalate. Combine pregnancy with other risk factors, such as an abuser being in possession of a gun, and it may even prove deadly.

The situation is bad for fetuses, too. More than twenty years ago, a large study conducted by a team of researchers from across the country looked at nearly 28,000 pregnant women's reports of violence in the twelve months before pregnancy and their use of prenatal healthcare. Women dealing with violence were nearly twice as likely *not* to have received prenatal healthcare until after the first trimester compared to non-abused women.[47] Since then, dozens of studies have shown that women abused during pregnancy are more likely to delay or never get any prenatal care than other women.[48]

Once babies are born, we have reason to worry about their health as well. Researchers call this the *intergenerational transmission of trauma*. Events that affect parents can impact the next generation, setting babies on familiar trajectories well before they can make choices about their own futures. For example, on my research team, Rebecca Babcock Fenerci found that mothers' feelings of shame and alienation about their own victimizations were linked to their young children's difficulties with problems like depression symptoms and acting out.[49] Researchers and health professionals have pointed out that the intergenerational effects of intimate violence can intersect with racialized trauma to leave wounds on the body and soul for generations.[50]

Some of the less obvious impacts of gender-based violence on sexual and reproductive health got a bit clearer to me several years ago when we were recruiting adolescent girls from the child welfare system for the Healthy Adolescent Relationship Project. Enrollment in the study was slow, and we were working hard to reach out to child welfare caseworkers to let them know that the research included classes on healthy relationship skills. One day, a tired-sounding caseworker asked "But can you provide childcare?" "Yes," I said. She explained that several of the girls on her caseload had infants or very young children, and programs in our community could rarely provide childcare. That meant the girls on her caseload couldn't take advantage of programming that might help them heal from abuse and parent their own children.

The next thing we learned from these youth was the insidious way that reproductive coercion played out in their relationships, as other research teams have reported as well.[51] One seventeen-year-old explained to me that her boyfriend, who had thrown her against the wall once before, was definitely going to change because she just told him that she was pregnant. Having grown up watching her own parents fight night after night, she was sure that having a baby now would put her on the fast track to building a different sort of family. Alienated from others, she imagined that the baby growing inside of her would become her best friend and that her boyfriend would stop hurting her because of the baby.

Moved by her optimism, I wanted so badly for her story to be different from the anonymous girls and women whose lives were condensed into statistics in dozens of studies about the challenges adolescent mothers and their children face, worsened by educational and economic hurdles. I don't know what happened to her in the years since that project ended, though I often wonder—and hope. I hope that the next chapter of her story was filled with connections to people and to her own sense of self because I was learning that those connections were essential to the story of health and wellness.

Psychological Health

My own path into research at the intersection of health and violence started with questions about the links between intimate violence and psychological symptoms. The most obvious psychological consequence of violence against women is PTSD. The diagnosis itself recognizes that traumas play a role in setting off a cascade of biological and psychological processes that manifest in a mix of symptoms that involve re-experiencing the trauma (such as through intrusive memories), avoidance, negative mood and thoughts, and arousal. However, PTSD isn't the only or even the primary psychological problem associated with violence against women. Depressive, dissociative, and eating disorders as well as anxiety among other symptoms, have all been linked with intimate violence.[52,53]

Interested in what might help explain the different kinds of psychological symptoms that can arise after intimate violence, my team began work to develop a measure of posttraumatic thoughts and feelings. In a study funded by the National Institute of Mental Health, we interviewed almost 200 people from the community, the majority of whom were women, who had survived a range of traumas—from sexual assault and domestic violence to combat and motor vehicle accidents. Survivors described that the trauma raised a mix of feelings—sometimes fear or shame, maybe anger and self-blame, or betrayal. One reaction stood out for how consistently people described feeling it, particularly after sexual assault and domestic violence: alienation. In interview after interview, survivors told us that they had friends, but still felt lonely; talked to people, but felt misunderstood; were offered support, and yet felt strangely set apart from the people who tried to help them. The feelings ran deep, with many describing feeling as if they had lost a part of themselves, lost their sense of being a person. They described being unmoored, disconnected from others and from themselves.

My research team had those findings in mind when we began the Triage Project, a study funded by the National Institute of Justice, carried out in collaboration with criminologists Joanne Belknap and Angela Gover. In the course of the study, our team talked with 236 women about their experiences in the criminal legal system after domestic violence, as well as about their health and well-being. Like women nationally coping with domestic violence, the women we spoke with were diverse. They ranged in age from eighteen to their mid-fifties and came from wealthy as well as poor families and from different ethnic backgrounds; some had children, some did not; some had high school educations, others had graduate degrees.[54] Interviewers spent hours with each woman, carefully listening to what she had to say about herself, what happened during the domestic violence incident that was reported to the police, what she was feeling, how other people reacted to the violence, whether her case was being prosecuted, where she lived, and more.

In the course of that study, we asked women about their feelings and thoughts—including alienation—using the measure we had developed earlier. In analyses conducted on my team with Ann Chu and Rheena Pineda, we discovered that women who felt more alienated also had more severe PSTD, depression, *and* dissociation symptoms.[55] Together, these symptoms make up a mix that would have been labeled hysterical by Charcot and Freud, yet we could account for it by taking measure of women's alienation from others. Since the Triage Project, this same pattern of alienation and psychological distress has shown up in study after study—among college students and older adults in the US, with trauma survivors in Northern Ireland and people diagnosed with dissociative disorders in the Netherlands.[56]

These studies of alienation reinforce the importance of thinking about interpersonal relationships when trying to understand the consequences of intimate violence. That's just what internationally recognized psychologist Jennifer Freyd did when she introduced the term "betrayal trauma" to describe abuse that is perpetrated by someone on whom the victim depends.[57] A robust literature now documents that betrayal traumas, such as intimate partner violence, are linked with worse psychological and physical health problems relative to other kinds of traumas.[58]

While betrayal can add to the harm of intimate violence, social connections can be critical to health and healing. For example, social support can play a protective role in decreasing PTSD symptoms after intimate violence.[59] In fact, social support may be particularly important after betrayal traumas.[60] Social support can come from friends and also from people in and around where we live, making the places where women live important also to understanding posttraumatic health.[61]

Taken together, research on alienation, betrayal trauma, and social support offer a resounding response to Freud's legacy: women's psychological responses to the trauma of violence should not be reduced to something about the women themselves. Rather, context matters: whether the violence was a betrayal by someone close, where women lived, and the quality of their connections to other people are all important to understanding the impact of intimate violence and working toward solutions together.

Brain Health

Hysterical women at the Salpêtrière complained of headaches, confusion, black-outs, and memory problems, and some went on to suffer seizures, depression, dementias, and suicidality. Their stories share an eerie similarity with those told on the pages of national media about athletes and combat veterans who have suffered traumatic brain injuries (TBIs). Profiles of football stars who died by suicide, struggled with depression, or developed neurological disorders after repeated blows to the head have left parents around the country wondering whether to sign their children up for football camp. Similar stories of debilitating symptoms have emerged from combat theaters where modern warfare has exposed soldiers to the impact of improvised explosive devices that rattle the brain.

That rattling can cause TBIs. TBIs happen when a blow to the head interrupts normal brain function. When the brain is injured, people lose consciousness, have memory loss for events immediately before or after the injury, or show neurologic deficits, such as muscle weakness or disrupted vision. They may have changes in mental state, such as not knowing their own names, where they are, the date, or who is the president.[62] The impact of head injuries can vary greatly across people and often be undetectable to observers. Many people who have a single TBI recover quickly without long-term consequences. Repeated and severe TBIs can be a different and more complicated story, though. People can suffer from a host of ills: poor overall physical health, problems paying attention or remembering information that gets in the way of school or work, difficulty managing the ups and downs of emotions, depression, and even suicidality.[63]

Around the time we started the Triage Project, I began to realize that some of the posttraumatic problems my team was studying—learning, memory, attention, and emotion regulation difficulties—might be caused by unrecognized TBIs. We tended to draw on *psychological* theories in our work, focusing on the impact that being betrayed might have on attention or emotions. Those theories are important to understanding the impacts of intimate violence, to be sure. However, looking back, I'm surprised at how long it took me and other trauma researchers to wonder about the impact of *physical* trauma to the head on women's health after intimate violence. Since then, I have come to think that head injuries are important to more than women's health alone. They are important to women's education, work, and even how they navigate complicated court systems to seek justice, as we'll look at in later chapters.

The Triage Project was the first time that my team started to screen for head injuries among the women interviewed. It's important here to note that women talked with us about domestic violence incidents that varied greatly in terms of physical violence. Some incidents involved life-threatening physical violence; others violations of protection orders and stalking—events that, in and of themselves, do not involve any physical injuries.[64] When 225 women told us about what happened during the incident that led to the police call, more than one in ten women reported being hit in the head or losing consciousness.[65] When we included the six months before that incident, 20% of women described head injuries arising out of a violent attack perpetrated by their intimate partners.

We also asked women about head injuries that might have happened at other times in their lives. Their answers startled us: 80% of women described head injuries at some point in their lives. More than half of women remembered a change in consciousness, such as blacking-out or being dazed and confused, which meant they met screening criteria for having a mild TBI. We recognized, though, that people who are hit in the head aren't always aware that they were dazed or blacked-out briefly. They might respond negatively to those questions, which would make us think they didn't actually have TBIs. Taking into account that we might, then, underestimate the seriousness of women's head injuries, we also asked women if they sought medical care. Another 12% of women who didn't remember changes in consciousness were concerned enough about their head injuries to seek medical help.

One issue that caught our attention was that all those lifetime head injuries were not necessarily due to incidents of domestic violence. We asked women to tell us the causes of all the head injuries they reported, which was often more than one. As we expected, a majority of women said at least one head injury was caused by violence that ranged from child and intimate partner abuse to other assaults. However, nearly a third of women also had head injuries caused by motor vehicle accidents. More than two-thirds had injuries arising from a different sort of accident, such as a fall or bike accident.

Since many women who had *just* been through domestic violence also reported histories of head injuries caused by something other than domestic violence, my collaborators and I started to wonder whether the consequences of head injuries are risk factors *for* abuse. Women with neuropsychological problems stemming from TBI, regardless of the source of injury, could be targeted by abusive people. After all, abusers would have good reason—and millennia of medical history—to think that women who seem confused or emotionally dysregulated when they disclose abuse will be written off as hysterical and not believed.

When I interviewed nine women who had just escaped sex trafficking, their reports of head injuries were even more startling. Eight of those women said they had been struck in the head at some point in their lives, some as recently as in the previous few weeks. They told me about multiple blows to the head that happened in their intimate relationships, during their sex work, when they were walking down alleys late at night and jumped by someone stealing their meager possessions. They all described losing consciousness or feeling dazed.[66] A similarly worrisome picture is emerging in our ongoing research with women seeking services after intimate partner abuse. In a research collaboration with psychologists Julia Dmitrieva and Kim Gorgens and community partners at the Rose Andom Center, TBIs are common. We're trying to understand how TBIs affect women's healthcare needs and access.[67]

A growing number of studies nationally reinforce what we have been learning in Denver. More than twenty studies have now documented shocking TBI rates among women after intimate partner abuse, ranging from a low of one in five women to three in four women.[68] As high as the estimates run, they are likely to underestimate the problem and impact of head injuries because the brain can also be damaged by strangulation. Sometimes mistakenly referred to as *choking* (which happens when something gets lodged in the throat), abusers who strangle their victims around the throat can cut off the flow of oxygen to the brain and cause significant tissue damage. The loss of oxygen can be so sudden that women may not be aware of what happened, such as whether they passed out or not. While early research suggests that strangulation is common in intimate partner abuse, researchers do not have a good sense yet of how frequently victims lose consciousness from strangulation or the impacts on brain health, in part because many TBI measures ask only about external blows to the head.[69] But screening for strangulation is important for more than understanding brain health: when abusive partners strangle their partners, the odds go up that they will eventually kill those women.[70]

Even when TBIs resolve relatively quickly, people can feel confused, have headaches, and experience memory problems. When TBIs are more complicated, though, a constellation of cognitive, emotional, and behavioral problems can interfere with many aspects of life. Imagine, for example, trying to access healthcare while struggling with TBI-related problems. Headaches and concentration difficulties might make figuring out how to schedule appointments or navigate insurance companies more of a challenge than usual. Memory problems might cause women to miss medical appointments. Shame or embarrassment at changes in mental abilities may lead women to hide their struggles from doctors. It's time to change how medical providers work with women after intimate violence to address these kinds of issues. Such changes would make navigating healthcare easier for all of us.

Adapting Healthcare Systems

When I show up at my doctor's office for routine gynecological care, a nurse checks my temperature and blood pressure before I go into the exam room. She points to a few questions, so as not to read out loud, that ask if I feel afraid at home. I shake my head no as she finishes taking my blood pressure and asks me to get on the scale. The nurse's question makes clear that healthcare professionals have a potential role to play in exposing and stemming violence against women. Yet I wonder how likely I would be to tell a nurse that I've never met before about abuse as the blood pressure cuff tightens around my arm. Thinking about the girls and women I've interviewed about abusive relationships, many of whom have never talked to anyone about what they survived, I suspect most of them would have said no, too.

Indeed, when asked questions about intimate violence during routine care, far fewer women say that they are being abused than are affected by violence. Given many false negatives in screening, the World Health Organization has raised concerns that asking all women about violence will leave health providers with the mistaken impression that violence isn't as common as it is—or isn't an issue for any particular patient who says no.[71] But it's not surprising that many women don't disclose when initially asked by providers—whether because of shame, self-blame, fear, and distrust, or because of *how* they're asked. Indeed, a major barrier to universal screening is that many healthcare providers haven't received training on how to ask about intimate partner violence and, in turn, how to respond when women do disclose.[72] This barrier is surmountable with education to prepare providers for conversations about intimate violence.[73] That's what sexual assault nurse examiners have shown in programs across the country where healthcare meets the criminal legal process.

Sometimes healthcare in the aftermath of intimate violence is also the start of a criminal legal process. Women's bodies may hold evidence about the assault, which can be critical to criminal legal responses. At the same time, women need healthcare and information. They may have injuries or questions about preventing pregnancy and sexually transmitted infections. They have also just been assaulted, so the administration of healthcare can be painful and confusing as well as evoke feelings of shame, embarrassment, and anxiety.

If a woman seeks medical care after an assault, she may be offered a forensic medical exam, providing what is commonly called a "rape kit." The advent of Sexual Assault Nurse Examiner (SANE) programs has helped victims to receive necessary and timely medical care while also preserving physical evidence. Biological evidence degrades rapidly, which means that women need supportive ways to learn about their options so that they can make informed choices about whether they'd like forensic evidence to be collected.

In SANE exams, a specially trained nurse collects biological specimens, takes photographs of the most private parts of a women's body, and documents the woman's own words to describe what happened to her. Nurse examiners facilitate the exam, helping women to have as much control over what is happening as possible at each step in a process that is deeply personal and invasive. Author and survivor Chanel Miller, in her memoir *Know My Name*, described the utter vulnerability she felt during this multihour forensic medical exam. And yet she recalled the profound care she also experienced, saying "the discomfort and fear are secondary. The primary feeling was warmth."[74]

With a clear chain of custody, the evidence that nurses collect can potentially be used in prosecution. This means that nurse examiners span systems, playing a critical role in providing healthcare while also doing work that is essential to any criminal legal response. Importantly, the nurse examiner is trained to bring a victim-focused, trauma-informed approach to a woman's care in the aftermath of violence. They are also often the first people to give victims information about resources and options. In many communities, nurse examiners work closely with victim advocates from community-based agencies who can support women as they make potentially life-altering decisions about reporting to law enforcement, prophylactic drugs for HIV, and disclosing the assault to friends and family.

In my home state of Colorado, nurse examiners help women understand their choices about what happens to the evidence collected in the rape kit. Women can report to law enforcement right away, often meeting with an officer right at the hospital. Or, they can choose to remain anonymous for the time being. In such instances, the evidence is preserved through an established chain of custody but not analyzed. The police do not learn women's names until and unless they decide to report. This anonymous option is critically important because women may not be able to make considered decisions about whether they want to proceed into the criminal legal system in the hours after an assault.[75]

Despite the critical role that SANE programs can play in the aftermath of sexual violence, access is a problem for many women. A 2020 investigative report by NBC News revealed that states vary greatly in how many SANE programs they have and where they are located, with particular gaps in rural areas. Imagine driving miles and miles after a rape just to access needed medical care. Even in urban areas, though, getting an exam can be difficult. NBC described one survivor's story of arriving at one hospital only to be told they didn't provide forensic medical exams. She had to make her way six miles across the city to another hospital to get an exam.[76]

Much can be learned from the SANE model about how healthcare systems can evolve. When survivors show up in healthcare settings, providers need to be ready. Training such as that which SANE examiners receive can equip providers to understand the consequences of violence on patients and take compassionate action. With training on how to respond to disclosures, healthcare systems have the potential to make a tremendous difference in identifying violence in the lives of their patients to improve short- and long-term care as well as help survivors access other resources that are critical to well-being, such as housing.[77] Recognizing this, some health systems and specialties have called for universal screening—that is, asking all women about violence during routine care. For example, the American College of Obstetricians and Gynecologists has recommended that all women be screened for intimate partner violence during routine care, and the Affordable Care Act included such screening and brief counseling among free preventative care services.[78]

Even if women do not disclose abuse, the act of *being asked* may still have an impact, even a life-saving one. During the Triage Project, we asked women if it was ok for victim advocates to call out of the blue to offer resources. Nearly every woman said that it was ok to call. One woman explained that she remembered getting just such a call from an advocate who left a message. She never called back, yet she said the call made her feel like she wasn't alone, that what had happened to her mattered, and that she lived in a community that cared. All that gave her hope and helped her cope, she said. Plus, now she knew where to call if she decided to reach for help down the road. In the same way that healthcare workers have started to routinely ask about violence, victim service providers begin a process of educating women that violence is not taboo or uncommon, someone is concerned that it might be happening, and resources are available if and when they want to talk. In this way, they can open the door for women to disclose later while reducing women's feelings of alienation in the short term.

Healthcare providers also have the potential to make a difference in preventing violence from happening in the first place. Consider, for example, nurse-visitor programs, which have been incredibly successful at supporting new parents with home visits from nurses after a baby is born. These programs take healthcare out of the office and into living rooms, which shows families that they aren't alone and brings resources right to their homes. The payoff is tremendous: home-visitor programs have been shown to decrease not only child maltreatment, but also intimate partner violence.[79]

It's time to apply what has been learned from these life-saving programs to preventing violence against women more broadly. In my own community in Denver, I think about how some public libraries now have social workers on staff because patrons come into libraries looking for more than books.

Sometimes they seek shelter from the cold or food or help with a resume or a computer connection to apply for a job. Together, perhaps we can imagine new ways for healthcare providers to connect with our neighbors to bring education and interventions that disrupt violence against women to whole communities, through libraries and community centers, coffee shops and places of worship.

Of course, funding innovations such as this would take an act of public will. Ordinary people paying taxes or fees through local governments would have to see that they benefit from supporting such programs, the stake that we all have in preventing violence against women.

Our Shared Interest

The idea that victimization is *both* a physical and psychological threat is one of the important discoveries of recent decades—and should be a driving force in pointing our attention to violence against women as a major health risk and a cause of exorbitant healthcare costs in the US. In the face of stressors, our nervous, endocrine, and immune systems all amp up to respond and adapt to challenges that confront us.[80] However, these systems evolved to help us maintain our health in response to short-term stresses. They did not evolve to manage the *chronic* stress that is often characteristic of violence against women—violence that happens over months and years of a relationship or the stress caused each time a survivor vividly remembers and feels as if she's reliving a sexual assault. That chronic stress takes a toll on health.

The price tag for medical care following sexual and physical violence is jaw-dropping. One of the earliest comprehensive cost estimates comes from the CDC, which, in 1995, set out to calculate the costs for direct medical services and lost productivity in the aftermath of violence against women.[81] The CDC estimated that more than 220,000 women were raped by intimate partners in a single year, approximately 1.3 million women were physically assaulted, and a half million women were stalked by intimate partners. From surveys with more than 8,000 women, they learned that about one-third of who were raped and one-third of those who were physically assaulted used some medical care. Most frequently, that care was delivered at the hospital. Some had multiple medical care visits in the aftermath of the victimization. From the survey results, the CDC estimated that physical and mental health-care resulting from victimization cost $4.1 billion dollars in 1995, which is about $6.7 billion today. In the twelve months after intimate partner violence, other researchers have estimated that healthcare costs run up to $7.0 billion.[82]

Since that seminal study, another CDC-led team has estimated lifetime health costs of intimate violence. In 2012, they conducted a national survey on intimate partner sexual assault, physical assault, and stalking to estimate how many women and men were victims. From other research, they estimated the probability that survivors would suffer a range of health issues, from rape-related pregnancies and alcohol abuse to heart disease and gastrointestinal problems. When they tallied the likely medical costs over survivors' lifetimes, the total was $2.1 trillion. The estimated cost for each woman was $65,165, fourteen times men's healthcare costs after intimate violence.[83]

Those billions of dollars annually and trillions of dollars over survivors' lifetimes have an impact on the cost of healthcare for all of us. Looking within a single healthcare plan, researchers calculated the costs of care for women victimized by their partners relative to other women. Among more than 3,000 women, those who were physically abused used more emergency, hospital outpatient care, primary care, pharmacy, and specialty services—especially if the abuse was ongoing. The higher costs weren't just for emergency or gynecological care. Rather, costs were higher across a broad range of services, from primary care, pharmacy, specialty, laboratory, radiology, and mental health services.[84]

Drilling down into a single healthcare provider system reveals a similarly pricy picture. Women abused in the past year faced costs that were more than *twice* that of other women. Those higher costs persisted over years because the health consequences of violence are not neatly resolved in a few months. Women who had histories of physical, sexual, and emotional abuse faced healthcare costs of $1,700 more than other women. Those higher costs came from services that spanned neurologic symptoms, injuries, and mental health.[85]

Reining in healthcare costs in the US will require stopping violence against women. Ensuring access to healthcare for all people, including reproductive healthcare, will require addressing the effects of violence against women. Failure to do so means that women will continue to bear the individual burden of physical and psychological consequences that affect their health—from gastrointestinal problems and pain to reproductive consequences and TBIs. Women from poor backgrounds and

Women of Color will pay an even higher price than White women and wealthier women.

Evolving healthcare systems to be responsive to the particular needs of survivors promises to improve care for everyone. For example, healthcare in the US is challenging on the very best of days. Patients have to figure out how to make appointments, find the physical location of offices, manage referrals, and decode insurance plans. All of those steps require significant focus, attention, and emotional wherewithal. Unfortunately, the health consequences of violence—from depression to TBIs—undermine women's ability to do what's required to get in the door. By reforming these access issues to care to be responsive to survivors' needs, we can make access easier for everyone.

Once survivors secure appointments, being touched and examined by providers can be emotionally triggering. Tolerating the stress of health visits and regulating emotions, in turn, can make it difficult for women to track and retain information—like instructions for follow-up care. SANE programs offer evidence, though, that healthcare professionals can incorporate trauma-informed practices and principles to understand and support women with histories of violence as they balance doing what is medically necessary with a host of competing demands and goals—providing information, empowering women, and facilitating their steps toward wellness. Orienting care to the emotional and cognitive challenges that victims face may inspire a roadmap to reforming and improving healthcare in the US for all of us.

And it may require greater empathy and understanding from all of us, which became clear to me when I led a focus group of women who had escaped sex traffickers. I was there to learn about the kinds of legal needs women had when trying to rebuild their lives. A woman not much older than me started telling a story about her dental problems, including how long she had waited to get to a dentist and how much harder it was to find ways to pay for dental care compared to other medical care. As her story unfolded, I remember thinking, we've got to get back to the point here—legal issues. I tried to gently redirect the focus of the conversation, to which she turned to me and demanded: "I *am* talking about legal needs. How am I supposed to go in front of a judge and be taken seriously without front teeth?"

And so my education about the ways that violence against women and health connected to myriad other issues continued—including issues that stoke national passions, such as gun violence.

2

When Gun Violence Is Gendered Violence

Most of us recognize that feeling when the news breaks: another shooting, another intake of breath as we map the location of the shooting to places where we have known someone, once lived, or live now. In 1998, not long after the country was trying to understand what had happened at Columbine High School, I was a graduate student in Eugene, Oregon, when a young man killed his parents and then opened fire at his school in the neighboring town.

By 2012, I lived in Denver, a stone's throw from Aurora, Colorado, when another young man murdered 12 people and injured 60 others at a movie theater in the middle of the night. My six-year-old next-door neighbor banged on my door the next morning in tears, telling me she was sure the little girl down the street was hurt in the shooting because her family wasn't answering the door. "You're banging on doors early in the morning," I told her, "and people are still asleep. I'm sure everything is okay." My reassurances were wrong. The little girl was dead and her mother grievously injured.

In 2016, a man opened fire at the Pulse nightclub in Orlando as I visited friends back in Oregon. We sat in stony silence scrolling as the morning news reports broke, each of us running through our own memories of LGBTQ spaces that had been our refuges for a few hours of dancing and laughter. In the morning quiet, those spaces didn't seem like ours anymore.

In November 2018, news broke that a man had barged into a yoga studio in Tallahassee Florida, with a gun, and my stomach dropped. My sister-in-law took yoga classes in Tallahassee now and then. A call, a text later, and I knew she was not at class that day. She was fine. The relief I felt was tainted by the unearned privilege that the murdered did not include my loved one. But someone's loved one died that day when the shooter killed two women and injured others. Another pin in a map, another community terrorized by mass gun violence, another set of families left to grieve.

In March 2021, it was a friend texting me to ask, "You didn't go grocery shopping today in Boulder, did you?"

We all know the script by now: pundits describe these killings as tragic and senseless. Politicians call for thoughts and prayers, but say now is not the time to talk politics. The platitudes whitewash a disturbing, consistent pattern: when men walk into yoga studios, nightclubs, concert venues, malls, and military complexes to open fire, there is—more often than not—a link to violence against women.

That's what policy expert April Zeoli and graduate student Jennifer Paruk discovered when they examined the backgrounds of eighty-nine shooters who killed four or more people in mass shootings between 2014 and 2017. Almost a third (31%) had histories indicative of perpetrating domestic violence, such as a history of domestic violence restraining orders, charges, and/ or convictions.[1] Their research was in line with a database of dozens of mass shootings that had resulted in at least three deaths since 2011, compiled by *Mother Jones* in 2019.[2] That database revealed that more than a third of those shootings were carried out by men who were targeting women or who had histories of domestic violence, stalking, or harassment. A subset of the men called themselves "incels." Incels blame women for so-called involuntary celibacy and tend to espouse violent and misogynistic views.[3]

In sorting through the many mass shootings that have happed in the US, we might be tempted to try to distinguish mass shootings in malls, yoga studios, and places of worship from school shootings; however, they are one and the same in terms of the inextricable links to violence against girls and women. Consider the twenty-year-old gunman who killed his mother before walking into Sandy Hook Elementary and killing twenty children and six adults in 2012 as the nation looked on in horror.[4] Seven years later, a twenty-four-year-old man killed nine people and wounded seventeen others at a bar in Dayton Ohio. He was already known by high school for his violent aspirations: he had hit lists targeting peers for rape and murder.[5]

Even teenagers who murder their peers with guns show this pattern of hostility to girls and women. The teenage boy who killed seventeen people at Stoneman Douglas High School in Florida in 2019 had been expelled after threatening to kill his ex-girlfriend and fighting with her new boyfriend, according to news reports.[6] When a seventeen-year-old adolescent boy opened fire at Santa Fe High School, in Texas, in May 2018, one of the ten people he killed was a girl who had rejected him.[7] Girls should not be dying for saying no to boys, yet they are—and so are those who happen to be near them in hallways and classrooms.

Today's young people have grown up with a new normal: active shooter drills, huddling together as friends bleed out, and watching the fortification of their schools. After each mass shooting, students, parents, and neighbors call for common sense gun laws while pundits and legislators distract us with talk of mental illness and catchy phrases about people killing people, not guns. Relatively lost in the din of the well-practiced post-shooting punditry is a path forward: if we want to stop mass shootings—whether in schools or yoga studios—we have a stake in working together to stop violence against women.

Femicide, American Style

Across regions around the globe, the number of women dying at the hands of intimate partners is on the rise.[8] This is true in America, too, though guns play an outsized role here in homicides generally and women's murders by intimate partners specifically: as gun deaths increased in the US from 2015 to 2017, women were the disproportionate victims, often at the hands of current or former intimate partners.[9]

An important aspect of American femicide is the sheer availability of guns in the US. Researchers have looked at gun availability using different kinds of metrics, from the number of gun owners and federally licensed dealers to indicators of illegal gun markets. Across metrics, more gun availability corresponds to more women murdered by intimate partners. For example, women are more likely to die at the hands of someone they know in states with greater proportions of gun owners.[10] In another study of gun availability, intimate partner homicides across 286 US cities were linked with the number of federally licensed firearm dealers. More legal gun dealers corresponded with more intimate partner homicides, even when taking into account the availability of *illegal* guns.[11] Once acquired, guns in the home significantly increase the risk that women will be killed by their intimate partners.[12]

Long before they kill their partners, though, abusers use guns to coerce and control, to make women feel vulnerable. By one estimate, 4.5 million women have had partners threaten them with guns.[13] To understand more about these kinds of threats, domestic violence researchers Kellie Lynch and T. K. Logan asked more than forty women about their abusers' use of guns. Women explained over and over to the researchers that abusive partners used guns to threaten and have power over them. One woman described, "If you've got a gun pointed to you and he's telling you you're going to do this or else, chances are you're going to do it. And he knows that." Another survivor described that verbal threats aren't even necessary when a gun is present because the threat that he is going to use the gun on you is there "at any time."[14]

After news of shootings break, we've become used to hearing gun advocates say that the answer is to train more people to use guns so that they can defend themselves. The women who talked to Lynch and Logan knew better, saying time and again that bringing a gun into their homes for their own protection would only put them in more danger or increase the risk that they would accidently or intentionally kill their abusers. They didn't want to kill their abusive partners, but also worried about their own survival. As one woman told the researchers, "You're going to end up dead or in prison."[15]

The experiences described by the women in those focus groups matched large-scale studies that combed through tens of thousands of police reports. University of Pennsylvania researcher Susan Sorenson looked at police reports for more than 35,000 domestic violence incidents in Philadelphia and found that more than 500 (1.6%) reports involved a gun.[16] Abusers used guns to threaten or intimidate their victims, often in the absence of physical aggression or injuries. Though injuries were less likely when incidents involved guns, victims were more likely to be afraid.

Removing guns from people who abuse women is necessary if you want to prevent women from dying because their partners shoot them. That's what researcher April Zeoli and colleagues discovered when they looked at data on intimate partner homicides over more than twenty years (1979–2003) from forty-six US cities. They evaluated the impact of laws that reduced gun access for people under domestic violence restraining orders or convicted of domestic violence offenses as well as those that allowed law enforcement to remove guns from domestic violence crime scenes. They found that those laws mattered for decreasing intimate partner homicide rates over time.[17]

However, other research highlights how pernicious and complicated domestic violence intervention can be when it comes to guns. Turning again to research by Sorenson's team on domestic violence reports in Philadelphia, the research team tracked cases where guns were removed from the home compared to other cases. When guns were removed, the odds of a subsequent police report for domestic violence went up considerably.[18]

A few things could be going on here, as Sorenson's team explained. Victims who have a positive experience when the police respond may be more likely to call the police again when violence continues. For example, the police who showed up, listened, and believed women and then removed the weapons. In such instances, removing guns might not change the risk of violence without that weapon; rather, the successful police interaction opens the doors wider for women to see the police as a resource. Alternatively, when men who used guns to coerce and control victims no longer have those weapons available, they may become more physically aggressive, leading to more incidents reported to the police. This explanation certainly fits with what women in Lynch and Logan's focus groups described—that abusers threatened to get their guns or brandished them as a means of coercion and control.[19]

If a policy has the risk of increasing physical violence, we might be tempted to avoid that particular policy. However, in this case, concluding that guns should *not* be removed from abusers would be an unfortunate take-away. Instead, policies must recognize that domestic violence is complicated, and removing guns can only ever be one part of larger, coordinated efforts to prevent and respond to violence against women.

Of Guns and Laws

According to federal law, a person cannot possess a firearm or ammunition after conviction for a felony or a misdemeanor domestic violence offense or once certain types of domestic violence protection orders have been entered against them.[20] As we'll review in Chapter 6, though, there are numerous reasons that women who are being abused by intimate partners may never request a restraining order or report domestic violence to the police. The people abusing those women will be able to continue to legally acquire guns.

For the smaller subset of domestic violence incidents that lead to a qualifying domestic violence restraining order or domestic violence conviction, there's still a high likelihood that abusers can acquire guns. Federal enforcement of gun restrictions related to domestic violence has been limited, driving more than twenty states to enact their own laws prohibiting possession, laws that can be enforced locally.[21] Nonetheless, loopholes remain that threaten the lives of women and our communities when intimate violence becomes mass violence. For example, background check requirements that could flag domestic violence offenses apply only to federally licensed gun dealers. People can avoid background checks by purchasing weapons from private dealers or at gun shows instead of from licensed gun dealers.[22]

The so-called *boyfriend loophole* is another problem. Federal laws on domestic violence gun restrictions do not apply to convicted abusers who dated but did not live with or have children with their victims.[23] Sorenson's work in Philadelphia shows why the boyfriend loophole is such a big deal. Out of more than 30,000 reports of intimate partner violence to the police, the majority (>80%) involved boyfriends and girlfriends—that is, people who weren't married and didn't necessarily live together.[24]

In 2019, the Republican-controlled Senate had their chance to take action to close the boyfriend loophole by taking up a House of Representatives version of a bill to reauthorize the VAWA. Closing the boyfriend loophole would have extended existing federal law to keep guns away from people convicted of domestic violence before they kill their dating partners and go on to become mass shooters. The reauthorization bill would have also chipped away at other long-standing problems separate from guns, such as accountability for non-Native people who abuse Native women on tribal lands. The Senate, however, failed to take up VAWA's reauthorization, calling for a "clean" reauthorization that did not expand the law at all.[25] Yet every reauthorization since the original bill was passed in 1994 included provisions to evolve the law as our national understanding of the realities of violence against women also evolved, making the call for a clean bill particularly disingenuous.

The call for a clean bill also ignored evidence that the kinds of changes proposed in the 2019 VAWA reauthorization would save lives. That evidence comes from research into the impact of two kinds of laws passed by several states. The first are *relinquishment laws*. While federal (and some state) laws prohibit some people convicted of domestic violence offenses from possessing weapons, that focuses on their *acquisition* of new firearms. Those individuals aren't necessarily required to surrender guns already in their possession. Relinquishment laws, then, have been passed by states to alert people convicted of domestic violence offenses that they are required to surrender their weapons for a defined period of time. By 2014, eleven states had passed relinquishment measures, with evidence suggesting those measures save lives.[26] A team of public health researchers compared rates of intimate partner homicide across states, looking at the particular configuration of laws in each state. The researchers discovered that states without relinquishment laws saw slower declines in homicide rates from 2005 to 2013 and *increases* from 2013 to 2015. Next door, states with relinquishment laws continued to see decreases in the number of murdered partners through 2015. The researchers estimated that relinquishment laws in those eleven states probably saved seventy-five lives in 2015 alone.[27]

The second set of laws are often referred to as *red-flag* laws. Passed by at least seventeen states and the District of Columbia, these laws give law enforcement a way to remove guns temporarily from people at significant risk of harming themselves or others. Such laws help entire communities, including families at risk of losing loved ones to deaths by gun suicide. Take Connecticut as an example. That state passed the first red flag law in 1999, which was called a *risk-warrant law*. Over the next fourteen years, 762 guns were removed, primarily from men. Nearly one in five of those individuals later attempted suicide. Of those 142 people, 21 died by suicide, including 6 by guns, even though weapons had been removed. The majority, however, survived. The research team estimated that for every ten to twenty guns seized, one suicide was prevented.[28]

Preventing suicide takes on a different meaning in light of intimate partner murder-suicides, which are nearly universally carried out by men who kill their women partners (and sometimes children) before killing themselves.[29] When journalist Rachel Louise Snyder investigated just such a case, she discovered a host of missed opportunities to avoid the tragic shooting death of Michelle Monson and her two children. In *No Visible Bruises*, Snyder detailed Monson's murder, which had the hallmarks of what researchers have identified about murder-suicide in the US.[30] Murder-suicides are most often carried out by men who aim their guns at their current or ex-intimate partners before turning the firearms on themselves. Typically, the murder follows some episode that left men feeling jealous or abandoned.[31] Though women shouldn't die for men's jealousy, hundreds do each year in the US.

Trying to understand more about murder-suicides, a team of researchers tracked down news stories from across the US.[32] Among more than 700 murder-suicides cases identified in a six-year period, they discovered that women victims were divorced, separated, or in the process of leaving that abuser in almost 40% of cases. Their research echoes other findings about murder-suicides, pointing out the very real dangers women face when leaving abusers.[33] These dangers are important to keep in mind the next time you hear someone reduce domestic violence to an individual choice or problem, asking "why doesn't she just leave?" We, as a community, have to decide to do something about the life-threatening risk she faces if she does leave.

In the wake of the murders of women by their intimate partners, many communities across the country have established multidisciplinary groups, often referred to as *domestic violence fatality review committees*. These committees typically bring together representatives from the criminal legal and healthcare systems, as well as community-based organizations that serve victims along with other community leaders, such as faith leaders. When domestic violence ends in homicide, the committee members bring together all the information they can find on the case to try to learn where actions could have been taken to try to stop the violence. This is grim and necessary work if communities are going to improve their responses to domestic violence generally and save lives specifically.

Where I live in Colorado, the domestic violence fatality review committee looks in depth at domestic violence murders in our state. Their 2019 report reflected many of the things documented about intimate partner homicide in national research: Frequently, perpetrators were jealous, had histories of domestic violence, and had access to weapons. Their report also pointed toward avenues for prevention. For example, co-workers commonly knew about the violence, which we'll take up in Chapter 5 when we consider ways that workplaces can be part of prevention efforts. Their report also made the case for starting much earlier than when people go into the workforce. We should start, they said, by preventing adolescent dating violence.[34]

Transforming Helplessness into Prevention

In February 2020, the two largest teachers' unions partnered with Everytown for Gun Safety to call for ending active shooter drills. A chorus of voices at the time argued that the drills terrified students, particularly when exercises simulated violence or were unannounced. As schools' investments in security continued to rise, Shannon Watts from Moms Demand Action for Gun Safety, argued for investments in prevention.[35] Assault simulations and dollars spent fortifying schools do not get to the root causes of school and other mass shootings.

There are many root causes of gun violence, including access to weapons. Another root cause is one that we're well equipped to address: rigid notions about gender and masculinity.

Traditional gender roles dictate that men should be dominant and powerful, women submissive. In the 1980s, researchers started measuring the stress that not living up to these rigid notions about gender causes some men.[36] That stress, it turns out, endangers women and communities. The more stress that men feel when gender norms are violated, the more they think that intimate partner violence is acceptable.[37] Even worse than just *thinking* that intimate partner abuse is okay, rigid gender views are linked with acting violently against women.[38]

The links between gender views and violence against women were clear when a team of researchers surveyed men arrested for domestic violence.[39] The researchers found that the stress men felt from violating traditional gender norms was linked with their reports of violence against their partners. There were other patterns detected by the researchers. For example, men who felt physically inadequate were more sexually aggressive against their partners, whereas those who felt intellectually inferior were more likely to have injured their partners.

The connections between gender views and violence show up in boys as well. Heather McCauley, a nationally recognized researcher from Michigan State University, led a team that examined views of gender equity among 1,699 boys who were athletes enrolled in a Coaching Boys into Men program. Nearly one in five boys (16%) reported perpetrating abuse, either physical, sexual, or emotional, on their dating partners in the previous three months alone. But the boys who had more equitable views of gender were less likely to describe abusing their partners.[40]

The good news is that there are effective tools for helping young people explore gender roles and relationship health. Often those tools come packaged as adolescent dating violence prevention programs, which research has shown have a positive impact on adolescents' beliefs about intimate partner violence and their own aggressive behaviors.[41] Consider the success of a program called Coaching Boys into Men. This program engages athletic coaches to be part of socializing boys and young men into more equitable views of gender. Boys who were athletes in schools that used the Coaching Boys into Men curriculum were less likely to abuse their dating partners compared to boys at other schools.[42]

Other programs that teach about healthy relationships and address gender also show terrific potential. For example, the Fourth R curriculum is integrated into health and physical education classes, adding relationship education into existing school programming. The relationship education components tackle issues of gender norms and behaviors, splitting girls and boys into different groups for discussion. This intervention decreased physical dating violence years later. Safe Dates is an interactive curriculum that engages the whole school community. The curriculum, which has been tested with eighth and ninth graders, tackles gender and dating norms, among other issues. Those tests show good evidence that Safe Dates reduces sexual and physical dating violence, including severe physical violence, also years later.[43]

Recent research hints at promising approaches for transforming boys' views of gender as early as in the middle school years. That's important because by middle school, boys are already well on their way to developing their notions of masculinity, and dating violence is already common.[44]

Healthy relationship and dating violence prevention are frequently integrated into schools.[45] Yet not all schools have the financial resources to offer high-quality programming to students. And not all youth attend traditional schools, such as many of the girls our team met through the Healthy Adolescent Research Project. Truly universal relationship education will require leveraging schools *and* other settings—faith communities, medical offices, and libraries for example. Maybe you know just the organization to bring these prevention efforts to your town. Or maybe you know just the space where people can convene to work on prevention. After all, this is your cause, too.

Finding Common Cause

There's a feeling of helplessness that comes with the veiled threat of gun violence, as I learned one day during the Triage Project. A graduate student researcher from my team called my cellphone during a block of time when I knew she had an interview, which signaled that this was some sort of urgent matter. When I picked up, she asked if I would come over to our research offices to join her in walking the woman she had just interviewed out to the street to meet her ride. "Of course," I said. "But why?"

The grad student—in the same pressured speech I imagine the participant herself used—began to explain that the woman's abusive partner was picking her up and that he often, but not always, kept a gun in the car. The woman reassured the grad student that he *probably* wouldn't be in a bad mood when he picked her up, so it would *probably* all be fine—and the grad student tried assuring me of the same. "But still," she asked, "can you come with us?" "Of course," I said again, with more ease and confidence than I felt.

So there we were: a psychology professor, a grad student, and a woman who had survived a beating days earlier. There was no imminent threat, but reason to be fearful. We had no reason good enough to break research confidentiality, so no one to call for help. Our only option was to press on, as so many women do every night. We walked in fear to a nondescript car as the rest of the world passed us by unknowingly.

None of us got shot that day, but I have learned that that feeling of helplessness doesn't have to be where things end. Instead, we can discover networks and communities of people who share interests with us, including a commitment to action. John Feinblatt, President of Everytown for Gun Safety, gave voice to our common cause this way: "You can't reduce violence against American women without also reducing gun violence—women in the US are twenty-one times more likely to be killed with a gun than women in other high-income countries."[46]

In recent years, ordinary citizens concerned with the dangers of guns in our communities have built up networks from coast to coast through organizations such as Everytown for Gun Safety to Moms Demand Action. They're not alone. Local officials have banded together in groups such as Mayors Against Illegal Guns. Volunteers put hours into phone banks to back electing officials who will vote for gun reform to save lives. Their work is inseparable from the work to end violence against women so that children can safely go to school and families to malls and places of worship.

Persuading elected officials to pass laws is important, but we have more options and more work to do. Once laws are passed, communities need resources to implement those laws. Colorado passed a red flag law in 2019. The next year, Denver made the news when they hired a full-time investigator dedicated to reviewing domestic violence cases to identify when abusers have guns.[47] Additional staffing, such as that investigator, will be necessary if prosecutors are going to have the information they need to go to judges to ask that the guns be temporarily removed in line with the law.

Relying on the criminal legal system alone to mitigate the links between gun violence and violence against women is just too late, though. It's also often fraught for People of Color, where a knock on the door or a traffic stop to ask about a gun carries different risks than for White families.

We need a different path, then, that heads things off long before that knock on the door. We share interests with gun reformers and prison abolitionists, with criminal justice reformers and police unions, in going upstream to stop gendered violence before it begins. In doing so, we have the potential to reduce the number of people (mostly men) who buy weapons to coerce and control intimate partners and who turn those weapons on their communities in malls, parking lots, schools, and places of worship.

We share an interest in getting relationship education that focuses on healthy gender development into schools and community settings as early as possible—and certainly no later than the middle school years. When we go upstream to change things before problems emerge, we're doing what health experts call *primary prevention*. In this case, primary prevention of gun violence means teaching boys and men that they have options for healthy, full lives that don't involve being trapped into dominating others. Offering boys and men the freedom to radically accept who they are instead of trying to live up to rigid notions of masculinity is a powerful intervention—one that just may save our lives.

Primary prevention, whether through relationship education or limiting availability of guns for use in intimate violence, will require political will and resources. The political will part is clear given the relative failure of meaningful federal gun law reform, let alone the reauthorization of VAWA. Even wading into seemingly less political waters to expand prevention programming education will require coalitions to agitate for money, time, and even space, whether through libraries and community centers, religious organizations and workplaces, or schools. And of course, there's sure to be resistance to programs for youth that focus on more flexible, less rigid and traditional gender roles as well as healthy relationships, particularly in today's divisive political environment where there's often controversy over what youth should be learning in the K–12 years.

One way to help people see their stake in prevention efforts with youth may be to show how the harms caused by gun violence ripple out to affect even those who were not in the direct line of fire. That's what researchers found in Texas when they compared data from students who attended schools where shootings had occurred to students from similar schools without shootings.[48] Students in the schools where shootings occurred were significantly more likely than peers at similar schools to be chronically absent and repeat a grade over a two-year period. That wasn't all. The impact of the shooting rippled out to negatively affect graduation rates, college attendance, and even their incomes in their mid-twenties.

Unfortunately, school shootings are not the only way that violence against women has an impact on education. Across development—from the earliest school years to high school and college—the trauma consequences of witnessing intimate violence or being victimized affect learning and education outcomes. Out of that dire situation, we have a chance to expand the coalition of people whose passions about education would be served by ending violence against women; for restoring and ensuring dignity, fairness, opportunity, and safety to our communities.

3

Lessons in Intimate Violence

I made my way from a downtown conference hotel to a park on the edge of East Chicago in the cold with thousands of people—young and old; Brown, Black, and White; all genders—for the student-organized 2018 March for Our Lives. On that overcast March morning, youth got up one by one and looked out at the crowd as they made the case for gun reform. They talked about violence in their schools and on the streets, and also in their homes. They told us about witnessing domestic violence and their victimization in dating relationships.

I had steeled myself for these sorts of stories—the ones that are so like what my research team hears from survivors. Stories of love and lives cut short, opportunities lost, indignities endured, holes in our social fabric. That particular day, however, hearing young people's modest ask jarred me: "We need counselors," they told us, speaker after speaker.

I stood in the cold trying to figure out why *that* was the thing that got to me out of everything else in their impassioned speeches. I had not prepared myself for the simplicity and indignity of a situation in which adolescents had to take to a stage in a park in the freezing Chicago winter to tell grownups that their mental health mattered for their learning. In hindsight, I realized what shook me was the collective failure in a situation where there was such collective possibility. We were teaching the wrong lessons, again.

After all, the students had it right: from coast to coast, schools have overwhelmingly failed to provide enough school counselors and psychologists.[1] Only about half of schools in the US have the one full-time registered nurse recommended by the American Academy of Pediatrics, and nearly a third of schools have no nurses on site to address students' needs.[2] Equipping schools with counselors and nurses isn't a wonky policy issue, nor is it an outrageous expense relative to installing metal detectors and paying for off-duty police officers to patrol school hallways.

The kinds of changes that young people called for that day have the potential to connect lots of our self-interests. From policy-makers, educators, and employers who see education access and success as among the most pressing issues of our time; to parents who want the best for their children's education, including being safe in high school cafeterias and college dorm rooms; and civic leaders who want to engage young people in the work of democracy.

Those collective self-interests run through violence against women, which is tangled up with education access and success at the roots of a host of social problems. The trauma of witnessing intimate partner violence and being victimized in dating relationships can affect the brain and body in ways that disrupt learning for victims *and* for the students sharing the same classrooms and hallways. When violence against women disrupts individual learning, students can't achieve to their potential and communities lose out on what they might otherwise have brought to offices, neighborhoods, and town halls. Tolerating harmful attitudes about violence and violent behaviors teaches the wrong lessons, ripping at the fabric of communities.[3]

If we can get a handle on the insidious ways that violence against women seeps into education systems through its emotional, cognitive, and behavioral consequences, we'll have a roadmap for taking steps to help *all* students. We'll also have a set of lessons that can help us make sense of the impact of violence against women later in life, from workplaces to legal proceedings. Those lessons give us a chance to answer the students who called on us to do better from the Chicago stage.

Witnessing Violence Against Women in Kitchens Matters for Classrooms

Early one rainy morning, I was scanning news headlines over a pot of tea when a smiling face looked out at me under a dystopian headline: "School Principal Was Victim in Apparent Murder-Suicide."[4] The article reported that the husband was suspected of killing her and then himself. The story assured readers, though, that the children, home at the time of the shooting, were not physically harmed.

The children may not have suffered bruises or gunshot wounds, but the traumatic stress of witnessing domestic violence can impact children's developing brains and the body's stress response systems without leaving outward physical signs. And, unfortunately, witnessing domestic violence is all too common among youth in the US.

When researchers asked more than 3,600 adolescents if they had seen or overheard physical violence between their parents, nearly one in ten (7.9%)

said yes. The physical violence that they witnessed was serious: punching or hitting with a fist, kicking hard, strangling, beating up, hitting with an object, or threatening with a weapon. Most often, the perpetrators of that violence were fathers or father-figures.[5]

Of course, people of any gender can be abused or perpetrate abuse in intimate relationships, and witnessing that violence can be a traumatic stressor for children regardless of the parent's gender. However, children are more likely to see or overhear women be victimized and injured, including serious injuries, than men.[6] In turn, witnessing domestic violence tends to coincide with children being victimized or exposed to other kinds of trauma themselves.[7]

The traumatic stress of witnessing domestic violence can lead to a cascade of stress-related impacts on the brain and behavior that disrupt learning, whether that learning is focused on reading in elementary school or philosophy in college. Those disruptions have the potential for lifetime consequences: researchers estimate that witnessing intimate partner violence costs children tens of thousands of dollars in lost productivity in adulthood because of impacts on education.[8]

However, domestic violence does more than impact individual student learning. When children witness domestic violence in kitchens and living rooms, the consequences ripple out to classrooms and communities. Understanding *how* witnessing domestic violence can affect individual learners and classrooms requires taking a step back to consider all that goes into learning.

Children learning their multiplication tables in grade school have to do far more than memorize some numbers. For example, children have to shift their attention away from the reading lesson that happened earlier to start focusing on math. Then they have to stay focused on math, *not* thinking about recess, which is in 45 minutes; *not* thinking about how they can't remember what 45 minutes looks like on the clock face or that there is a bug buzzing by the clock right this second. Oh, right, focus. Then their brains have to begin the long haul of laying down memories, the process for which will run long into the night while they sleep. They have to retrieve old memories, too, recalling one plus one, for example. They also have to keep exerting control over their bodies to sit still until the moment when the teacher tells them to grab the blocks they need for this lesson. Then their brains have to signal their bodies to initiate action, but not *too* much action. Once they have the blocks and a crayon to write down the answer (using their fine motor skills to pick up the crayon and write), they cannot take their actions too far. They absolutely cannot write on their neighbor's worksheet, pants, or desk. All the while, they also have to watch for social and emotional cues from their peers and the teachers to figure out what they feel and how they're *supposed* to react if they don't know the answer; and how to respond when they figure out the answer. They have to learn that there is a sweet spot where they can be excited, but not jerks, when they achieve something.

The good news is that the brain has all this covered. Human biological systems come ready for rapid development so that infants who are utterly dependent on caregivers in their first months of life can become relatively independent adolescents in a matter of years. From birth on, the human biological system is oriented toward figuring out how to navigate the world—physically, emotionally, cognitively, and behaviorally. This covers ABCs and 123s as well as how to be a good friend, self-aware, handle conflict, and manage difficult emotions. However, these systems can get knocked off course by witnessing violence, particularly when violence is repeated, as is often the case in violence against women. Some children then face a double challenge: the traumatic stress of witnessing violence as well as posttraumatic psychological symptoms can both affect learning.

Witnessing violence against women, like other childhood trauma, can affect at least two major pathways in the brain that are important for succeeding in school and later in life.[9] The first is a stress pathway. When confronted with a stressor, stress hormones are released to prompt action across the body, affecting everything from how fast the heart beats and blood pumps to the speed of metabolism. During this biological response to stress, hormones called *glucocorticoids* bombard the hippocampus, an important structure in the brain for memory. Bombardment by glucocorticoids over time, as can happen with the chronic stress of domestic violence, can influence the overall structure and function of the hippocampus.

The hippocampus plays a central role in creating new memories and then accessing them. Memory is important to all that humans do—from remembering the autobiographical details of our lives to learning facts and figures in school. Children facing chronic family violence, though, are trying to learn at the same time that this sensitive region bears the burden of the body's biological stress response to that violence. The biological responses to stress are automatic, entirely outside the child's conscious control. Teachers cannot tell children to sit still and stop pumping glucocorticoids through their systems. Parents cannot will glucocorticoids into submission at homework time.

Glucocorticoids do what glucocorticoids do, with consequences for learning and memory when stress is chronic.

The second path involves brain regions that work together to identify and respond to emotions. Connections that feed back and forth between several brain regions allow people to figure out if a shadow in the room warrants a scream or a sigh. For example, the amygdala alerts the whole system when there is a potential threat, and then the prefrontal cortex makes decisions about whether the threat is real. The prefrontal cortex sends the amygdala signals to settle down when that shadow isn't really a threat.

Perhaps not surprising given the number of brain regions involved, growing evidence shows that childhood trauma affects both the physical structure of the brain and the way that brain networks work. For example, several brain regions are smaller in youth with PTSD relative to peers, such as the prefrontal cortex and hippcampus.[10] After traumas such as witnessing domestic violence, youth have trouble regulating emotions and frequently see threat where it may not be.[11] When youth are overly sensitive to potential threat cues, the whole world can seem dangerous. If the world seems dangerous even when it isn't, children can have a hard time trying to learn in their classrooms or focus on their homework.

Disruptions in that emotional regulation network, particularly the prefrontal cortex, can also mean problems for attention. Attention is essential to academic learning as well as to complex social-emotional learning. In the school years, children have to learn how to build and maintain relationships with peers and adults as well as how to control their own behaviors. From the playground to group assignments, they have to figure out how to cooperate and manage conflict. These social tasks require children to think flexibly about their perspectives and others', about potential solutions to problems, all of which involves attention. These different kinds of attention skills are sometimes referred to together as *executive functions*. Executive functions tap a diverse set of abilities to shift, inhibit, and focus attention; maintain focus in the face of distracting information; update new information in the working memory system; think flexibly about potential solutions; and plan and initiate actions.

Several years ago, my research team looked at links between trauma and executive functions in the Children's Attention Research Project.[12] We welcomed more than 100 mothers and their school-aged children to our research offices, where we asked the children to play games that tested their executive functions. Meanwhile, their mothers filled out surveys next door, including questions about their children's exposure to trauma. We asked about different kinds of trauma, from witnessing or experiencing family violence to medical trauma, disasters, and car accidents. About a third of children hadn't experienced any trauma. Another third had witnessed domestic violence or been abused directly in family violence. Another third had experienced other kinds of non-family traumas, such as medical traumas, natural disasters, and car accidents.

We compared children's executive function performance based on their mothers' reports of children's trauma histories. Children's attention looked the same regardless of whether they were exposed to *no* trauma or traumas *outside* the family, such as natural disasters and car accidents. However, children exposed to family violence did significantly worse on the attention tasks compared to *both* groups. Since then, several other research teams have documented similar attention patterns after family violence.[13]

Witnessing violence against women can impact more than attention. The regions and pathways of the brain affected by trauma also play a role in how children (and adults) process and regulate emotions. During a single day of school, children face ups and downs, frustrations and excitement, situations that are clear (a bad grade on an assignment) and situations that are ambiguous (was that person making fun of me?). Children who have witnessed domestic violence or been directly abused can have difficulty navigating the emotions that arise from those ups and down, made worse by reminders of the trauma and ambiguous situations. Emotion reactions, especially when they are big and take a lot of time to wane, make learning difficult.[14]

On top of attention problems, children (and adults) commonly feel irritable as well as have problems with memory and sleep in the aftermath of traumas, including witnessing domestic violence. Feeling irritable or having intrusive memories of violence that happened a few days before can make it difficult for children to tolerate sitting in classrooms. Feelings of sadness or helplessness, stomachaches and headaches, and feeling physically unwell may compete with math problems for children's attention.[15]

Given the many ways that trauma can affect the brain and emotion regulation, it's not surprising that children who witness domestic violence as well as those who are directly abused are at risk for worse school performance than other children. Relative to their peers, youth who have lived through such traumatic stresses have lower academic achievement.[16]

Untangling the particular impact that witnessing intimate partner violence has relative to other forms of trauma and adversity has been challenging for researchers because these things often occur together. However, one research team went a long way toward parsing these influences in a study of academic outcomes among nearly 3,000 children. Using state child protection and education records, they identified four groups of children, ages seven to thirteen. Three of those groups had gone through child protection investigations that determined whether children had been abused, witnessed intimate partner violence, or both. A fourth group was comprised of children who came from similar backgrounds but who hadn't been involved in any child protection investigations. The children who had been abused, witnessed intimate partner violence, or both *all* had worse school attendance as well as lower math *and* reading achievement than the peers who came from similar backgrounds. Those who witnessed intimate partner violence had the worst attendance and achievement scores of the three child protection groups.[17]

Witnessing intimate partner violence is also linked to behaviors that psychologists refer to as *externalizing problems*—things like lying, aggression, hyperactivity, and bullying.[18] These behaviors make sense given the impacts of trauma on the brain and learning. For example, when children perceive ambiguous situations as threatening, they may be more likely to respond defensively, perhaps lashing out at or withdrawing from others. When they've learned from watching domestic violence that a way to solve conflicts is by being aggressive, they're more likely to treat their peers badly. When their attention and emotion regulation systems are dysregulated, they may squirm in their seats, be impulsive, and otherwise disrupt what's happening in the classroom.

Teachers, then, have to manage this constellation of trauma reactions in their classrooms. One child struggling with overwhelming anger or impulsive behavior can take a toll on the learning environment for everyone. And so the intimate partner violence that *one* child witnessed has the potential to quickly become an impediment to learning for *everyone* in the class.

Unfortunately, things can get worse for children when schools penalize these kinds of trauma responses. Since the 1990s, zero-tolerance policies have carved out well-worn paths to principals' offices across the country. Over thirty years, schools have seen increases in suspensions, expulsions, and juvenile justice referrals for student behaviors that range from disrespect and classroom disruption to violence. Despite promises that zero-tolerance policies would prevent violence, suspensions and expulsions have not made schools safer.[19] Instead, these policies have punished students for the kinds of dysregulated behaviors that arise from having witnessed intimate partner violence and being abused by other people without addressing or remedying that root cause. Thus, the policies punish youth for the reactions they have to violence and abuse perpetrated by other people, failing to restore or ensure dignity, fairness, opportunity, or safety.

Such policies have also stacked the deck against ethnic minority and low-income children who are more likely than peers to be exposed to multiple adversities.[20] Consider that schools expel Black girls and boys at rates exponentially higher than White peers, beginning as early as preschool and kindergarten.[21] Getting pulled out of class, suspended, or expelled means less instruction, time to learn, and access to education as well as more contact with the criminal legal system. A school-to-prison pipeline perpetuates racial injustices and the loss of human potential in our communities.

Zero-tolerance policies are all about punishment. From a behavioral perspective, punishment happens when we do something (such as yell) or take away something (such as playground privileges) to try to decrease an undesired behavior (a child speaking disrespectfully). Punishment is an incredibly ineffective way to try to change behavior, according to decades of research.[22] In part this is because yelling and skipped allowances do not teach children new skills or what to do *instead* of whatever they did to elicit the punishment.

And so schools face a bind where the consequences of witnessing domestic violence and other traumas in children's lives impact classrooms, but punishing those trauma-related behaviors disrupts education access for the children who most need support. This bind reminds me of the girls we met in the Healthy Adolescent Relationship Project. Many had been kicked out of neighborhood schools because of behavioral problems. Relocated to general education development (GED) or residential treatment programs, the girls no longer disrupted other students' learning in the neighborhood schools, but that wasn't really a solution when we take a long view. Some of those young people were already raising children. Fending for themselves and their children, they were likely to spend time living in poverty and at risk for revictimization, maybe by the same partners who sabotaged their birth control and got them pregnant or maybe by new partners. That adversity and the potential that their children will witness them being victimized puts their children at risk for problems, thus perpetuating the intergenerational transmission of trauma.[23] And so the violence endured by these adolescent girls that contributed to them getting kicked out of school will ultimately make its way back into those same school hallways through their children.

Recognizing the limits of zero-tolerance and punitive policies, some schools have started to refocus their attention on restorative justice approaches to children's problem behaviors. Restorative justice practices emphasize relationships among students, teachers, and administrators. When a child behaves badly, for example, their behavior is treated as a violation of relationships and thought about in terms of the harm caused. Responses, then, focus on what needs to be done to repair the harm. Thus, the individuals harmed, the child who caused harm, and the larger community are all involved in figuring out how to correct the harm. Relative to punishment, this value-focused, collaborative response to problem behaviors has much potential for restoring and ensuring dignity, fairness, opportunity, and safety. Restorative approaches have the potential to teach students critically important skills for navigating relationships and participating in communities for the rest of their lives.

Of course, such programs require that schools rework policies as well as invest in training and ongoing professional development for the staff who facilitate restorative justice responses. Facilitating restorative justice responses requires skill and time to do well and can be fraught with difficulties depending on what the problem behavior was. For example, victim advocates have had serious concerns about using restorative justice processes to respond to sexual harassment and dating violence, where victims might feel compelled to participate in processes that fail to meet their needs. Nonetheless, community models and research are continuously expanding, providing a foundation for the implementation of restorative justice programs that are survivor-centered and build on an understanding of intimate violence and its dynamics as well as consequences.[24]

In restorative justice models, there is potential for rethinking approaches that have the potential to benefit *all* students. After all, learning to resolve conflict, remedy wrongs, and invest in one another's well-being are key lessons for life and relationships. Those lessons are urgently needed to prevent and respond to the adolescent roots of intimate violence.

Uncovering Adolescent Roots of Intimate Violence

Anonymous student Instagram accounts started to go live, one by one, in 2020. Student survivors of all genders described sexual coercion, harassment, and assault across tiled galleries in assorted pastel colors. Many of the stories, though not all, described coercion and violence perpetrated *against* adolescent girls and women *by* adolescent boys and men. Their stories came from communities across the US and in the United Kingdom, from small liberal arts colleges to large universities. Despite geographic differences, the details were similar. Survivors recounted sleepless nights, physical illness, anxiety and depression, and thoughts of suicide. They also described vigilance and dread in school hallways, declining grades, and withdrawal from school activities.[25]

The Instagram posts illustrated that the same kinds of cognitive, emotional, and behavioral harms that arise from witnessing domestic violence can also come about after intimate violence in dating relationships. Furthermore, the accounts started by high school students pointed out that the gendered roots of intimate violence often lay in adolescence.[26] By adolescence, young people's understanding of gender is unfolding against the backdrop of rapid social and biological development. Young people begin to explore sexuality and intimate relationships in a world that is also changing quickly—from technology to cultural messages about intimacy and gender expression.

Despite so much technological and cultural change, however, the sexual assault of girls and women persists, just as it has for millennia. That's what a team of researchers reported in the fall of 2019, when their research made national headlines for showing that archaic traditions of forced sexual initiation remain wretchedly common in the lives of girls and young women. The researchers asked more than 13,000 women about their first intercourse with a man. A majority of the women surveyed reported their first intercourse happened in adolescence, somewhere between the ages of eleven and seventeen. For one in sixteen women, that first intercourse was rape. The women who were forced into sex were two years younger, on average, than other women in the sample at the time of their first intercourse. Earlier intercourse has many implications for health, from risks for unintended pregnancy to sexually transmitted infections.[27]

For some participants in that study, a dating partner forced them to have sex. That fits with decades of research showing that aggression and violence are common in adolescent dating relationships. However, the degree to which dating aggression is gendered has been a source of much consternation in the research literature, driven by questions about whether girls or boys are more physically aggressive in heterosexual relationships.

The short answer is that some studies find that girls are more physically aggressive and others find that boys are more aggressive, depending on how aggression is measured. When a research team combined 101 studies of dating violence among adolescents aged thirteen to eighteen in a meta-analysis, they found about 21% of girls *and* boys report physical victimization.[28] The researchers explained that the relatively high rates of physical aggression—including things such as pushing and shoving—probably reflect some degree of normative learning. Young people don't start romantic relationships knowing how to handle conflict, for example. With little experience in managing intimate relationships, the researchers argued that girls adopt typically masculine aggressive behaviors as they're learning to navigate intimate relationships during this developmental period. In turn, many of those physically aggressive behaviors in girls go relatively unnoticed or unpunished during adolescence because girls' aggression is more easily dismissed than boys'.

The idea that people respond to girls' and boys' behaviors differently fits with theories about gender, such as work by psychologist Jacqueline White.[29] A groundbreaking gender and violence researcher, White argued that gender does not cause aggression. Rather, acting aggressively gives young people a sense of themselves as traditionally masculine or feminine. As adolescents use aggression in relationships—particularly opposite-sex relationships—behaviors get interpreted in ways that line up with societal views of gender. Girls who act aggressively are seen as emotional or "mean-girls." Boys are seen as tough and taking what they want.

White's work on gender turns my thoughts again to the girls in the Healthy Adolescent Relationship Project. Over the twelve weeks of healthy relationship classes, the girls told all sorts of stories about being aggressive in their intimate relationships, with no shortage of adolescent bravado. They'd say things like: "I showed him I was the boss—I pushed him against the wall just like that." Or, "He was messing with my texts, so I took his phone and shattered it and laughed at what I'd done." Or, "I could kick his ass if I wanted to, and he knows it." More often than not, underneath the bragging was something wrenchingly vulnerable. These girls—thrown out of homes and schools, some with babies of their own—seemed to be trying desperately to regain a degree of control in relationships and a world in which they were otherwise disempowered. They wanted to be respected and did not have many other means to be powerful beyond sometimes shoving someone or breaking a phone.

The girls' bravado was a poor cover for the fact that, beneath all the shoving and pushing, was a real lack of skills. Even late into their teen years, the girls and their dating partners didn't seem to know how to do things that are important to healthy relationships, such as resolving conflict without resorting to aggression. They may not have had healthy models for or access to basic information about relationships, such as consent. For some girls, our project was the first time that anyone told them that relationships could, in fact, *not* involve abuse. Some had learned that the nature of love and relationships included emotional, physical, and even sexual harm. Across weeks of healthy relationship classes, some of the girls talked about relationships as never-ending struggles for control—of their phones, their birth control, their contact with friends—in the face of pressures from their dating partners, who were mostly boys.

Once learned, beliefs that intimacy involves harm can persist beyond the adolescent years into adulthood. I think of interviewing a woman in her twenties after domestic violence. Upon finishing a survey that asked about self-blame, shame, and other reactions to the violence, she shoved it back across the table and said, "Do people really tell you they feel this shit?" My team had spent years developing that particular instrument over the course of interviews and surveys with hundreds of trauma survivors, so I said "Yeah, some do." She went on to explain to me that violence just happens—that's what relationships are, so why get so shameful about it?

The Healthy Adolescent Relationship Project wasn't designed to test hypotheses about girls' motivations for using physical or psychological aggression, but other research was so designed. For example, Vangie Foshee, a groundbreaking researcher of adolescent dating violence, and her colleagues interviewed girls and boys in opposite-gender dating relationships about their uses of violence.[30] They found that girls used violence for a few different reasons: as a response to past or current violence from their boyfriends, in anger at their boyfriends, and when their boyfriends did something wrong. Boys, too, described using violence in response to girls' violence, but, beyond that, the researchers couldn't identify many clear themes. While boys' explanations in that study varied a lot, other researchers have uncovered links between men's aggression and their motivations for power as well as beliefs that power and sex are linked together.[31]

Given that both adolescent girls and boys can be aggressive in relationships and that they sometimes give similar reasons for that aggression, it be can be tempting to assume that gender doesn't matter much for understanding

adolescent dating violence. However, equating girls' and boys' intimate physical aggression masks ways that *gender* does indeed matter. Consider, for
example, dating violence perpetrated against gender and sexual minority
youth. LGBTQ+ youth are victimized in dating relationships significantly
more than their peers, and LGBTQ+ Youth of Color are at even higher risk of
victimization than White LGBTQ youth.[32] Bisexual adolescents and young
adults face especially high risk for sexual victimization.[33]

These findings point to problems addressing victimization in isolation
and the need to, instead, work at the intersection of gender identity, sexual
orientation, and ethnicity. Take, for example, the hypothesis that adolescent
dating aggression happens because adolescents just don't yet have adequate
relationship skills to manage conflict other ways. Relationship skill deficits
alone, however, cannot explain why bisexual youth and LGBTQ+ Youth of
Color are victimized more often than their peers. There are sure to be more
complex dynamics at play. For instance, intimate violence may be used as a
means of controlling youth who violate heterosexual and cisgender norms.
LGBTQ+ Youth of Color may be targeted for their skin color *and* gender
or sexual identities. When violence is motivated by racial bias or to control
youth with nonconforming gender identities, teaching relationship skills
alone will not work. Rather, prevention will have to take into account racial
and gender biases, too.

Prevention will also require attention to the ways that gender intersects
with sexual violence. Turing back to that meta-analysis of 101 studies of
dating violence, researchers found that 14% of girls reported sexual victimization compared to 8% of boys.[34] Furthermore, boys and men were significantly more likely than girls and women to perpetrate sexual assault,
including rape.[35] Differences in sex-related victimization persist into digital spaces.[36] Both girls and boys report being aggressive toward and trying
to control their dating partners through phones, social media, and the like;
however, girls are significantly more likely to be sexually coerced and victimized than boys.[37]

The consequences of dating violence can be gendered, too, in ways that
matter for understanding education access and success. When boys are violent, girls are more likely to suffer injuries than when girls are violent, particular as youth get older.[38] More adolescent girls die at the hands of intimate
partners than do boys. Of 150 adolescent homicides in the US attributed to
intimate partners from 2003 to 2016, 90% of victims were girls.[39] In nearly
all (94%) cases, the perpetrators were current partners, usually adolescent

boys or young men. More than half of the deaths involved guns. The most common antecedents to the murders had to do with the relationship—a break up, a jealous partner, a fight. About one in fourteen murders had to do with a pregnancy.

So while some degree of pushing and shoving may be normative during dating relationships as young people learn the skills necessary to be more interpersonally effective, more severe physical and sexual violence are gendered. The negative health consequences of dating violence can be gendered, too, as seen in increased risk for suicidal ideation and suicide attempts among girls and sexual minority youth after dating violence.[40]

Dating violence and sexual assault in adolescence have been linked to a host of trauma-related problems, from depression and substance use to PTSD and suicidality.[41] This constellation of psychological symptoms can be terribly disruptive to learning and academic performance. For example, PTSD, depression, and substance use can all involve poor concentration, memory problems, and disrupted sleep. Concentration, memory, and sleep are necessary for learning and thriving at school. Adolescents cannot meet their learning potential if they cannot concentrate or sleep, if they miss school to give birth or care for baby, or if they are dead.

The good news is that there are effective prevention programs that can help *both* girls and boys learn the skills necessary to handle conflict in relationships in healthy ways.[42] In Chapter 2, we looked at dating violence prevention approaches, including those delivered in schools.[43] Going beyond this primary prevention to stop dating violence before it happens, researchers have pointed to the importance of delivering interventions that treat the trauma symptoms caused by dating violence that has already occurred. Treating trauma symptoms is important for students' learning, health, *and* future victimization risk: girls' trauma symptoms after adolescent dating violence predict revictimization in young adulthood.[44] In college, then, intimate violence continues to diminish young women's educational opportunities.

Violence Against Women on College Campuses

The turning of late summer to fall brings the sights and sounds of young people moving into dorms across the country's four-year colleges. Brightly colored university t-shirts, showing off a new campus pride, blend with the optimistic banter of first-year students. Parents and loved ones wave out the window as cars pull away, leaving young people to explore this new begin-ning, a critical juncture on their way to adulthood and the American Dream.

About two out of five of the women unpacking boxes in their new dorm rooms have already been sexually assaulted or raped before getting to col-lege, according to one study with 750 women in their first year of college. Compared to their peers, young women who start college with histories of sexual victimization face academic disadvantages from the start. On average, they enter college with lower high school grade point averages and receive lower grades in that first year.[45]

Beyond that unequal start to college, victimization in adolescence begets intimate violence once at college, often in the first year.[46] From there, inti-mate violence and stalking insidiously chip away at that move-in day opti-mism. A study of more than 6,400 college students, the majority of whom were women, found that students victimized during college felt less confi-dent about their ability to do academic work and more stressed about school. They were less likely to be committed to re-enrolling at the school in the next semester and more likely to show signs of disengaging, such as showing up late.[47] Indeed, trauma consequences such as PSTD have been linked with leaving college before the end of the second year.[48]

These academic realities affect an enormous swath of women. Looking at sexual assault alone, one in five of the young women arriving on campus will be victimized during college. That one in five estimate has been remarkably consistent across decades of research, reaching back to two of the earliest studies of campus sexual assault and aggression in the 1950s.[49] Since then, researchers have studied campus sexual assault at small private colleges, his-torically Black colleges, and big public universities. The available research clearly shows that campus sexual assault happens to women with terrible frequency and serious consequences. No campuses or students are immune, though research suggests that women are at particular risk if they are in their first year of college, have a disability, or are bisexual.[50]

For student survivors, depression and PTSD symptoms, cognitive problems, social withdrawal, isolation, emotion dysregulation, and aca-demic difficulties make navigating college difficult. Those challenges are magnified by sharing dorms, food halls, classes, and clubs with the people who victimized them. Long after college is over, survivors are left to weigh the risks of encountering abusers at reunions or when they open the pages of alumni magazines. All of this is made worse when colleges cover up or ignore sexual assault, as catalogued in documentaries such as The Hunting Ground.

Psychologist Jennifer Freyd and colleagues gave a name to schools' failures: *institutional betrayal*.[51] When institutions create the circumstances in which assault is likely to occur or fail to respond appropriately when assault does happen, they betray the members of their community who depend on the institution. These kinds of betrayals regularly make the news, such as cover-ups of sexual assault allegations against star athletes.[52] But many betrayals happen quietly, such as those we heard about in our research with more than 200 women who were sexually assaulted in the previous year and who disclosed the assault to a healthcare provider, counselor, law enforcement officer, or the like. About a quarter of those women talked with us about sexual assaults connected to campuses, and a third of those women described betrayals by their schools. Some told us that their universities had contributed to creating the very environments in which sexual assault was common, seemed like no big deal, and was likely to happen. Some indicated that universities made reporting difficult and failed to respond adequately when they did report. Half who reported institutional betrayals said their universities had covered up the assaults.

Thanks to student activism and organizing, the Obama administration came to recognize the problem that schools' failure to respond to sexual harassment and assault caused for education equity.[53] In a now-infamous "Dear Colleague" letter in 2011, the Administration recognized what women had long been saying: that being sexually assaulted made learning difficult, led them to drop out of activities, and affected their psychological and physical health. Because sexual assault and harassment have an impact on education, the Obama administration said that schools were accountable to respond.[54] Recognizing the gendered nature of campus sexual assault, the Dear Colleague letter put Title IX at the center of a battle over defining and responding to campus sexual assault.

Title IX, a provision of the Education Amendments of 1972 that applies to institutions receiving federal money, specified "No person in the United States shall, on the basis of sex, be excluded from participation in, be denied the benefits of, or be subjected to discrimination under any education program or activity receiving Federal financial assistance."[55] Best known for changing the landscape of athletics for girls and women, the Obama administration argued that Title IX obligated schools to conduct adequate, reliable, and impartial investigations following reports of gender-based sexual harassment and violence. Where education institutions previously responded (or not) as they liked to assault and harassment reports, the Dear Colleague letter made clear that schools' failure to respond could affect their federal funding. The letter also laid out expectations that schools would conduct their own investigations, *separate* from any criminal investigations because what constitutes a Title IX violation may differ from a crime.

The Dear Colleague letter brought about significant college investments in the prevention, investigation, and adjudication of sexual assault and harassment cases. Campuses hired investigators and built their capacity to gather and respond to reports.[56] College task forces developed policies for handling reports that aimed to take into account both the complainant (campus language used to describe the person alleged to have been assaulted) and respondent (the person alleged to have committed the assault) and trained their employees.

While taking action to address serious, long-standing problems in how schools handled sexual harassment and sexual assault, the implementation of Obama-era Title IX policies also created a host of thorny problems. For example, campuses created mandated reporting policies that required employees—faculty, staff, teaching assistants—who learned of sexual harassment or assault to report the incident through the school's Title IX process regardless of what survivors wanted.[57] The logic was that when a campus employee learned of an incident, then the school officially knew and became responsible for responding. In the aftermath of serial abuse that came to light at institutions such as Pennsylvania State University and Michigan State University, there seemed to be some wisdom in trying to minimize risks of cover-ups or turning the other way. However, the blunt-tool approach of mandating all employees to report took agency away from survivors while putting faculty and staff in the precarious position of being required to break student confidentiality.

Campuses and law enforcement agencies have faced challenges, too, struggling to avoid working at cross-purposes when their co-occurring investigations triggered two separate sets of procedures and ways of approaching cases. Even their language differs: campuses refer to complainants, police to victims, and advocates to survivors, as my team heard when we documented the work of multidisciplinary groups trying to improve co-occurring investigations.[58] Each group has to manage its own legal and ethical obligations as well as timelines for investigations. Criminal investigations can take months and prosecutions years, whereas the Obama administration directed campuses to take immediate action, with the exception of allowances for brief delays related to time-sensitive law enforcement activity, such as executing search warrants. In the face of complexities and frustrations such as these, as well as a lack of support from campus administrators, Title IX offices have been plagued by alarming turnover nationally.[59]

Many of these problems are fundamentally addressable, such as rethinking the scope of mandatory reporting policies to support survivors and building multidisciplinary collaborations to respond effectively to sexual assault. What has proved (and will likely continue) to be more difficult is overcoming the creeping prioritization of criminal legal concepts and approaches in the Title IX process. The Title IX process is supposed to be about civil rights and educational access, but that focus has been eroding over time. The slide away from social justice and civil rights to criminal legal thinking was already under way when graduate student McKenzie Javorika and Dr. Rebecca Campbell, a national leader in sexual assault research, interviewed twenty Title IX experts between 2014 and 2017.[60] The criminal emphasis became more prominent and further entrenched, then, as part of the backlash over the Obama administration's approach to Title IX. Pundits and parents of accused students mounted lawsuits and public relations campaigns calling for criminal legal-like procedures.[61]

The emphasis on criminal legal system priorities became enshrined in rules put into effect in 2020 by the Department of Education under the Trump administration. The rules laid out requirements for cross-examination, much like a criminal courtroom. Unlike a criminal courtroom, though, the cross-examination provision was designed in a way that offered people accused of sexual assault and harassment an easy loophole: if they refused to be cross-examined, then none of their prior statements could be considered, even if those prior statements were confessions.[62]

Rationalizations for the new rules' emphasis on procedures more like criminal legal processes have centered on claims that the previous Obama guidance was too survivor-centered and, therefore, inherently anti-male. But here's the thing: ending and responding to violence against women promises to be good for all students, regardless of their gender. This is because the pathways to ending violence against women can make schools more inclusive and equitable spaces that treat all students holistically.

Righting the Wrong Lessons

Since the turn of the twenty-first century, the US has tried various approaches to reforms to improve education access and success. We've raced to the top, redefined common curricula, promoted school choice, increased standardized testing, and demanded greater teacher accountability. Over the course of those reforms, student performance has dropped compared to peers worldwide as inequities across the country increased dramatically. The top quarter of students gained ground, measured by standardized tests, while the bottom 10% fell even further behind their peers.[63] Schools have been driven to focus on those students who are cheapest to teach, not all students nor the students who most need support.[64]

Unfortunately, most approaches to reform have ignored the impact of witnessing violence against women or intimate violence by a dating partner instead trying to improve education by focusing on disciplinary practices, teacher tenure policies, and testing. We need a new approach that recognizes that many students passing through school cafeterias and across campuses have witnessed or been victimized by intimate violence. Instead of waiting for any individual student to come to the attention of guidance counselors or academic advisors because of trauma-related problems, we have to design proactive policies and practices to mitigate the impact of violence on individual students *and* the entire learning community. In so doing, we can improve schools for *all* students.

This kind of proactive approach is the centerpiece of the call for *trauma-informed schools*. The idea behind trauma-informed schools is to recognize that many students have witnessed or experienced violence. The impact of those traumatic experiences on individual students *and* the entire learning community are then addressed proactively through school-wide policies and practices. Further, collaboration and teamwork are emphasized among school personnel along with work to ensure that students feel connected to the school community. Thus, proponents argue that trauma-informed approaches have the potential to make schools more responsive, better learning environments for *all* young people because they focus on supporting *all* students to feel emotionally, physically, socially, and academically safe and treating each student's needs holistically. Even if the impetus to design schools in this way comes from addressing trauma in the lives of *some* students, *all* learners stand to benefit.[65]

As a practical matter, trauma-informed approaches are generally organized around a handful of central principles, such as those espoused by the federal Substance Abuse Mental Health Services Administration (SAMHSA).[66] SAMHSA has described six trauma-informed principles, beginning first and foremost with physical and psychological safety. The importance of this principle is obvious now that we know more about trauma's impact on the brain. When the brain redirects cognitive and physiological resources to respond to threat, learning is more difficult. Creating safety for learners and school staff, then, has to be a priority.

One component of safety is *physical space*. Students and staff need to know that they will be safe at school, whether in hallways, dorm rooms, classrooms, or activities. This is about more than well-lit parking lots. Researchers Jennifer Hirsch and Shamus Khan, for example, described how their study of campus sexual assault revealed ways that the physical set-up of dorms and social spaces affected students' perceptions of power and safety and, in turn, risk for sexual assault—a phenomenon they called *sexual geographies*.[67] A trauma-informed approach, then, would use physical spaces in ways that maximize real and perceived safety. Research shows that such aspirations are possible, such as when New York City schools worked with researchers to test a building-based intervention that involved three components: increasing the presence of school staff at "hot spots" identified by students as places where aggression happens well as implementing boundary agreements and displaying posters about dating violence and reporting. These relatively modest changes in the school's physical space had an impact on reports of youth violence.[68]

Physical space is only one dimension of creating safety, though. Institutions also have to create *psychological safety* through their cultures and procedures. Students need to know that they will be treated with respect and dignity; that they will not be harassed and abused. This means that institutions have to convey a commitment to relationships and treating people well. In so doing, schools have opportunities to show that threats to safety will be taken seriously and responded to in ways that restore dignity and promote safety for the whole community. Developmental psychologist Kathryn Becker-Blease often holds out Oregon State University's (OSU) past president, Ed Ray, as a model here for his leadership in 2014. Years earlier, in 1998, Brenda Tracy disclosed a gang rape by OSU athletes. She went through a forensic exam and reported to the police, though decided ultimately—like many women do—that she did not want to continue in the criminal legal system. Back on campus, coaches knew what happened and yet the only action taken was that two athletes were suspended for one game.[69] Years later Tracy contacted OSU to ask about her case. Instead of denying, ignoring, or minimizing all those years later, President Ray publicly apologized, acknowledged the emotional and physical harm, and took action.[70]

President Ray's response also gets to the second principle of trauma-informed schools: *trustworthiness and transparency*. Here, SAMHSA and others have urged leaders to consider the degree to which students and staff can trust schools to give them clear information about rules and procedures and be trusted to follow those rules. Unfortunately, schools have a long way to go to combat the perception and reality of Title IX failures across the country. For years, high-profile investigative reporting has spotlighted schools' failures to respond to, minimizing of, or downright covering up of sexual assault and harassment.[71] This means schools have to do better and regain public trust.

A third principle of trauma-informed schools focuses on *support* for survivors of violence and their families. Support might involve counseling and nursing services, which the young people in Chicago called for. Yet there's more to integrating support across school systems, such as making sure that teachers understand and are responsive to how violence and trauma affect learning so that they can design classes that support *all* students' learning. Such an approach is in line with movements toward universal design in classes that take into account different learning styles and neurodiversity. Part of responding to the diversity of a class full of learners is recognizing and teaching in ways so that students impacted by the trauma of violence against women can learn also.

Trauma-informed principles also emphasize *collaboration and mutuality*. My research team saw this in action when we studied the multidisciplinary team of professionals who came together from campuses and the criminal legal system to find a better way to carry out co-investigations. Month after month, they dedicated their time to building relationships, explaining policies and procedures to each other, and problem-solving to find ways to do their jobs better.[72]

The final principles articulated by SAMHSA calls on institutions to focus on *empowerment, voice, and choice* as well as to *recognize culture and history* as part of being trauma-informed. These principles translate to expectations that schools will center student needs even amid pressures to navigate the needs and priorities of alumni, donors, and funding agencies. Further, they will analyze power structures to work toward change that both helps individuals and dismantles systems that have created and maintained educational inequities based on gender, ethnicity, ability, sexuality, and other identities. In so doing, schools recognize and work against systemic forces that have marginalized and minoritized some students, adding to the flow of school-to-prison pipelines and other inequities.

Across the country, educators, education advocates, policy-makers, and researchers are working to put the principles behind trauma-informed schools into practice.[73] To date, much of the promise of trauma-informed schools remains just that. Many schools and districts aspire to be trauma-informed but haven't yet had the resources to evolve their institutions.[74] Nevertheless, trauma-informed principles offer a blueprint for policies and practices that can move schools toward coordinated, holistic, institutional responses to violence that also create more equitable learning environments. Here we can find new opportunities to collaborate with others invested in education equity.

Collective Action, Student Edition

The impact of violence against women on education is bad news for girls and women whose educations are diminished by violence. It's also bad news for people of all genders, regardless of whether they've ever been victimized, because our communities need girls and women to have access to education and a chance to realize their potential. When they don't, the civic fabric of our communities weakens. Indeed, another part of the story of why the educational success of each and every student is important to all of us is because education is, at its roots, about democracy itself. Our educational system plays a critical role in socializing young people into the norms and values upon which our communities and democracy depend. When educational systems sidestep responding to violence in the lives of their students, we teach young people that violence is a victim's problem, not a community's problem. When educational opportunities are cut short for individual students, the civic health of our communities is diminished, too.

Today, students and alumni across the country are reviving civic health, having built organizing capacity to advocate for ending violence and the restoration of dignity, fairness, opportunity, and safety for students. Organizations such as Ending Rape on Campus (EROC) and Know Your

IX take up space in the digital and real worlds to educate and act. Students and alumni have used the courts and turned to investigative journalists to tell stories of institutional betrayal, inequity, and women's lost potential.

College student organizing has unfolded as teachers' unions have taken to the streets and inspired collective action. In 2018, images that streamed onto our phones and televisions from West Virginia made visible the collective self-interests Americans share in education. Thousands of schoolteachers, clad in red, marched on picket lines and at the state capital. The urged us all to wear Red for Ed as they closed down every single public school in the state.

By April, people in Denver put on their red in solidarity with area teachers who voted to strike. Charter school teachers in Chicago took to the picket lines in December. Strikes unfolded in Los Angeles just after the New Year.

Nearly a year of national attention to teacher strikes from one end of the country to the other offered many opportunities to talk about the factors that drive, constrain, help, and harm the US education system—factors such as lack of investment in teachers and technology disruptions, seniority and tenure policies, class sizes in underresourced schools, and the perils of standardized testing. Yet there was no widespread conversation about the impact of violence against women on education.

We're left, then, with a few important lessons and opportunities to keep in mind. First, education reforms that fail to address intimate violence are missing a root cause of education challenges and inequities and will therefore only ever have limited impact. Second, students and teachers have shown that it's possible to organize in ways that galvanize the political will and funding for change. They have also shown that organizing successes depend, at least in part, on the coalitions they bring together. That's what Hava Gordon, a social movements scholar, pointed to, using the example of the Los Angeles teachers unions that built relationships with community groups long before the 2019 teachers' strike.[75] Those long-standing relationships meant that teachers brought interests that they had in common with community groups, such as immigrant rights, to the table under a frame of bargaining for the common good. Community groups concerned with immigrant rights, then, had a stake in supporting teachers because progress for one group would mean progress for both.

You and I have a similar opportunity to foster shared interests at the intersections of immigration and violence against women in our work for the common good.

4

The Local Cost of Global Pain

The call to turn the night purple came in September 2019 with #NocheVioleta. Women and allies poured onto streets across Spain, wrapped in the color of the feminist movement, to protest the murder of women by their intimate partners. The forty-second woman had just been killed that year, joining the corpses of more than one thousand women since the government began keeping statistics on intimate partner homicides in 2003.[1]

What happened in Spain wasn't unusual in a growing sea of global protests. Another scene unfolded in Paris in late 2019, with signs proclaiming #NousToutes (All of Us). Women across Mexico declared #UnDíaSinNosotras (A Day Without Us) in March 2020, in the aftermath of high-profile killings of women by current and former intimate partners. UN Women called on us all to #OrangetheWorld with 16 days of activism against gender-based violence.[2]

Country by country, women took up a common song: "It wasn't my fault; not where I was, not how I dressed."[3] From the New York courthouse where Harvey Weinstein stood trial for multiple counts of sexual assault to Istanbul, Kenya, India, and across Central America, they chanted and danced to these words written by Chilean women feminists.

The demonstrations, activism, and unrest in countries around the globe felt more personal when I visited Paris not long after their national march. My plans included a walk to the old Salpêtrière building, now part of the Pitié-Salpêtrière University Hospital, a teaching hospital in the Thirteenth Arrondissement. I wanted to see the building itself after spending so much time with the stories of the women who occupied those halls. The building had become a character in the background of my work as a trauma psychologist. Like returning to the scene of something important, I wanted to walk up that drive and feel the place that I had seen in paintings and photographs.

After an exhausting couple of days with cancelled flights and travel woes, I arrived in Paris with my partner, bleary-eyed but ready for that much anticipated walk to the Salpêtrière. We arrived at the hospital grounds and promptly took a wrong turn, ending up lost on campus. Tired from travel and feeling silly for wanting to stand outside a former insane asylum, I tried saying "Never mind. We can skip it," but the words rang hollow, untruthful. I *really* wanted to see the building.

We gave the campus one more pass and spotted the historic building through a doorway that led to the back of the old hospital. Making our way around to the front of the building, there was the expansive drive, the looming windows, that entrance that I had imagined so many women passing through. The exterior was in a state of decline, with paint peeling and windows covered, signs fading, but the building still stood—a testament to a history of hysteria that ignored the violence and trauma women had survived.

As I traversed the city over the subsequent days, I discovered messages that lingered on walls near busy boulevards and quiet streets. On the Left Bank, black spray paint decried "Leur Haine, Nos Mortes"—their hate, our dead women. Across the river, another wall proclaimed, "Feminicides: Etat Coupable, Justice Complice"—Femicide: Guilty state, justice complicit. A flyer plastered to a lightpost urged President Macron to commit money to ending femicide.

With each message, I found myself wondering more urgently: How is it that women in Paris and around the globe are still fighting this same fight—a fight for dignity, opportunity, safety; a fight for our lives? That fight, whether in Chile or Kenya, in Mexico or France, is not some other country's problem, though. It is #NousToutes. All of us.

Governments Failing Women Worldwide

In early 2020, as the novel coronavirus pandemic hit, governments around the globe ordered people to stay at home to slow the spread of the virus. Not long into this health crisis, the world began to notice that lockdowns at home meant some women were trapped with abusive intimate partners. In France, reports emerged that domestic violence incidents were spiking, though women shut in apartments with abusers couldn't call for help. The government initiated plans to have phone lines available at pharmacies for women to use to call the police. If women's abusers were with them, they could ask pharmacists for "mask 19" to indicate that they needed police help.[4]

France wasn't unique in reporting new dangers from intimate violence during the pandemic. Similar reports emerged from China, Brazil, Spain, and other countries, including the US.[5]

Lockdowns made the logistical barriers to connecting women with services stand out, but women around the globe have long faced such challenges: abusers monitor victims' movements, shelters are prohibited from providing emergency contraception, and communities lack adequate resources to help victims escape. That's why activists and policy-makers around the world have tried to find ways to get services *to women* where they are.[6] The phone lines in French pharmacies were but the latest example of work done before and during the pandemic by UN agencies, international nongovernmental organizations, and grassroots groups to leverage technology and other creative problem-solving to address violence against women.[7]

We'll need innovative work to continue long after the pandemic because rates of sexual assault, domestic violence, and trafficking of women around the world have been persistently high, since well before the novel coronavirus emerged. The World Health Organization estimates that more than one-third of women globally have been victimized by intimate partners or sexually assaulted. Nearly 40% of murders of women globally are perpetrated by intimate partners. Those women who survive intimate violence suffer a host of health consequences, from increased odds of having a low birthweight baby to sexually transmitted infections.[8]

Today, current events—from armed conflicts and natural disasters to extreme weather caused by climate change—amplify the dangers facing women. When current events lead to scarcer resources, for example, women often pay a price. Consider research on natural resources and intimate violence in sub-Saharan Africa, for example.[9] Women living in countries with limited economic opportunities and rigid gender role expectations have tried to sell fish to provide for their families. With boats largely controlled by men, women have been forced to trade sex for fish. When coerced into sex, women endure sexual trauma as well as incredible health risks, including for HIV. In Kenya, a program that built boats for women increased their economic opportunity and changed community perceptions of women. Improving women's economic opportunity became a way to halt pressures for transactional sex, decrease sexual trauma, and improve public health by preventing HIV and sexually transmitted infections.[10] Expanding economic opportunities for women is good health policy. Indeed, the World Health Organization has argued that preventing gender-based violence must involve economic interventions that work towards equality.[11]

Yet many governments around the globe continue to fail women in terms of economic policy and basic safety. Investigative reporting has shed light on governments that have yet to take seriously women's reports of violence and hold perpetrators accountable. For example, *New York Times* reporter Azam Ahmed told Lubia's story.[12] Pregnant and sixteen years old in Guatemala, she fled her violent boyfriend to her parent's home. Her boyfriend chased her to her parent's house, where he killed her mother. Unlike most murders in Guatemala, which go unsolved, Lubia's boyfriend was apprehended and sentenced to four years in prison. When released, he will have the right to visit their son under Guatemalan law, despite having abused Lubia and murdered her mother. With his release approaching, Lubia's father made his way to the US to make an asylum claim, hoping this would protect his family.

Lubia's story is like too many others, where the abuser targets a woman for being a woman and her family for being her family. To escape abusers, women, their children, and other family members have fled their home countries, only to face new dangers in their migration. Angela Me, the chief of research and trend analysis at the United Nations Office on Drugs and Crime told the *New York Times* reporter, "Despite the risk associated with migration, it is still lower than the risk of being killed at home."[13]

Danger During Migration

Each year, millions of people cross international borders for a host of reasons, perhaps to reunite with families, seek better opportunities, or flee persecution based on "race, religion, nationality, political opinion or membership in a particular group."[14] For many women, the impetus for migration is to escape intimate violence perpetrated against them by spouses and romantic partners or gangs. This has been especially true for women from Honduras, Guatemala, and El Savador, where femicide rates are among the highest in the world.[15]

Climate change and other economic disruptions also drive migration patterns, circumstances that are becoming more common with more frequent extreme weather. Changing temperatures and weather patterns, for example, will increasingly disrupt people's abilities to make their living through agriculture. In turn, families will have to make difficult decisions about whether to move elsewhere to seek out work and opportunity. Sometimes their moves will be across national borders.

When events—whether related to climate or persecution—force people to flee their homes, girls and women are at risk of intimate violence and exploitation during migration, sometimes perpetrated by those who are supposed to protect them.[16] As chronicled in *New York Times* reporting, women who set out to seek safety in the US instead endured harrowing sexual assaults. One woman, a mother of three migrating from Guatemala, described to the reporter, "They raped us so many times they didn't see us as human beings anymore." The women disclosed assaults that happened on both sides of borders—before arriving in the US and after. For many women, reporting the sexual assaults to authorities wasn't possible: smugglers hid their identities or told women they would be killed or their children sold if women reported the violence. For many women who had been smuggled into the US, being undocumented silenced them for fear that, after being raped repeatedly, they would be deported.[17]

Health providers and researchers have long pointed out that victimizations that happen during migration to the US harm women's health.[18] This isn't surprising because intimate violence, wherever it occurs, has serious consequences for health. However, women victimized during migration face additional uncertainties that can worsen the impacts, such as a lack of social support as well as the ongoing risk of detention and deportation back to their countries of origin. Women who are detained then confront the stress of imprisonment as well as new risks of intimate violence. Harrowing reports of the sexual assault and rape of women have emerged from US immigration detention facilities.[19]

Women may also face the stress of having to retell their stories of victimization, sometimes as part of the process of seeking safety in a new country.

Seeking Safety

Women seeking asylum in the US from domestic violence in their home countries arrive to find an ever-changing political and legal landscape. Over the past thirty years, refuge has become possible with the recognition of gender-based violence as grounds for asylum; however, that progress has been punctuated by twists and turns in policy and law.[20] While the ins and outs of asylum law are beyond the scope of our discussion, the changing landscape gives us a chance to see how policy-makers' understanding of and beliefs about intimate violence influence policy and create hurdles for our work toward effective responses to violence against women.[21] Indeed, even the asylum-seeking process itself is fraught because of the ways that the dynamics of intimate violence and its consequences can be either misunderstood or ignored. These issues came into stark view in the case of *Jimenez Ferreira v. Lynch*, as described by Alana Mosley, a jurisprudence doctoral candidate at the time.[22]

According to Mosley's summary and analysis, Ana Veronica Jimenez Ferreira fled the Dominican Republic to escape her common-law husband who had repeatedly beaten, raped, stalked, and threatened to kill her. In 2007, he beat, strangled, and raped her when she returned home from a Christmas party with her children. She fled to a friend's house, got medical attention, and made a police report. Though her partner was arrested, he was released four days later, at which point he started to stalk her and made threats to kill her if she didn't return to their relationship. She eventually quit her job and relocated about fifty miles away, to the city where her mother lived. When her former partner found her, he broke into her apartment and beat her until her mother called neighbors for help. He returned two months later, kidnapped her off the street, and raped her in the woods. Afterward, he continued to threaten to kill her and her children. Ana gave up on the police, who had done nothing to stop him. Fearing he would make good on his threats to kill her, she fled to the US, leaving her children with her mother. He continued to harass her mother and threaten the children after she fled.

When Ana entered the US in Texas, she went through a *credible fear interview*. These interviews are one of the early steps in the asylum process. As the name implies, the asylum officer uses the interview to determine if the interviewee is credible with regard to a fear of persecution because of their "race, religion, nationality, political opinion or membership in a particular group."[23] The interview is used to make critically important decisions, including whether or not to grant asylum.

To evaluate credibility, judges can use the asylum-seeker's demeanor, candor, and responsiveness; the plausibility and internal consistency of their descriptions; or any falsehoods.[24] Unfortunately, pervasive myths about intimate violence also focus on these same things, creating expectations that "real" victims will behave in certain ways.[25] For example, people expect women to be consistent in their emotional displays and the narratives they provide about the violence; that "real" victims will be distraught and cry while telling the same story over and over in the same way. Even many professionals, such as in law enforcement, buy into these myths.[26]As we'll look at in Chapter 6, though, the stereotypes don't line up with research on the impact of stress and trauma or even the ways that typical autobiographical memory is prone to errors. After intimate violence, some women cry, others appear numb; some tell the story of what happened in a relatively coherent way, others do not. PTSD symptoms can leave memory feeling jumbled, such that women appear unsure as they tell their stories, even though the gist of what happened—being beaten and raped—is accurately relayed.

In Ana's case, Mosley pointed out that she didn't speak English, so her credible fear interview was done through an interpreter. The interview took place by phone, not in person. As is practice for such interviews, the call was not recorded or transcribed. Instead, the officer took notes about what was conveyed through the interpreter. So Ana, in detention in Texas, was asked to tell the intimate details of being raped, beaten, stalked, kidnapped, and threatened by her common-law husband to two strangers, one of whom did not speak her language.[27]

Some perspective-taking is important here: I'm writing and you're reading a book about violence against women, so we're getting pretty comfortable together talking about these things. But imagine a woman whose life and body have been horribly violated and now she has to somehow make her way through the shame and fear lingering from the assault on top of the stress of being in detention to tell the story consistently with the right amount of emotion to seem credible. Despite the circumstances, the immigration officer found that Ana's claims could be credible in a *full asylum* or *withholding of removal hearing*, the next step in the asylum process.

At that next step, though, the immigration judge who heard Ana's case found that there were "glaring inconsistencies" in her testimony. The judge took issue that the notes from the asylum officer's phone interview, conducted through an interpreter, and police notes said that Ana had been raped and beaten before the Christmas party, but Ana testified in front of the judge that the rape was after the party. The immigration judge weighed that inconsistency more heavily than the fact that she made a police report and went to the doctor and that the medical notes confirmed that Ana had injuries from the attack.[28]

The judge's expectations and ultimate disbelief weren't unique to asylum proceedings. Women are met with this kind of skepticism in the criminal legal system, too, as Chanel Miller described poignantly in her memoir about being raped and the aftermath. During the trial, she wondered what behavior was acceptable for a victim: "If you're flat, you're apathetic. Too upbeat, you're suspect. If you weep, you're hysterical. Being too emotional made you unreliable. But being unemotional made you unaffected."[29] For women seeking asylum, the price of not fitting into stereotypes of good victims of violence could be nothing short of being sent back to the country where their abusers have threatened to kill them.

The good news for Ana was that her case was appealed. On appeal, the Court found that notes (vs. transcripts) of credible threat interviews may not be reliable. The Court also found that the judge had overlooked corroborating evidence, such as the medical exam. These wins were important, but did not erase the issues facing or harm done to women like Ana who fight an uphill battle to be taken seriously when asking for asylum. Imagine if she hadn't gone to the doctor or reported to the police, like so many women. Women have to make a lot of "right" choices in harrowing moments with their credibility on trial in the future.[30]

Even if women make all the "right" choices, twists and turns in the legal landscape of asylum-seeking can put them at the mercy of US officials' beliefs about intimate violence. Consider, for example, what happened when Attorney General Jeff Sessions stepped in to deny asylum to a woman from El Salvador who was a victim of domestic violence in a case that dramatically changed US asylum policy for a period of time.[31]

In that case, Sessions argued that domestic violence was "private" violence, and asylum was not an appropriate solution for a private matter.[32] The idea that domestic violence is a private matter, of course, has been used across history to justify dismissing intimate violence as a family matter best handled within family relationships. The Attorney General also said that a woman could not claim to be a member of a persecuted group—a requirement for asylum—if she had a preexisting relationship with the perpetrator, as is necessarily the case in intimate partner violence. As lawyer Elisa Vari and University of California Hastings Law Professor Richard Boswell explained, the logic went that a preexisting relationship meant that the perpetrator might have other motives to harm her, beyond that she was a woman.[33]

The Attorney General's reasoning challenges us to ask a larger question: Why *are* women targeted for violence? Is it coincidence that one in three women around the world are sexually or physically victimized by (mostly) men? Is it also coincidence that girls as well as gender nonconforming groups are frequent targets of intimate violence, too?[34] It's really hard to imagine making a case that global patterns of intimate violence against girls, women, and gender nonconforming groups are unrelated to gender, especially when we consider the ways that countries around the globe reinforce cultural messages and policies that perpetuate gender inequities across all aspects of life.[35] Consider, for example, high-profile stories about girls and women being denied access to education simply because they are girls, such as Malala in Pakistan. Or the persistence of pay inequities in the US, which were on display when the US Soccer Federation said that the women's team—who had just had a global stage as the World Champions—did not perform work of equal skill, effort, and responsibility to the men's team. Women and girls aren't denied access to school or equal pay for some reason that differs radically from the reason they are commonly victims of intimate violence: they are denied because of their gender.

In addition to what Sessions's reasoning revealed about the tendency to downplay the gendered nature of violence, his arguments also illustrated the potentially deadly consequences when key dynamics in intimate violence are ignored. Here, Sessions argued that when persecution is driven by only a few people—such as an abuser and their friends or relatives—relocation is more reasonable within the home country than asylum in the US.[36] Of course, as Judith Herman made clear in *Trauma and Recovery*, context is everything. Let's use Guatemala as an example here. Geographically, Guatemala is about the same size as Tennessee. The population of Guatemala is about 15.5 million, which is less than the population of Tennessee and its neighbor North Carolina combined. With that context in mind, imagine a Guatemalan woman fleeing an abuser who has told her that he will hunt her down and kill her if she leaves with their child. It's easy to picture that a determined abuser could find her in a region the size of Tennessee, particularly in an environment where the police and others in positions of authority are frequently unwilling to intervene.[37] After all, think of the many ways that we each telegraph our locations—from government documents that require addresses, such as drivers' licenses and school registration forms, to digital footprints left in cell phone records, IP addresses, and on social media. In the US, address confidentiality programs have been developed precisely because of the danger that abusers can hunt down their victims. Address confidentiality programs allow victims of crimes such as domestic violence, sexual assault, and trafficking to apply for a post office box that becomes their address on all government and business documents, such as water and phone bills. These programs exist in the US because simply relocating is often insufficient to keep women safe from predators.

Even if relocating within a country was a good solution, women's movements in many countries are constrained by gender norms and laws. Familial, community, and cultural norms as well as laws can make it difficult for women to escape abusive partners at all, let alone to relocate. Abusers can leverage those rigid gender expectations in their control and coercion, making it even more difficult for women to leave abusive marriages.

Those same dynamics can continue in the US, even if women are able to eventually settle in their new country. Once here, they may face barriers to accessing services, from language and financial to anti-immigrant sentiment that is isolating and fear-inducing. On top of those barriers, their risk for victimization continues.

Navigating Intimate Violence in a New Country

Under the Trump administration, anti-immigrant sentiment became a staple of daily news. Stories painting migrants as dangerous to US citizens were common fare, particularly if the migrants were Black or Brown. Those stories were not only wrong, they also distracted us from a crisis that needs our attention: the US can be a remarkably dangerous place for immigrant and refugee women. Intimate violence can be common. For example, across research studies, 17–75% of women who immigrated to the US from South Asian countries reported intimate partner violence in the current year; one-third to half of Latinx and Spanish women who immigrated to the US disclosed intimate violence in the past year.[38]

Immigrant women are also at higher risk than US-born women of dying at the hands of their current or former intimate partners. That's what a research team discovered when they analyzed approximately 147,000 homicides that occurred in nineteen states between 2003 and 2013, and looked closely at 3,641 cases where women were killed by current or former intimate partners. Immigrant women were younger, more likely to be married to their murderers, and more often killed after a fight or some episode in which partners were jealous, relative to US-born women. Immigrant women were also more likely to be killed by something other than a gun— such as stabbing, suffocation, or strangulation.[39] Strangulation is a particularly brutal and intimate form of violence, one that requires perpetrators to be in victims' personal space to squeeze their throats as life leaves women's bodies.

Many factors converge to affect foreign-born women's risk of intimate violence in the US. For example, language barriers can make accessing victim services and support difficult. Victim service agencies vary in their abilities to provide interpreters, and working through an interpreter to talk about intimate harm can be difficult, to say the least. Language barriers can also mean that victims don't have accurate information about their legal rights and options if they are being harmed. Someone might be conversant enough in English to navigate much of their daily lives, but understanding legal and medical terms is another matter. To many monolingual English speakers who grew up in the US, legal terms are impenetrable, and that situation can be far worse for women for whom English is not their primary language.

I recall sitting in a focus group with Spanish-speaking women to discuss their legal needs. My language abilities only include English and tenth-grade French, so I was there only to support the graduate student facilitators who were new to working with interpreters. Twenty minutes or so into the group, I noticed that one of the graduate students who was conversant in Spanish was getting agitated. I also noticed that, to my ear, the interpreter's comments seemed like they didn't match the length of what the facilitators or participants were saying; however, I chalked that up to my own language inabilities. After the group, though, the graduate student explained that she understood enough to know that the interpreter was adding and leaving out things relative to what the facilitators and women said. As a team, we headed back to the office and had to grapple with what it meant for the science and ethics of our work. To not include Spanish-speaking women in our research would be a failure to understand the very things—like language barriers— that make it difficult for immigrant victims to access legal services. And yet our own language limitations as a team meant that we couldn't communicate directly with women to make sure we understood, in real time, what they wanted us to know.

In the end, a bilingual undergraduate research assistant on our team transcribed and translated a recording of the focus group so that we could rely on women's own words instead of the interpreter's words. That was a fix for a concrete part of the problem—making sure we accurately understood what women said. But it wasn't a fix for all the things women might not have said because they, too, picked up on their words being changed or left out in the translation. It wasn't a fix for how chilling and isolating it can be for victims to see that an agency or team isn't properly equipped to navigate language barriers for any number of reasons, including questionable or no interpretation. Agencies might not be able to afford interpretation services or may not have interpreters in their community who speak the same dialects as victims.

Regardless of the cause of lack of access to interpretation services, the consequences for victims can be serious, as researchers Filomena Critelli and Asli Cennet Yalim learned from Marta, who was taking steps to leave her abusive partner. When the partner saw her packing to leave, he threatened to kill himself with a gun. Marta fled in a friend's car and called the police. The responding officers didn't speak Marta's language and didn't call for interpretation services. Instead of grasping the immediate danger, the officers spent time criticizing Marta for not using a car seat for her child. Eventually, she found a way to communicate the gravity of the situation to the police, who discovered an unregistered gun in the abuser's possession.[40]

Beyond the impact of language barriers, gender roles can also play a role in women's isolation and risk for intimate violence after immigrating to the US. This was clear when Edna Erez, a criminologist from the University of Chicago, led a research team who interviewed 137 immigrant women from thirty-five countries to learn more about immigration's intersection with domestic violence.[41] Most of the women interviewed described clear-cut gender roles in their families, with women charged with home-related responsibilities, such as parenting and housework. That's not necessarily surprising or unique to immigrant women. After all, gendered divisions of labor leave US-born women with more housework and child care responsibilities than men. What was notable was other ways that gender played out that affect women's mobility and ability to literally navigate in the US. For example, six out of ten women didn't have access to a car or a driver's license. Those women face additional layers of isolation in many US communities where infrastructure makes people dependent on cars for transportation.

Rigid gender roles increase the risk that women will end up economically dependent on abusive husbands if, for example, they aren't allowed to work. Economic dependence can quickly get tangled up, then, with social isolation. Work often gives people a chance to connect and meet others, in addition to giving a reprieve from the constraints of home life. Women who are not allowed to work outside the home miss opportunities to build social networks. Those networks are important for mental health in all of us, but especially critical when trying to cope with trauma such as violence. Women can end up socially isolated, unable to make social connections in their new country.

Isolation is difficult psychologically, but can also have social, legal, and economic ramifications. For example, not having friends and social networks may make it difficult for women to learn about places to turn for help, including what to expect in system responses to intimate violence. After all, many survivors talk to informal supports—friends and family—long before they reach out to formal services through social services or the police. Those friends and families can help survivors figure out where to go for help and what to expect. I think back to college conversations in dorm rooms about who to talk to at the counseling center, where to get a emergency contraception. Or, more recently, times when a friend of a friend asks what to expect if their daughter calls a crisis line or the police. Lots of us pass along information to help friends and loved ones enter and navigate systems, maybe without even realizing we're doing so.

When victims are isolated, abusers can take advantage of women's lack of knowledge about or familiarity with legal, medical, and social service systems. Women's ability to effectively advocate for themselves—and their children—are hindered when they don't know how those systems work. And, worse still, abusers can use women's lack of knowledge against women. One victim told Erez's team, "he has become more abusive. He knows the system. I don't. He speaks English. I don't. I don't have family support or someone living with me, so he can lie about me."[42]

Even when women are familiar with systems, navigating them can be intimidating and difficult and may not lead to the outcomes that women want. I think of what we learned from women in the Triage Project, all of who had some familiarity with police responses because an incident of domestic violence had been reported to law enforcement. When new incidents of violence happened over the subsequent year, many women did not call the police again. They had lots of reasons for not re-engaging the criminal legal system. A quarter had negative impressions of the police. Nearly one in five didn't want to deal with the courts or didn't think that that the legal system offered the right options. About one in ten of those women didn't call because of worries about legal consequences for themselves.[43]

Often the police aren't even the kind of official help women need. To leave an abuser, women might need social services related to housing, food, employment, or their children. Those systems, too, can be difficult to navigate. When those systems are government agencies, survivors may worry about the negative consequences of interacting with authorities. Some women immigrating to the US arrive with fear of authorities and government, given the circumstances that led them to leave their home countries or experiences they had during migration. One woman told Erez's team, "He has had more power to manipulate in the US because I am illegal and depended on him and I didn't have any rights here."[44] Under the explicitly anti-immigrant sentiment communicated by the Trump administration, those kinds of fears were validated, particularly for women who were not in the US legally.

Still other migrant women who speak out about abuse face alienation in their communities. As one victim service provider told researchers Filomena Critelli and Asli Cennet Yalim: "People are finding themselves ostracized from their support network because they are taking a stand against violence in the house. A lot of our victims have to wrestle with that in terms of moving forward and continuing on staying out of the abusive relationship."[45]

Of course, intimate violence can happen in workplaces, too. When Unite Here surveyed some 500 of their Chicago union members working in the hospitality industry, they discovered that many members were migrants and that sexual harassment was common.[46] Recognizing just how commonly workers were sexually harassed, organizers in California and Chicago took action. In a Hands Off, Pants Up campaign, they demanded panic buttons for cleaning staff so that workers who faced chronic harassment and abuse by hotel patrons could call for help. Together, immigrant and non-immigrant women showed that the workplace can be made safer for everyone when they took action together.[47]

A Stark Reminder That Political Context Still Matters

You and I have seen this story before: The shifting socio-political context of nineteenth-century France mattered to whether or not doctors at the Salpêtrière Hospital recognized the impact of intimate violence on women patients or wrote them off as hysterical. More than a hundred years later, the third wave of the US women's movement ushered in changes in how violence against women was viewed and treated, from legislatures to medical offices. And, in recent years, anti-immigrant sentiment in the US has intersected with violence against women in ways that make the world more dangerous for migrant women and our communities.

Donald J. Trump was elected President in November 2016, after a campaign that featured anti-immigrant rhetoric. Prior to that campaign and Trump's inauguration, my research team had worked with a multidisciplinary group of victim service providers as well as survivors to identify the barriers crime victims face when trying to get their legal needs met. We identified fifty barriers—problems such as not knowing enough about the criminal justice system or how it differs from the civil legal system or not having access to an interpreter or enough money for a lawyer.

In 2015, we started to ask victim service providers around the area to fill out a survey to track those barriers. At the time, we were interested in whether a program designed to improve legal services in our community decreased barriers; however, the data ended up giving us insight into the impact that the new administration and anti-immigrant action were having on the problem of violence against women in our community, particularly for immigrant women and their families. One of the barriers on our list was victims' fears that seeking legal services might result in deportation or changes in legal status for themselves or their loved ones. Thus, we were able to track changes in perceptions of deportation fears before and after the Trump administration came to power.[48]

Before Trump's inauguration, victim service providers rated their clients' fears about deportation or legal status as a medium-to-big problem (on average) for getting legal services. With the inauguration of the new administration in 2017, providers began to rate victims' fears about deportation or legal status as a big-to-very-big problem.[49] Across the Trump years, fears about deportation and legal status remained stubbornly high—so high, that when we surveyed providers about barriers each month, deportation-related fears were often among the top few barriers from the long list.

The fears we tracked reflected an increasingly terrifying situation for victims nationally. Across 2017 and 2018, reports emerged about Immigration and Customs Enforcement (ICE) personnel showing up at courthouses.[50] People who had to go to court for any number of reasons—such as seeking a protection order against or filing for divorce from an abusive partner—suddenly had more reason to fear that they might be detained. Other US policies, such as the dramatic sight of detention camps filled with immigrants along the southern border, amplified fears across immigrant communities with threats of roundups and deportations.[51]

Perpetrators leverage fears to control victims. Long before Trump took office, three out of four women interviewed by Erez and her team said that their husbands used immigration status to coerce women. Abusers commonly told women that they would call ICE, have them deported, or take away their children. One woman described, "He would tell me that without him, I was nothing in this country."[52]

And so, one of the insidious parts of ICE's actions at courthouses, as well as the detention camps, was the way that the threat of being detained and deported fell right in line with threats that abusers make to control victims. The government gave abusers additional ammunition to use in the psychological control and coercion of their victims.

When the acting director of ICE, Matthew Albence, visited Denver in 2019, he was asked about domestic violence shelters' reports that service requests were up among Latinx women. He said he didn't necessarily believe that abusers threatened foreign-born women with deportation.[53] Of course, you and I know better—and that's what Executive Director of the Rocky Mountain Victim Law Center Emily Tofte Nestaval, graduate student Naomi Wright, and I cautioned in 2019.[54] Abusers routinely try to amplify victims' fears, alienate them from friends and family, and cut off paths to getting help.[55] For example, abusers commonly tell victims that the police won't believe them or will take their children away. Anti-immigrant sentiment reinforced another way to threaten victims, this time with detention and deportation.

Connecting Issues

The threat of round-ups and deportation has the potential to affect migrant women's willingness to disclose domestic violence to formal service providers, whether police or magistrates, healthcare providers or social workers. When women can't access emergency and other services that they need, this isn't an isolated problem. It's a problem that intersects with a host of issues, like gun violence, and diminishes our collective health and safety. After all, imagine a woman who doesn't petition for a restraining order against her husband who perpetrates domestic violence against her because she fears what impact that will have on her own or her children's legal status. Without a final protection order entered, gun laws that would have otherwise regulated the husband's possession of firearms and ammunition aren't in play. Her husband can legally acquire a gun, and, if he does, her risk of being killed goes up. So does ours if he kills her and then turns that weapon on those of us who are at the local Walmart or movie theater that day.

The potential of a scenario like this one was made real during the 2019 El Paso mass shooting, when immigration-related fears seemed to affect people's decisions about whether or not to access emergency services. On that day, a gunman shot and killed twenty-two people, injuring at least another twenty-four. But was it only twenty-four people? We don't know because reports quickly emerged that Latinx victims were afraid to seek medical care for fear of being deported. Juliette Kayyem, who worked previously for the Department of Homeland Security, told CNN, "It's clear that there are people not unifying with their family and that there are people who are worried or injured that did not go to hospitals likely because of their immigration status."[56]

In the wake of the tragic consequences of anti-immigrant sentiment and policies, people passionate about immigrant dignity and rights have taken action. I think of neighbors, friends, and strangers who protested the Trump administration's immigration policies at Colorado's capital and in front of a detention center in nearby Aurora, Colorado. Their public actions drew attention, in social media feeds and local reporting, to the mass detention of human beings and illustrated the cruelty of immigration policies—not in some distant place, but in our community. Across the country, more and more people seemed to see the relevance of global immigration and human rights movements in their local communities. Other actions may be less visible than protests but also reveal people's passions and potential for taking action together. I've seen this firsthand at the University of Denver, where faculty, staff, students, and community members have worked together to pilot new and innovative ways to tackle the root causes of immigration-related injustices.[57] Where anti-immigrant sentiment has torn at the fabric of our communities, their collaborative work weaves a tapestry of potential: the potential to make progress on immigration reform *because* we're also working on intersecting issues that can't be separated out, such as economic insecurity. And, in the problem of economic insecurity, we find another thread that connects to violence against women and our collective self-interests.

5

The Price of Intimate Violence

McKinsey and Company—the American management firm and global giant—published a report on gender parity in 2016.[1] The report concluded that realizing the economic potential of women and advancing gender parity could add more than $2 trillion to the gross domestic product (GDP) by 2025. Each state had the potential to add some 5–10% to their GDPs, the authors concluded. Six things would have to change to unlock this level of economic growth, from addressing unpaid care work and teen pregnancy to—you guessed it, violence against women.

Here we are, years later, without perceptible progress toward unlocking that potential. Instead, near-daily commentaries about the modern economy raise fundamental questions about who benefits and who doesn't. The COVID-19 economic crisis put a spotlight on the persistent problems that leave many women in the US behind. Women bore the brunt of childcare responsibilities when schools shuttered, adding to long-standing inequities, from wages to the composition of executive management teams.

And then there's violence against women. You and I already observed that violence against women can affect education to set in motion a lifetime of career and other economic consequences. Yet there's much more to intimate violence's role in the tangled roots of economic inequity: violence against women diminishes economic opportunity for individual women, contributes to housing and other economic insecurity, and drains potential from our communities. But that's not all. Economic problems also make women vulnerable to abuse.

If you're one of the many Americans who think that widening economic disparities have dire consequences for everything from our local businesses' ability to succeed to our national politics, then we share an interest in addressing the price of violence against women. Whether we want to add $2 trillion to the GDP or make meaningful progress toward ending economic inequity, we have a chance to make progress by tackling violence against women. We share a self-interest in policies and approaches that recognize the tangled web of economics and violence against women because, in that complexity, are solutions for improving economic opportunity for all.

Economic Insecurity Takes Its Toll

In April 2020, after several weeks of coronavirus lockdowns and rapidly worsening unemployment, stories started coming out of Hawaii about landlords. A few more stories followed in May. The economic nosedive opened the door for unscrupulous landlords to exploit tenants who couldn't pay their rents. Even the Trump administration, not known for advocating to prevent or respond to violence against women, saw Attorney General William Barr call on US attorneys to investigate reports of landlords sexually harassing women.[2] At the time, Yale psychologist Joan Cook and I reached out to Kazi Houston, Legal Director at the Rocky Mountain Victim Law Center to get her take. She described that "a large number of our clients have concerns about housing instability, and we're hearing that even more right now. When victims of crime do not have access to safe and affordable housing, their options to leave dangerous situations, to safely seek assistance from law enforcement, to enforce protection orders, and to prevent additional exploitation and victimization are limited. Ensuring housing protections and resources are expanded is a vital part of addressing public safety."[3]

The links between housing and violence against women have been clear for years. Back in 2005, a reauthorization of VAWA made it illegal for landlords to kick victims out of federally subsidized housing because of domestic violence perpetrated against them.[4] Despite such efforts, reports have continued of landlords who threaten to evict victims or are reticent to take victims as new tenants.[5] Some states have tried to expand protections to victims beyond those living in federally subsidized house, though laws have not necessarily gone far enough. In Colorado, for example, protections were in place to prevent women from being evicted due to domestic violence, but it was years before those same protections were extended to women after sexual assault. Imagine being sexually assaulted by someone who lived down the hall from you and having to return to that hall each evening after work. Then imagine a landlord telling you that you will lose your deposit if you break your lease to move. You would have to choose between the anxiety and terror you feel each day on returning from work and the deposit money that you need for a new apartment. In 2017, Colorado extended protections to sexual assault and stalking victims.[6]

In the shadow of emerging harassment during the pandemic in mid-2020, Cook and I called for actions that are still relevant now to curbing housing instability for women after violence.[7] We argued for public education about tenants' rights and housing options so that people would know what to do if their landlords harassed or took advantage of them. We also argued that better public–private partnerships were needed for fast innovation in the wake of changing housing burdens and opportunities. The pandemic showed, for example, the importance of having systems in place to make use of empty hotel rooms to stop exploitation and staunch the flow of women being turned away from emergency shelters. Yet, in many communities, domestic violence victims quarantined with their abusers because of lack of shelter space even as individuals experiencing houselessness died in crammed conditions or were left to sleep in parking lots while hotel rooms sat vacant.[8]

Like so many other inequities—from racial injustices to food insecurity among school children nationwide—COVID-19 revealed and worsened the ways in which individuals and communities around the country were *already* hurting. For instance, the National Network to End Domestic violence conducted its fourteenth annual one-day census of the country's domestic violence on September 12, 2019. The census documented that domestic violence programs served more than 77,000 victims nationwide on that single day. Approximately 40,000 of those victims got some kind of housing support, such as emergency shelter or transitional housing. On that very same day, however, more than 11,000 victims who needed assistance were turned away as they sought help with emergency shelter, housing, transportation, childcare, and legal representation. Programs just didn't have enough resources—long before the novel coronavirus increased domestic violence and complicated service delivery.[9]

Given the unmet needs on that single day, it's not surprising that domestic violence drives economic insecurity generally, and houselessness in particular among women and their children.[10] Housing issues echoed loudly in the early days of a legal services needs assessment my team did in collaboration with victim service agencies in and around Denver. The needs assessment became the foundation for a program called the Legal Information Network of Colorado (LINC), which we'll look at more closely in Chapter 6. In the early days of that research effort, we did interviews and focus groups, asking service providers and survivors about a host of legal issues. Over and over, service providers and survivors alike circled back to describe that housing was tangled up with legal needs. Without stable or safe housing, how can victims handle phone calls, make and keep appointments, file away papers they might need later to apply for benefits, or track their case in the criminal justice system?

Yet, for some women and their children, the danger posed by their abusers means they have to flee their homes. Sometimes they flee to get respite from relentless abuse. Other times, women leave their homes to begin the arduous process of healing and starting over—without a house. No matter the reason, emergency shelters play a critically important role in community responses to domestic violence. Shelters also reveal the kinds of service and support women need to move toward economic stability for themselves and their children.

Shelters are what they sound like: facilities for emergency situations that focus on short-term stays, typically thirty to sixty days. Because of the dangers abusers can pose to women who are fleeing, programs rely on confidential, secure locations. Shelters offer women and their children much beyond immediate physical safety, though. Advocacy programming within shelters helps women with myriad needs, such as coordinating with workplaces or children's schools. Women might get help accessing legal information, such as how to file for protection orders or divorce, and help with safety planning for when they leave shelter. Research points to the importance of shelters for women's safety. For example, two large studies with more than 3,500 women accessing emergency shelters found that women felt safer and had more strategies for staying safe when they left shelter. They also had more hope, which is no small thing in the aftermath of fleeing a violent relationship and facing incredible uncertainty.[11]

The sheer number of needs women face while living in shelters reveals the overall uncertainty caused by intimate partner violence and the challenges inherent in moving towards stable, safe housing. A research team led by domestic violence scholar Cris Sullivan looked more closely at the issues facing more than 500 women in shelters at eight sites across the US. Not surprisingly, women's needs were diverse and far-reaching. While some women needed help with one or a handful of things, other women faced complex, interconnected needs that would make pathways to safe housing more difficult—from disabilities and health problems to financial concerns and complications related to education for themselves or their children. Women needed help figuring out how to plan for their own safety and for their children's or how to leave the abuser or get their injuries addressed. Some needed help figuring out financial next steps. A majority of women needed emotional support, including to cope with overwhelming stress. Still others needed assistance to find community resources to solve a host or problems: how to get into affordable housing, find a job, get enrolled in school for themselves or their children, access government benefits, get transportation, or file for divorce.[12]

Sullivan's research found that a quarter of women stayed a week or less in shelter, but more than one in ten women stayed longer than sixty days. A minority of women ended up living in emergency facilities for hundreds of days. The more complex their needs, the longer that women stayed.[13] When agencies take the time to work with women with complex needs over months and years, there's no letup in the arrival of new clients, which brings us back to the situation revealed by the National Network to End Domestic Violence's census: the US shelter system is taxed to the point that thousands of women and children are turned away each year when seeking emergency services because there just isn't space for them.

As much as shelters are urgently needed, they are also challenging places to live. Sarah, for example, described to *The Guardian* in 2017 the lack of accessibility to shelters in England.[14] As a woman with disabilities, getting into beds and showers in shelters was difficult and sometimes impossible. She snuck into a library to sleep and stayed on friends' couches when she could to avoid the challenges that faced her at shelters.

Accessibility is not the only challenge of living in emergency shelters. All residents, by definition, are experiencing traumatic stress, loss, and uncertainty at the same time that they are living in close proximity to strangers. Shelters vary greatly in their capacity to support survivors with disabilities and serious health conditions or women who do not speak English. Immigrant women and Women of Color as well as lesbian women have described the sting of fear and discrimination in shelters.[15]

Outside the emergency shelter system, transitional housing programs also seek to support women moving toward housing security. Not yet permanent housing, these programs typically support women for one or two years and often involve a range of services, some of which may be required as a condition of housing. A central goal of such programs is to give women the time and support needed to eventually establish stable, permanent housing.[16] Transitional housing programs can look quite different—from communal living arrangements to individual apartments owned by the domestic violence agency and leased to program participants.[17] The National Network to End Domestic Violence's 2019 census estimated that 35% of domestic violence programs nationally offer some sort of transitional or other housing program beyond emergency shelter.[18]

When researchers interviewed thirty survivors in transitional housing programs about their housing needs, nearly all of the women said that they didn't have enough money to pay rent. The majority faced hurdles trying to come up with security deposits or first/last month rent. For many others, poor credit history and lack of current employment created insurmountable challenges to stable housing. The confluence of these issues was worse for women with disabilities and immigrant women. Immigration barriers to employment, for example, left women who were trying to leave domestic violence in need of expensive services like transitional housing. Women also described numerous safety and employment factors that continued to weigh on them. Some described that their abusive partners had gotten them fired from jobs, stalked them, and chased them to the transitional housing programs where they were living in other cities. More than half of women worried they wouldn't be safe when they left the transitional housing.[19]

This kind of housing instability, common among women surviving domestic violence, arises out of many overlapping factors.[20] The violence may have contributed to a host of red flags that will concern landlords as they review rental applications. For example, women may have moved around a lot or broken leases to flee abusers. Their abusers may have caused evictions that are a strike against the women themselves in markets with limited affordable housing. Women may have poor credit history thanks to abusive partners who sabotaged their credit or prevented them from working outside the home. In the face of financial stresses and strains, women may not be able to afford first and last month rent or other application fees and deposits. For women who manage to get into stable housing, making monthly rent payments can mean having to choose which other bills aren't going to get paid.

Sometimes by design and sometimes by consequence of not having space, programs provide hotel rooms in lieu of emergency shelter or voucher or rent assistance programs instead of transitional housing.[21] These resources can be useful and life-saving, but they come with a different set of challenges with regard to safety and isolation. Hotels don't have the same safety measures in place as confidential shelters. In the absence of communal living and program activities, some of the isolation that may have been a hallmark of abuse can feel ongoing when women don't have access to advocates, counselors, and peer survivors.

To gain some perspective on what would be required to support women to get to stable housing, Sullivan's team interviewed eleven advocates working from rural to metropolitan areas. The in-depth interviews revealed a few key takeaways for policy and practice. First, stable housing has to mean safe housing. For example, an affordable apartment that is a block from where the perpetrator lives will not be a safe option for many women. Moving safely within the same community may not be possible for women whose abusers have power in that community, such as police officers. Second, advocating for women who need housing after violence is time-intensive work that intersects with everything else that women are going through. Advocates estimated that long-term housing solutions took from days to months to piece together, frequently requiring the dedication of many hours per week. This level of investment is necessary for a host of reasons, not least of which is that the psychological and physical consequences of intimate violence can make it difficult for women to manage the many details required to find, secure, and move into affordable housing.[22]

You and I already know from looking at education and violence against women (Chapter 3) that the traumatic stress caused by intimate violence can affect attention and memory. Attention and memory play a big role in the organization required to rent a house and move. Think about the last time you had to move, for example. You might recall that there was so much to do and coordinate. You had to organize where you looked for new places to live, and figure out different financial scenarios for what you could afford. Maybe you could afford to spend more on rent for a place near your work if you could walk to work and didn't have other commuting costs. If, however, you picked a place further away, you'd have to budget for the cost and time of commuting, maybe having to sign your children up for after-school care because of the commute. You had to call to schedule times to look at places, remember what you saw, fill out applications, dig out reference information for landlords who want to talk to former landlords or employers, and on and on.

On my research team, we suspected that the sorts of logistics required to get basic needs met, such as housing, would be impacted by attention problems that can arise after violence. We tested that possibility in work led by Michelle Lee.[23] We discovered that, as physical abuse got more severe, women's performance on tests of attention got worse. In turn, those attention problems had an indirect effect on getting their basic needs met a year later— putting food on the table and finding housing. Even when we took into account women's income, poorer attention continued to contribute to women's difficulties getting basic needs met. This means that the story is about more than poverty alone; cognitive difficulties that are common after intimate violence also play a role in the struggle to meet basic needs.

Getting basic needs met can be further complicated by the limitations of agencies themselves, such as where they are located, their hours of operation, and their staffing capacity. Women living in rural communities who don't have reliable access to a car might not be able to get to service sites. Agencies might not be able to staff weekend or evening hours, making it difficult for women with nine-to-five jobs to use their services. Or they may not have childcare available on site, creating barriers for women with childcare responsibilities.[24]

Many communities have some of what is needed to respond to the pressing problem of housing instability and houselessness after intimate violence, but not all. For example, communities may have domestic violence programs but not enough capacity for emergency shelter or transitional housing. Communities may have homelessness initiatives, but discover that housing programs are not designed to address the safety concerns specific to intimate partner violence. For example, communal living in homeless shelters may not have confidentiality and other safety procedures to keep women safe from abusers searching for them.

Meanwhile, an affordable housing crisis has worsened across the US in recent years, which means that advocates are trying to help women find housing solutions in increasingly tight markets with fewer and fewer affordable options, which brings us back to landlords. Advocates described to Sullivan's team the importance of building relationships with landlords who would be willing to work with their clients despite poor credit histories and other application weaknesses, even when other applicants might have stronger rental applications. The advocates also hoped that, through relationship-building, landlords would know how and be willing to refer their tenants for services, if those tenants seemed to be struggling.[25]

A world where landlords know how to spot when a tenant needs help because of intimate partner violence and make referrals has the potential to make housing more stable—and so much more. It's an opening to other creative connections—networks and partnerships where industries that have a stake in ending and responding to violence against women can each do a part. After all, both nongovernmental and governmental agencies have a shared interest in thwarting the kind of economic insecurity that leads to houselessness. To see that shared interest, all we have to do is listen to public health experts who have warned about the dire impact of houselessness on individuals and communities.[26] Once individuals and families end up unhoused, the road back to a stable roof overhead and food on the table is arduous. When communities fail to prevent houselessness, many end up turning against their unhoused neighbors in policy and practice—from urban camping bans and laws prohibiting panhandling to hostile architecture that blocks people from sleeping in public spaces. That doesn't make good sense for the health and well-being of our communities. If we keep digging, we'll discover options that make a lot better sense for individuals, businesses, and communities.

Losing Ground, Losing Wealth

I had a bad run of three parking tickets in a row. I didn't know you could get a ticket for being eighteen inches from the curb, to which my sister unhelpfully asked: "How bad is your parallel parking?" In my defense, I was rushing for a meeting and more focused on how long the security line would be than distance from the curb. For the second ticket, I should have moved my car instead of just feeding the meter when I ran outside in the middle of interviewing a participant. I took my chances even though the sign on the meter clearly said the vehicle had to be moved after two hours, and GPS sold me out. I don't remember what I did to get that third ticket.

The first two times, I thought: "Doesn't a portion of traffic tickets go into the victim compensation fund? My parking woes might be helping survivors." By the third time, I just wanted to make a donation myself to a victim emergency fund, which seemed more efficient than going through the government. But, it turns out, the government counts on some of us behaving badly to fund victim services.

After intimate violence, all kinds of costs can pile up for victims. They might need to pay to fix a broken lock or replace a smashed window, for therapy or an ambulance to the hospital. Under some very specific conditions, victim compensation funds may be available to crime victims to help with bills related to the crime. In Colorado, for example, a Crime Victim Compensation Program was established by the Colorado General Assembly. Fines from some adult and juvenile crimes, along with some traffic offenses, go into the fund—and are administered by each judicial district. In Denver County, near my house, for example, the District Attorney's (DA) Office administers the funds with a three-person board appointed by the DA.

The fund can be a lifeline for victims who cannot pay bills from the victimization, but some requirements also put those life-saving funds out of reach to many victims. Consider Colorado, where crime victim compensation funds require that the victim notify the police within seventy-two hours of the crime and then *cooperate* with law enforcement.[27] The term "cooperation" has a lot of baggage, as we will see when we talk about criminal legal responses in Chapter 6. Often things that look like lack of "cooperation" actually reflect systems that have failed victims and survivors. And never mind that the vast majority of intimate crimes, like sexual assault, are never reported to law enforcement. Marginalized women can be further marginalized economically. For example, Women of Color who do not want to call the police because of the risk of police violence won't be eligible for victim compensation.

For the sake of argument, though, let's say that a woman was assaulted, reported to the police within seventy-two hours, and planned to cooperate with law enforcement. She still has to navigate a lot of waters that can be difficult in the aftermath of the assault, including because of the cognitive consequences of traumatic stress. For example, in Colorado, she has to know the judicial district where the crime occurred and find information about the Administrator in that district. She has to remember to collect and organize itemized receipts to submit with the request for compensation. Then she has to wait around thirty to forty-five days to hear if she gets the compensation that she requested.

As helpful and important as victim compensation can be, funds may not be available (say, to women who haven't reported the violence to the police) or enough to address the long-term financial consequences of violence. Consider, for example, a woman whose abusive partner sabotaged her work and credit. As she looks for new employment and a place to live, she is likely to have worries about feeding herself and her children. Back in 2017, the National Resource Center on Domestic Violence surveyed more than 1,000 advocates nationally to learn more about the role that public benefits played in their clients' lives and decision-making. The vast majority said that funding provided through the Temporary Assistance for Needy Families (TANF) and the Supplemental Nutrition Assistance Program (SNAP) were critical to survivors. TANF is a federal welfare program for families with children. TANF and SNAP resources focus on putting food on the table, which is essential to establishing safety and building stability. One advocate told the researchers that their clients "tell us that access to these programs has been a factor in planning how they afford to leave."[28]

Unfortunately, accessing such resources, which can be essential to leaving and surviving an abuser, can be complicated. Some of that complication goes back to 1990-era tropes about "welfare queens" and calls for personal responsibility. In that political context, the federal government made significant changes to the TANF program in 1996. Though each state manages its own TANF program, the federal government added rules about work requirement, time limits, and seeking child support. At the time, Senators Paul Wellstone and Patty Murray recognized that domestic violence victims might end up falling between the cracks in an ever-shrinking social safety net. For example, victims might not be able to meet the work requirements due to injuries or because they were hiding from the abuser. They might need benefits for more time than the program allowed or not want to seek child support from an abusive ex-partner. The Senators championed a Family Violence Option (FVO), which allowed states to make exceptions to the TANF rules when the recipient was a domestic violence victim.[29]

Over time, all states adopted the option or set up comparable rules. However, implementation varies wildly across the country, as documented by a research team from Rutgers University.[30] The researchers found that workers evaluating benefit applications sometimes asked clients about domestic violence, but not always. Sometimes workers made referrals for support services or told clients that waivers for time or work requirements were possible with domestic violence, and sometimes they didn't. This unevenness matters for survivors. One advocate in the National Resource Center on Domestic Violence study described, "SNAP [helps my client] because it is accessible. TANF could be a vital support, but the barriers to accessing it are a real problem."[31]

In that same National Resource Center on Domestic Violence study, advocates described a host of problems with screening, starting with lack of privacy. Victims are sometimes asked domestic violence screening questions in settings that don't allow for privacy, making disclosures that may already be difficult even harder. Some offices required legal documents to prove abuse, such as police reports and protection orders. Women who did not report to police or seek protection orders could not prove their abuse using those kinds of documents.[32] Other research teams have noted related concerns: efforts to create consistent procedures and processes can introduce or mask biases in who gets selected for resources.[33]

The importance of accessing benefits also reveals the many ways that intimate violence causes incredible economic insecurity, often as a direct result of economic abuse. Economic abuse can take many forms involving economic control and exploitation, such as when abusers take money from bank accounts or other shared resources. Economic abuse can also happen when abusive partners sabotage women's employment, leading women to have to change jobs or leave the workforce for periods of time. Those disruptions, in turn, can affect women's salaries over the long run. Economic abuse can make saving money more difficult or impossible, and, depending on timing, divorcing the abusive partner may mean not being able to access their Social Security benefits down the road. Taken together, there's ample evidence that violence against women is a root cause of persistent economic gender inequities.[34]

The McKinsey report from 2016 pointed to the potential for private-sector collaborations to increase women's financial independence. The Allstate Foundation, for example, has a curriculum that provides online modules with educational information about financial abuse, financial fundamentals, credit basics, financial foundations, and long-term planning. The online information bypasses critiques of some community-based educational programs that can be difficult for women to attend in person.[35] And yet learning by reading online documents will be useful for some women and challenging or impossible for others. Furthermore, a focus on teaching women about finances and money management makes many assumptions, including that women have capital to manage instead of living day-to-day. While some women do have capital to manage, others are dealing with the consequences of intergenerational economic insecurity or having had their money and resources stolen by abusers. To tell them to learn about finances is akin to the old adage that they should pull themselves up by their bootstraps.

Indeed, when Sara Shoener, author and policy advisor, interviewed thirty-one women about their perceptions of domestic violence services, she heard that they often had to navigate chasms between financial and domestic violence worlds. Financial planning workshops recommended taking abusers off of bank accounts, for example. That might be a great idea for some women and deadly for others, depending on the abuser. An abuser who discovers they've been removed from an account might guess that the partner is preparing to leave, and the danger facing that woman might rise dramatically. Thus, even something as simple-sounding as financial planning has to be coupled with safety planning.[36] This is our reminder that no specific curriculum or program is going to be *the* answer. Instead, we'll need more flexible, wrap-around thinking, including about how workplaces connect to our growing coalition of people with a stake in ending violence against women.

Imagine, then, what we could accomplish in our communities if people with expertise in financial matters built curricula in consultation with those focused on career and educational development alongside survivors and professionals knowledgeable about abuse dynamics. Imagine if separate workshops on financial literacy were transformed to become seamless opportunities to connect survivors with interventions related to education access for themselves and their children, career development, and safety planning. We can't build those kinds of curricula locally without bringing together the expertise and human potential of diverse people.

Our Workplaces

In her memoir *Know My Name*, Chanel Miller poignantly described moments when her work world collided with her life as a sexual assault survivor, which she was trying to keep private. Miller was unconscious when she was sexually assaulted, which meant that she did not know what precisely happened to her. She was waiting on results from a forensic medical exam to piece together what had been done to her. She described, "One day I received a call at work: no semen found . . . 'Thank you!,' I said, my co-workers in close proximity, 'You have a nice day, too.'"[37] When the DA called to tell her the trial was delayed, "My company was small, how would I explain my strange absences? Everyone thought I was taking off in June, but now I'd have to tell them I'd be gone in July or August or September."[38] Her sister, a key witness, would have to make new plans with college instructors during her fall quarter.

Waiting on news about details from an investigation, managing physical injuries, and weathering psychological distress can all affect a survivor's work life—as can an abuser's controlling tactics. When abusive partners block access to education, healthcare, and friends, they can impede women's access to job training, gainful employment, and meaningful careers. Consider, for example, what researchers discovered some women go through just to get to work, let alone what they contend with once at their desks.[39] A study that asked more than 500 women about tactics abusers used to disrupt work found that it was common for abusers to do things that made it difficult to get to work—from taking car keys to preventing women from leaving the house or not showing up for childcare.[40]

Once at work, abusers commonly harassed and stalked women there. For example, they made frequent phone calls to interrupt women, or they made threats or told lies to coerce women into leaving work. Women described also having to contend with abusers bothering, threatening, or lying to co-workers.[41] Nearly two out of three women who participated in a study of domestic violence in Maine said that they quit or got fired from jobs because of the abuse.[42]

Persistent phone calls can interrupt women's concentration, but that's not all. Stalking can amplify the psychological harm of intimate violence, adding to fear and psychological distress. Interruptions, fear, and psychological distress are a toxic combination for job performance and can contribute to absenteeism as well.

When women miss work due to intimate violence, their supervisors may not know the reason, believing instead that the women don't care about their performance or aren't capable of performing well. "We hear from women on a regular basis that domestic violence prevents them from going to work," Katie Ray-Jones, the CEO of the National Domestic Violence hotline, told Fast Company in 2016.[43] Ellen Bravo from Family Values@Work described that when women have visible injuries, like black eyes, they're more likely to call in sick than risk having to answer questions about what happened.[44]

The National Domestic Violence Hotline has some straightforward advice for employers for figuring out when intimate violence might be affecting job performance.[45] For example, when employees use up their sick time, seem withdrawn, are distracted by persistent texts and phone calls, employers should consider whether their employees are dealing with violence before jumping to the assumption that they are just bad performers at work. This is part of managing the downstream consequences of violence in ways that support workers and minimize the costs businesses pay when they lose talent because team members get fired or quit jobs.

Of course, employers, like any number of people, may feel hesitant to bring up domestic violence at work. We have a long tradition in the US of thinking violence is a private matter or that survivors won't want to talk about it at work. To be sure, talking about violence has to be handled carefully and skillfully, but avoiding the conversation isn't the answer—because those conversations are already happening in your workplace. Researchers from the University of Kentucky interviewed more than 500 women about the intersections of domestic violence and workplaces.[46] They discovered that about two-thirds of women had already disclosed the abuse to someone at work. That finding comes from the early 2000s, long before the #MeToo movement dealt a blow to long-held taboos against talking about intimate violence. The number may be even higher today.

Women's reasons for disclosing abuse at work varied. Sometimes they just needed support from friends and co-workers. Others thought their supervisors knew anyway or needed to ask for time off for things like going to court. Some women had to disclose after their abusers showed up at work. A minority of women disclosed at work because they were afraid. They told the researchers things such as "I was afraid to leave work because I thought he would be waiting outside for me" or "If anything happened to me, I wanted her to know as much as possible about him." Some women were worried about more than their own safety: "I was afraid for their safety." The safety and well-being of a whole office could depend on what co-workers notice and how the organization responds.[47]

The staff at Mercy Hospital in Chicago know this all too well.[48] As the rest of the country looked ahead to holidays, news reports described that shots rang out in the parking lot. Dr. Tamara O'Neal lay on the ground as a witness from an upper window watched a figure fire multiple shots into her still body. Juan Lopez's fingers were on the trigger. Lopez killed O'Neal, his ex-fiancé, outside the ER where she worked. Next, he went inside and kept shooting, causing more injuries and more deaths. Dayna Less, a first-year resident from the pharmacy, was in the wrong place when the elevator doors opened up. Samuel Jimenez, an officer, wore a bulletproof vest that didn't matter because Lopez shot him in the neck.

Lopez's backstory isn't surprising. He had been kicked out of a firefighting academy after harassing a woman cadet. An ex-girlfriend filed a protection order against for stalking, yet he had a concealed gun permit. Had people known about the protection order when reviewing the permit applications? Thoughts and prayers won't help us figure out the answer to that question as the interconnections between gun violence, intimate violence, and workplace safety come into sharp relief. O'Neal, Less, and Jimenez lay dead, shot down at a hospital where they showed up to do the work of healing and protecting others. Their co-workers were left to grieve and begin a chapter of dealing with the trauma that had unfolded in their hallways.

Sadly, there is no shortage of stories like Mercy Hospital's. Together, those stories and lost lives show that businesses of all sizes and types have a stake in keeping workers safe from intimate violence. The price of failing to do so is too high, sometimes weighed in lost productivity from an individual employee and other times in bodies in the hallway.

We have an opportunity to connect the tragedies faced by places like Mercy Hospital to forces that can be leveraged for change. Consider, for example, that many corporations are eager to demonstrate their corporate social responsibility. Lots of us are probably used to thinking about corporate social responsibility in terms of whether businesses donate to the local Little League, let employees use work time for annual service days, or have workplace wellness programs. Alice de Jonge, a business scholar from Monash University in Australia, though, made the case that addressing domestic violence should be a key component of corporate social responsibility.[49]

Her case for domestic violence and corporate social responsibility opens with the situation you and I have been dealing with: intimate partner violence rates have persisted and/or risen while social services and social safety nets haven't kept pace or declined. The needs of women and children affected by family violence go unmet year after year. This social failure, de Jong argues, means that the burden for dealing with domestic violence is one that businesses must bear. After all, businesses have an interest here. As we've seen, intimate violence leads to lost productivity for individual workers and has an impact on other workers. For some workplaces, the abuser is the one employed there, bringing violence and abusive behaviors into the office, plant, or board room. Responding to domestic violence is good business practice, offering a way for companies to build morale and demonstrate tangibly their care for employees. de Jonge described this as a virtuous cycle that can benefit businesses and the bottom line. After all, it's less costly for businesses to respond to intimate partner violence than to fire employees (whether they are victims or abusers) and rehire new employees.

Back in 2012, the Obama administration made a similar case for the federal government, the largest employer in the US.[50] The President argued that the government's policy to promote the health and safety of federal employees included addressing intimate partner violence. The President directed agencies to take a multiprong approach that included prevention and early intervention for domestic violence committed by or against employees, building up employee assistance programs to respond to domestic violence, specifying leave policies related to domestic violence, developing guidelines for when disciplinary actions should be taken against those who commit domestic violence, and improving workplace safety.

Researchers have identified a host of things that individual workers and workplaces can do to support women.[51] Each of us can listen to or spend breaks with survivors. We can help out with non-work responsibilities or safety plans. Supervisors can support survivors directly by being as flexible as possible with scheduling and workload or helping to get calls screened and escorts through the parking lot at night. Structurally, businesses can develop security plans for workplaces that are responsive to domestic violence and make information about resources highly visible—from human resources offices to bathroom stalls. The majority of women who got some kind of help in their workplaces credited those efforts with helping them stay employed. Your actions and your workplaces' actions matter.

What happens, though, when the workplace is at home? As more sectors of the economy give people options to telecommute and the gig economy becomes a larger piece of the puzzle, we have relatively little research on how intimate violence plays out in these new work spaces. Telecommuting, for example, relies on technology. On the one hand, this might create flexibility for women navigating violence who need to get to court and health appointments. On the other hand, technology has a dark side that offers a means for abusers to stalk and monitor victims.

We also have to contend with the problem that workplace abusers are not necessarily women's intimate partners. Sometimes they are colleagues, supervisors, and acquaintances. The serious problem of workplace sexual harassment and violence captured national attention in 2017, when landmark reporting by Jodi Kantor, Megan Twohey, and Ronan Farrow revealed multiple allegations against media mogul Harvey Weinstein. In their 2019 bestselling book, *She Said*, Kantor and Twohey recalled, "on October 5, 2017, we watched with astonishment as a dam wall broke. Millions of women around the world told their own stories of mistreatment. Large numbers of men suddenly had to answer for their predatory behavior, a moment of accountability without precedent. Our work was only one driver of that change, which had been building for years, thanks to the efforts of pioneering feminists and legal scholars; Anita Hill; Tarana Burke, the activist who founded the #MeToo movement; and many others, including our fellow journalists."[52] Indeed, #MeToo had been introduced more than a decade earlier, in 2006, by Tarana Burke as a way to bring attention to how dreadfully common are sexual abuse and assault. Overnight, their reporting, though, awakened choruses of #MeToo on social media.

Over time, more than eighty women accused Weinstein of sexual harassment and assault. Eventually charges were filed in New York and California on multiple counts of sexual assault. Weinstein's New York trial in early 2020 brought the problems of workplace sexual harassment and assault into the media spotlight. Weinstein was convicted of two counts of sexual assault after his defense team dusted off seemingly every myth about sexual assault ever invented. They said women lied, remembered incorrectly, couldn't have been abused because they stayed in relationships with Weinstein, weren't injured enough for what happened to have been rape, and on and on.

The Weinstein trial was something to behold as a trauma psychologist. The narratives and counter-narratives were fast and furious. Against the more jaw-dropping claims—such as when Weinstein's lawyer Donna Rotunno claimed that women needed to prevent their own victimization—it was easy to lose sight of how harassment and abuse chip away at women's career opportunities and economic well-being. And yet, the point was right there in what Rotunno said when asked if she had ever been sexually assaulted: "I have not because I would never put myself in that position. . . . I've always made choices from college age on where I never drank too much. I never went home with someone that I didn't know. I just never put myself in any vulnerable circumstances ever."[53] According to Rotunno's logic, women should give up on career opportunities in offices and industries where abusers work because otherwise they are responsible for being abused and harassed.

Rotunno isn't alone in holding on to outrageous views about harassment, assault, and responsibility. In March 2017, a few months before the Weinstein case broke open, the *Washington Post* reported that Vice President Mike Pence would not eat dinner with a woman unless his wife was there, nor would he go to events that served alcohol without her.[54] The social rules perpetuated by the Rotunnos and Pences of the world diminish women's opportunity, turning them into sexual objects who must avoid dangerous men or be avoided by susceptible men. Either way, the result is the same: women pay career and economic prices for abuse and harassment—damned if they do keep working in places with abusers and damned if they don't because they lose access to opportunity.

The silence breakers who bravely spoke out about Harvey Weinstein, such as Ashley Judd, helped the world see how abuse and harassment diminish women's contributions and curtail their opportunities.[55] Whether movie stars or warehouse workers, sexual harassment costs women and workplaces.

That much was clear when the Select Task Force on the Study of Harassment in the Workplace, convened by the US Equal Employment Opportunity Commission (EEOC), released a 2016 report after a year and a half of effort. The Task Force brought together diverse stakeholders, from academics and legal experts to employers and employee advocacy groups as well as organized labor. They studied EEOC data as well as academic research and heard testimony.

The bottom line? Harassment is terribly common in US workplaces. For example, 45% of the complaints made to the EEOC in 2015 alleged harassment based on sex and 34% on race. The Task Force shared Jacquelyn Hines's story to bring those numbers to life. Hines was a single mother with a GED. When a supervisor made ongoing sexually explicit remarks and gestures toward Hines and her co-workers, the women asked him to stop. The supervisor told them that he ran the place; those who complained would be fired. He made good on his threat: Hines's co-worker was fired after reporting the harassment to an anonymous hotline. Hines herself was confronted by the temp agency she was working through about alleged attendance problems. When Hines found work elsewhere, she was fired when her new HR manager recognized her name from the incidents at the previous job.[56]

The Task Force found that most harassment isn't reported. With their jobs on the line, victims are more likely to try to avoid the harasser, ignore the abuse, and downplay the situation. Victims, then, pay a price for this harassment—in terms of their psychological and physical health as well as their economic stability and career trajectories.[57] Harassment is *also* bad for co-workers, taking a toll on productivity and morale.[58] Workplaces pay for harassment in terms of the costs to employees who are victims as well as witnesses, even if companies haven't yet faced legal and reputational consequences.

Despite the clear costs of harassment to businesses, the problem persists. After the Weinstein case broke, a Virginia-based organization worked with researchers and a survey firm to gather information from about 2,000 adults who reflected the demographic makeup of the US.[59] Rates of sexual harassment were jaw dropping: three out of four women had been sexually harassed verbally, one in two had been touched in an unwelcome, sexual way; and one in three women were exposed to someone else's genitals.

"Hands-off, pants on."[60] That was the message from women hotel and hospitality workers in Chicago and California trying to do their jobs—cleaning rooms and serving drinks—while exposed to men's genitals, grabbing, and harassment. They crafted a message that works for any industry. Now it's our job to connect that message to help others see that intimate violence and harassment impact work stability, which is bad for women and our communities. Whether the abuser is at home or in the workplace, violence affects work performance. Losing one job because of absenteeism or other violence-related consequences makes getting the next job that much harder. That instability matters for women's safety: our research team found that women who were unemployed shortly after an incident of domestic violence was reported to the police were more likely to be revictimized with severe violence in the subsequent six months.[61]

Indeed, violence begets economic problems, and economic uncertainty begets violence. You and I share an interest in disrupting this vicious cycle.

Economic Drivers of Violence Against Women

As the 2020 coronavirus pandemic unfolded, states across the US and countries around the world issued stay-at-home orders. The actions taken to slow one public health crisis—the spread of COVID-19—seemed to accelerate another one—the victimization of women and children. Women around the world were now shut in their homes with their abusers, and the media was paying attention. Something in the public discourse seemed palpably different. Instead of asking outright (or implying) "why does she stay?" people were realizing "she can't leave." Long before a novel coronavirus circled the globe, however, many women couldn't safely escape abusive relationships, often due to economic barriers.

Early in the COVID-19 crisis, piecing together what was happening with domestic violence rates was difficult. Some communities seemed to have increases in calls to law enforcement while others did not. National hotlines were inundated with calls, but local hotlines varied in whether or not calls were on the rise. Since then, researchers have estimated that domestic violence incidents went up about 8% with lockdown orders.[62] But in those early weeks, when the situation was unclear, reporters were asking experts across the country whether the stress of the virus and lockdowns was causing domestic violence.

Stress does indeed play a role in some crimes. From examples, criminologists have demonstrated that strains are particularly important to people's propensity to commit property crimes.[63] But, what about the reporters' hypothesis that dramatic changes in the macroeconomic land-scape seed intimate violence in particular?

Economists and criminologists alike have turned to past economic downturns and unemployment data to try to understand this complex land-scape. One team of researchers from the University of London made use of national data on crime as well as regional unemployment rates to tackle questions about gender, economic stress, and domestic violence.[64] The researchers started with a couple of premises, including that men predis-posed to violence toward their intimate partners could either hide those ten-dencies or not. They imagined that, under some economic conditions, men would have good reasons to hide abusive tendencies in order to be more like non-abusive men. For example, a man who doesn't have much earning po-tential married to a woman who makes a good living might try to hide his violent tendencies from her lest she leave him. Yet another man with more earning potential than his wife might *not* have reasons to hide his violence. She'd be likely to end up stuck in the relationship whether or not he revealed his abusive tendencies, so he wouldn't have much incentive to keep those tendencies in check. Based on this logic, the researchers predicted that these probabilities and pressures would show up in national trends, such that men's and women's unemployment would be linked with different rates of domestic violence across the United Kingdom.

To test their predictions, the research team looked at data from the British Crime Survey. The crime survey included nationally representative samples of people living in England and Wales who were age sixteen and older with unemployment data by geographic police force areas. They then asked whether domestic violence went up as unemployment did in those specific regions. Using data from 2004 to 2011, they found that rates of violence did not go up as unemployment went up overall. However, the devil was in the gendered details. When men's unemployment went up, incidents of domestic violence against women went down. In fact, an increase in men's unemploy-ment of less than 4% corresponded to a 10% to 12% *drop* in domestic vio-lence. Yet when women's unemployment went up, so did domestic violence against them. A 3% increase in women's unemployment translated in a 9% to 10% *increase* in domestic violence. This pattern was unique to domestic vio-lence—it didn't hold up for things like theft or more general violence.

In the US, one of the frequently cited studies of economic stress and do-mestic violence was research funded by the National Institute of Justice. Researchers combined individual data on household resources and intimate violence from a nationally representative study with Census information about the neighborhoods where women lived. The researchers then looked at the combination of individual circumstances facing women in the context of the communities in which they lived. Like my team's research from the Triage Project, they found that neighborhood context mattered. Women living in economically stressed areas were more often and more severely victimized than their counterparts living in more economically advantaged places. In fact, the combination of being in a stressed community and struggling with money themselves was the most dangerous for women.[65]

Next, they peeked behind the curtains into individual households. The resources in the household also mattered. For example, women living in high-income households were less likely to be victimized than other women. As the ratio of a household's income relative to the family's needs went up, violence went down. They also discovered that one aspect of men's employment in particular was tangled up with danger to women. When men were unemployed two or more times in the span of the five-year study, women were three times more likely to be victims of intimate abuse. This pattern, they argued, wasn't a straightforward one about men's unemployment. Rather, what really put women in danger was men's job instability—being in and out of work—combined with the economic health of the neighborhood.[66]

If that's the case, what is it about job instability that influences intimate partner violence? Claire Renzetti, a leading violence against women scholar, argued that one way to understand this picture is to consider traditional beliefs about gender. For example, beliefs that men should be the breadwinners, the ones with greater career achievement than women, the ones in control and in charge. For men who buy into these rigid beliefs about gender in relationships, job instability and unemployment challenge the world order and their notions of masculinity and being a real man. Men who don't think they're living up to what it means to be a man in terms of making money and providing for their family may start doing other things to regain their sense of masculine power. They may start exerting power and control over their partners.

Control ended up front and center when a national team of researchers studied the interplay of macroeconomic trends and domestic violence from 2001 to 2010. During that period, the Great Recession resulted in dramatic and unexpected changes in labor and unemployment conditions in the US. The researchers paired local labor statistics with data from the Fragile Families and Child Wellbeing Study, a longitudinal study that interviewed parents of nearly 5,000 children across the US. Much like the National Institute of Justice study, the team was able to analyze individuals' reports of their household economics and experiences of domestic violence while taking into account the rapidly changing unemployment conditions around where people lived.[67]

They set out to test routes by which the recession might have an impact on violence against women in families. The research team discovered that the upheaval and uncertainty in local economies increased men's coercive control of their intimate partners, but not necessarily physical violence. This pattern held even when taking into account what was happening in individual households, whether it was unemployment or struggles to meet basic needs. The findings suggested that as men faced uncertainty and anxiety from the roiling economy, they tried to regain a sense of power and control in their relationships. When broad economic instability leads to uncertainty and fear, traditional gender norms dictate that men should be in control. In the face of feeling out of control, the data suggested men may try to reclaim a sense of power in other areas of their lives, say, by exerting control over their partners.[68]

A team from Massachusetts, led by criminologist April Pattavina, discovered a similar pattern of links between uncertainty and aggression when they examined community-level data on mortgage foreclosures and police incidents. Increases in foreclosures were followed in time by increases in police reports of domestic violence involving current or former intimate partners or other family members. However, violence among strangers or nonfamily members did not follow the same pattern, suggesting economic strain plays a unique role in domestic violence.[69]

Women *and* our communities pay a steep price for that uncertainty. In 2018, a research team tried to estimate the economic impact of intimate partner violence against adult women and men across their lifetimes.[70] They tallied about $2.1 trillion in healthcare costs and estimated $1.3 trillion for lost productivity by both victims and perpetrators. The criminal legal system cost another $73 billion, on top of $62 billion in other costs, such as property damage. While the research looked at violence against both men and women, the majority of those losses and costs were tied to cases where women were the victims of domestic violence or sexual assault. The price tag, though, did not include other forms of gender-based violence, such as sex trafficking and sexual assault perpetrated by people other than partners. Nor did it include violence that begins in the adolescent years, yet those other forms of gendered violence also add to the economic burden. For example, researchers from the University of Texas at Austin estimated the costs of minor and youth sex trafficking in their state alone at $6.6 billion in health, social service, and criminal justice costs.[71]

Back to that 2016 McKinsey report's conclusions: we can do more than simply cut back on the price tag for healthcare and legal systems if we focus on economic policies that prioritize gender parity. Brown University labor and health economist Anna Aizer examined changes in labor market conditions for women along with changes in domestic violence from about 1990 to 2003. To understand rates of domestic violence, she looked at women's assault-related hospitalizations in California alongside women's earning potential in the labor market. Looking at actual wages or other related indicators, she argued, conflated abuse and income because we already know that women who are abused are less productive, miss work, and so forth. Thus, she wanted to understand whether the potential in the labor market had an impact on domestic violence rates.

Aizer discovered that shrinking the wage gap between men and women had an impact on domestic violence. In fact, the narrowing of the wage gap from 1990 to 2003 was responsible for a 9% decline in domestic violence hospitalizations. Policies, then, that improve wages for women promise to improve their safety, too. And more.

That's what my University of Denver colleague Jennifer Greenfield has argued when she champions paid leave as good for workers and businesses alike.[72] A social worker, she has pointed out through scholarship and advocacy that businesses, workers, and communities all have something to gain with paid leave. Policies that improve the safety net have the potential to save the lives of our neighbors, sisters, and friends—whether increases in the minimum wage, universal childcare, or extended sick time. Organizing together to agitate for changes to the social safety net that address violence *and* other problems is the kind of change that just makes sense.

Yet the US is one of the few nations that does not have universal paid leave. Instead, a patchwork of state and municipality rules dictate whether paid leave is available to workers.[73] This means that whether a safety net exists, let alone how big it is, depends on where you live. Areas that have paid leave vary in whether that time covers so-called paid safe time—time when victims and survivors of domestic violence, stalking, and sexual assault can do things that keep them safe and often require work-hour time—going to court to testify, filling paperwork for a protection order, getting therapy. This kind of resource makes sense because we know that being unsafe affects work performance, absenteeism, and job turnover. It's a win-win for companies and employees. We can find other win-wins too.

Innovating Through Collaboration

A few years ago, I got a call at the office where I directed my university's community engagement center. A refugee resettlement agency rang with an unusual request: Did my university have a kitchen that they could use to teach a food safety class? The program director explained that refugee resettlement programs required individuals to meet timelines for gaining employment. The food safety class was one step in a path to helping newcomers to Denver find jobs as they resettled.

I said I'd look into it and reached out to my colleague Cheri Young, a professor in the Daniels College of Business. She worked in a beautiful building on campus that is home to the Fritz Knoebel School of Hospitality Management. The building happened to have a kitchen.

Cheri could have hung up the phone, but she heard an opportunity for innovation, learning, and collaboration in a simple question about a food safety class. She wondered if there was a win-win here for her students in a human resource management class and the organization. Down the road, her students would be supervisors in settings where the clients of the refugee resettlement agency, or others around the country, worked. What if the agency did their food safety class on campus and also worked with Cheri's class? Cheri and the agency hashed out a mutually beneficial game plan. Her students would serve as mentors to clients in the food safety class. As mentors, students would apply the things they were learning in their human resource management course—such as evaluating resumes and conducting job interviews—while helping the agency's clients learn about the US workplace and job placement in addition to food safety. Importantly, the students would also have a chance to learn about the refugee resettlement process and challenges facing individuals who might be on their work teams down the road.

Fast forward from 2012 to now. Cheri's class was such a success that other faculty and students across her department started getting involved. Today, the University of Denver Ready for American Hospitality (RAH) program is a robust partnership between hospitality classes and a refugee resettlement agency, meeting needs of both groups.[74] Students leave the hospitality program knowing more about people resettling after fleeing their homes and are better prepared to make workplaces responsive to the strengths and challenges facing that community.

What if this sort of model became how we prepare people to think and work across disciplines in ways that advance our collective self-interests? Imagine business programs intentionally teaching students about signs that employees might be experiencing violence and how to respond in a way that supports survivors and helps businesses thrive. Or imagine the same programs cultivating their students' understanding of why hotels, property managers, and developers should care about being responsive to the housing needs of women and their children escaping violence.

In short, my colleague's work shows that we can educate and prepare professionals in ways that serve the common good. We can move to an approach where professionals across industries and communities have access to the information and training they need to spot the impact of violence and related challenges, such as housing instability, in order take action. Of course, not every professional or agency can meet the needs they identify themselves. Rather, the opportunity here is to prepare employers, co-workers, and supervisors to spot issues and make referrals.

This approach is similar to what my colleagues have built through the Legal Information Network of Colorado model, which we'll explore in Chapter 6. The premise of that model is to help victim service staff develop the capacity in their *current* jobs to notice legal issues—whether their jobs have anything to do with the law or not—in order to help victims get access to information and resources. The same could be done in other fields to prepare advocates, lawyers, law enforcement, therapists, medical providers, hotel staff supervisors, and property managers to spot the fallout from domestic violence, such as housing instability and point survivors to resources. Their actions may feel small in the moment, asking an extra question, spotting an issue, and making a referral. These small actions, caught or missed in a matter of moments, may head off the kind of instability that is bad for individuals and communities.

The tremendous potential in taking small actions became clear to me a few years ago when a woman told me she was sure she knew what people would say when she didn't show up at court: that she was just another woman who cried wolf by calling the police, only to stand by her man. She had indeed called the police after her boyfriend assaulted her. Far from standing by him, though, she was incredibly relieved to be taken seriously and encouraged when a prosecutor moved her case forward. The prosecutor asked her to testify. Despite being nervous, she wanted to play a role in holding her abuser accountable so that he wouldn't do this again to her or anyone else. She asked for time off from her job on the day of the trial and planned the bus route she would take. She'd have to make several connections, but justice seemed worth the better part of a morning.

The day of the trial, the bus pulled up at the bus stop. She handed her fare to the driver, who told her she was fifty cents short. She pleaded with him to allow her to board, explaining why she needed to get to court. He refused. No one who witnessed the exchange offered her help with the fare, and she didn't get on the bus that day or make it to court. The price of justice was fifty cents too high.

Her story is like so many others. Problems with transportation, getting time off work, childcare. You and I could probably have covered the fifty cents. Now it's time to pool more than our loose change. Domestic violence is an economic justice issue that is inextricably tangled up with our local economies, workplaces, and neighborhoods—and with our legal systems also. It's time to pool our shared interests, too.

6

A Question of Justice

More than eighty women had accused media mogul Harvey Weinstein of sexual assault by the time his trial began in New York City, where he faced multiple counts of assault related to three victims. Over the waning days of the trial, psychologist Joan Cook and I worked on two versions of op-eds. Despite the sheer number of women who told remarkably similar stories about predation, we prepared one version if the jury returned acquittals, another for guilty verdicts. At the time, I put the odds in favor of needing to use the acquittal version. After all, his legal team had done what worked so well for other defendants: they impugned women's memories, motivations, and behavior.

When the news broke, a jury of peers had convicted Weinstein of two counts of sexual assault, but acquitted him on more serious predation charges. Everyone had an opinion, including me and Joan.

For some, the verdict pointed to a new day when even powerful men could be held accountable for violence against women. The dawning of a time when prosecutors might take on cases that they would have previously turned away, opening criminal legal doors for victims. Indeed, the same prosecutor's office that won the day in 2020 had declined to charge Weinstein a few years earlier in another case, despite having wiretap evidence.[1]

For others, the same story line revealed the persistent un-justness of the criminal legal system. After all, Weinstein was prosecuted for charges related to assaults of three White women only after more than eighty women came forward. The jury convicted Weinstein on two counts, but acquitted him of the most severe charges. For still others, the outcome didn't change the fact that the criminal legal system was the very same system that causes irreparable harm to Communities of Color through abusive policing practices and mass incarceration.

Looking back on that recent history, did the Weinstein trial or the larger #MeToo movement at the time bend the arc of history toward justice? The answer depends on what we mean by justice.

Justice is "the restoration of choice and safety," according to Sarah Deer, a citizen of the Muscogee (Creek) Nation of Oklahoma and legal scholar. Her book *The Beginning and End of Rape: Confronting Sexual Violence in Native America* traces legal responses to rape in the US beginning with what is known about the history of sexual assault of Native women. Before colonization, rape and other forms of intimate violence appear to have been extremely rare among Native American tribes. Such violence would have violated deeply held beliefs about the treatment of other beings. Responses to the rape would have been victim-centered in today's jargon, focused on women's emotional and spiritual healing. Survivors would have had a say in the consequences, and those who perpetrated rape would have paid high costs, such as banishment or exclusion from their community.[2]

This would all change with colonization, which brought the widespread rape of Native women and sexual abuse of children by White men. Over time, sexual violence was wielded as a weapon to subjugate entire Native communities and to reinforce white supremacy over Black women and communities. This deeply personal and intimate form of violence has been used to control and harm whole communities across history.[3]

The laws and courtrooms that come to mind when we invoke the word *justice* fall far short of restoring safety and choice for individuals or communities. The short-falls have been there from the start, as Deer traced. The earliest legal responses to rape in the US were based on European property laws. These early conceptualizations of rape focused on the harm caused to *men's* property, which happened to be women. Rape was held to standards not seen in other crimes. Into the nineteenth century, most states required two witnesses to convict a man of rape. Through most of the twentieth century, husbands could lawfully rape their wives because wives had no grounds to object to sexual behavior.[4]

Well into the twenty-first century and with decades of advocating for the reform of federal and state laws behind us, a woman is still sexually assaulted, beaten, or otherwise victimized at least every ninety seconds. After abuse, individual women may find temporary relief in the criminal or civil legal systems. A call to the police may result in the abuser having his gun taken away so that she doesn't get murdered with that weapon on that particular day. A civil attorney may help ensure a woman doesn't get evicted from her apartment when her landlord claims that domestic violence makes her a nuisance. These temporary reliefs are unequally distributed to individual women, affected by factors such as ethnicity and income. Failing to restore safety and choice, these reliefs are a minimum that come nowhere near justice for individual victims and communities.

Legal systems fail perpetrators of violence, too. In recent years, racial disparities in policing and punishment have led to more urgent calls for criminal justice reform, from news headlines and marches to politicians' talking points. Congress passed the First Step Act in 2019, which reduced some sentences for good behavior among people in federal custody. By the 2020 election season, political candidates up and down tickets called for reforms that would give people convicted of crimes a second chance. Presidential candidate Joe Biden critiqued the Crime Bill that had been so central to his Senate record and promised a host of policy changes to address disparities in the criminal legal system. Conservative voices urged reforms that recognize the need for law and order, echoing back to 1990s frames used during the years leading up to the VAWA while also acknowledging that punishments don't fit the crimes for Black, Brown, and poor people in America. People of Color pointed out that the criminal legal system works as designed, built on racial and economic inequities that won't be remedied with incremental reform efforts.[5]

Though news coverage has focused on the *criminal* legal system, there is also a *civil* legal system in the US. The civil system addresses issues between people, such as divorce, and harm to people and property.[6] Though the criminal and civil systems differ, they have in common a long history of failing women after intimate violence.

Out of these failings, we have an opportunity to leverage collective self-interests to work toward justice—the restoration of safety and choice—for all. To do so, we will have to build on lessons learned from legal responses to violence against women.

The Illusion of Choice

The US has long faced an untenable, unsustainable situation in terms of services for victims of intimate violence. We spend billions of dollars in victim services each year and still don't come near meeting the needs of communities across the country.[7] Worse, the investments have largely been built on a house of cards: The government collects fines from people after some misdeeds, such as white-collar crimes, in order to give money to agencies to meet the needs of survivors of intimate violence. Enough people have to do bad things in order for communities to do the right things for victims and survivors. When people don't do bad things or aren't held accountable, then funds for victim services disappear.

For example, federal investments in victim service programs come largely from the Crime Victims Fund. Established after the 1984 passage of the Victims of Crime Act (VOCA), VOCA funds get distributed to states. In turn, states grant them out to victim service providers. The Crime Victims Fund coffers get filled from fines for white-collar crimes, which means the funding available at any given time is tangled up with how seriously a given administration's Department of Justice takes white-collar crimes and the collection of fines. By late 2019, three years into the Trump administration, Congress was cutting VOCA funding, due in part to declines in the federal penalties collected by Trump's Department of Justice.[8] By summer 2021, Congress finally passed the VOCA Fix to Sustain Crime Victims Act Fund of 2021 at the urging of victim service agencies around the country.

The VOCA Fix was urgently needed because cuts and inconsistencies in VOCA funding matter in the lives of victims. That's what my team concluded when we evaluated changes in victim services in Colorado from 2015 to 2019. We analyzed grant reports and interviewed program directors from across the state to figure out what, if anything, changed when the state saw an increase in funds around 2017. We found evidence that the increases in funding corresponded with significant growth in the number of clients served, including increasing services to marginalized and minoritized clients. Increased funding enabled agencies to expand the number of services that they provided even as agencies saw their clients facing increasingly complex problems and struggled to keep up. Unlimited growth was not possible, however. Even in the years of highest funding, agencies couldn't keep up with needs. As agencies grappled with the stresses and strains of their communities' growing demands for victim services, funding sources started to shrink and disappear. Communities across the country have had to plan for significant cuts to VOCA and other social service funding.

Lack of adequate services strikes at the heart of choice and safety in the aftermath of violence. When communities lack victim and other social services, women's only option may be to call the police. When there's only one option, however, that's not a choice. Whether women have no other options or want to engage the criminal legal system, my research team and others around the country have tried to understand how the system can better support them—and work towards real choice.

A few years ago, my team asked whether the reactions women got when they disclosed sexual assault opened (or closed) the doors to police reporting in the Sexual Assault Support Services Project. Figuring out what keeps the doors open to police reporting is important because a woman cannot ever get recourse from the criminal legal system if the crime is not reported in the first place. In Colorado at the time, a relatively new law allowed victims who had forensic medical exams to have their evidence collected anonymously, which meant the police did not know who they were. Would those women or others who had not reported want to talk with the police someday?

To learn more about social reactions and police reporting, we analyzed interviews with about 200 women interviewed during the Sexual Assault Support Services Project who were sexually assaulted in the past year and who *also* disclosed the assault to a community-based service provider, such as a medical professional or counselor. The majority of women had also told a friend or loved one, but only about half had reported the incident to the police.[9]

When we first interviewed women, those who had reported the assault to the police also said they received greater tangible aid from both friends and loved ones as well as community-based providers. Tangible aid is what it sounds like: practical help with things such as access to information and resources. Because we measured whether they had reported the assault and the social reactions at the same time, at least two interpretations were possible. Practical help from family and friends or community-based providers might have increased women's likelihood of reporting to law enforcement. Or, friends and family as well as community-based providers might have rallied to provide practical help *after* women made a report to law enforcement.

We tried to untangle whether tangible aid led to law enforcement reporting or vice versa. Recall that about half of women had *not* reported to law enforcement when we first interviewed them; however, about 10% of women made a report to law enforcement over the next nine months. For these women, we were able to ask whether tangible aid from family and friends or community-based providers increased the likelihood that women reported the sexual assault to law enforcement down the road. We discovered that receiving more tangible aid from community-based providers (but not family and friends) predicted reporting the sexual assault to law enforcement over the next nine months. This finding is a big deal for policy and practice: despite sexual assault being drastically underreported, when community-based providers provided practical help in the aftermath of the assault, women's engagement with the criminal legal system increased through reporting to the police.

While our study didn't answer *why* more tangible aid from community-based providers led to law enforcement reporting, we saw several possibilities. The tangible aid that community-based providers offer might include information women need about reporting, such as what's involved, where to go, or how to make a report. In addition, positive experiences with community-based providers may demonstrate to women that formal responses to the assault can be useful, which might encourage women to try engaging with the criminal legal system. Furthermore, the practical help women receive from community-based providers may reduce barriers to reporting for women who want to report.

I hope that these findings mean that when women have access to community-based services, they get to make real choices to engage or not with the criminal legal system. Real choices should be a policy priority; however, as we look closer inside both the criminal and civil systems, choice remains elusive.

Did You Call the Police?

One holiday season a few years ago, my partner decided to have a neighborhood get-together. She sent me out one wintery day with directions to put a flier on every door for several blocks inviting people to come by on a Thursday evening for holiday cheer. I did as instructed, and, a few weeks later, we had a house crammed full of people. As the evening wore on, many people wandered back to their homes. A few more hung around talking about life, politics, and such. I was in the kitchen chatting with someone as I loaded the dishwasher when suddenly my attention was dragged to the living room. I could hear a neighbor explaining that if his daughter invites a man back to her dorm room, she deserves whatever happens. Ergo, he tells her never to invite a guy to her room.

"Stop women from drinking . . . If I had a daughter I would say, 'don't drink; don't put yourself in those situations.'"

"I strongly believe that the use of alcohol and drugs by victims put [them] in jeopardy of being sexual assaulted. A lot of the time . . . victims will drink too much to where they can't control their surroundings and make right decisions and defend themselves."

These quotes weren't from my holiday party, thankfully. That night, several women in the room intervened to counter the victim blame and assert that sexual assault was the responsibility of the assailant, never the victim. Instead, the quotes come from interviews with fifty-two detectives conducted by Sam Houston State University researchers Eryn Nicole O'Neal and Brittany Hayes. A quarter of the detectives interviewed blamed women for their victimizations.[10]

Whether in living rooms or police stations, victim blame is common because those spaces are connected by a long history of myths about intimate violence that permeate our culture. Those myths perpetuate stereotypes of "real" rape and "real" victims, conjuring images of women turning to police, prosecutors, and Special Victims Units after intimate violence. However, sexual assault, domestic violence, and sex trafficking remain among the most persistently underreported crimes in the US. Nevertheless, the lack of an immediate police report gets wielded like a weapon to damage women's credibility, reinforcing the myth that any woman who was *really* raped would have called the cops.

Women's decisions to call (or not call) the police today are tangled up in the problems of engaging a legal system built on fundamentally flawed views of violence against women. After a woman makes a report, the police can do a few different things with a case.[11] They can leave cases open as investigations continue or they can "unfound" them if they do not think crimes happened. For example, the police might think an incident was really a civil matter, not a criminal act (more on civil vs. criminal systems soon). There may not have been evidence of a crime, so the report was considered *baseless*, although not a fabrication. This might be a situation in which someone passed out at a party and woke up unsure if they been assaulted, but there was no forensic evidence of assault. Cases can also be *unfounded* when there is evidence the report was a false allegation; however, false allegations of rape are quite rare. When two different research teams looked respectively at reports made to the Los Angeles Police Department in a single year and to a large university police department over ten years, they found that only 4.5–5.9% of cases were false.[12]

The FBI's Uniform Crime Reporting Handbook lays out two other paths for clearing cases. Down one path, cases are cleared by arrest "when at least one person is (1) arrested, (2) charged with the commission of the offense, and (3) turned over to the court for prosecution (whether following arrest, court summons, or police notice)."[13] Down the other path, cases are *cleared by exceptional means*. In these instances, a suspect has been identified *and* located, but the police drop the case because of factors out of their control. According to the FBI Handbook, cases can be cleared by exceptional means if the answer is yes to four key questions:[14] First, has the investigation definitely established the identity of the offender? Second, is there enough information to support an arrest, charge, and turning over to the court for prosecution? Third, is the exact location of the offender known so that the subject could be taken into custody now? And finally, is there some reason outside law enforcement control that precludes arresting, charging, and prosecuting the offender?

As the name implies, exceptionally cleared cases are supposed to be rare—because something *exceptional* happened outside law enforcement control. For example, an offender made a deathbed confession and could not be arrested; or the offender was in custody in another jurisdiction that would not allow extradition. The FBI list of extraordinary circumstances mentions that the victim "refuses to cooperate with the prosecution," though there's a note that this isn't reason enough on its own to clear a case by exceptional means.

Clearing cases by exceptional means turns out to be rather common for sexual assault. A landmark study led by Cassia Spohn and Katharine Tellis found that one in three sexual assault reports made to the Los Angeles Police Department between 2005 and 2009 were exceptionally cleared.[15] That's an awful lot of known offenders and no arrests.

Spohn and Tellis identified a few different things that seemed to contribute to the sheer volume of cases cleared by exceptional means. One had to do with how the police and prosecutors work together. Instead of police doing their investigation and making their decisions separate from the prosecutor, in LA and elsewhere, it's common for the police to present their cases to a DA before an arrest to get feedback from prosecutors, such as whether there was enough evidence for the prosecution to move forward. The rationale makes sense insofar as once the police make an arrest, prosecutors have only a small window of time to file their charges. Often the DA's office wants additional information before they file their cases for prosecution. If they are surprised by an arrest, they may not be able to do the additional investigation before the window for filing charges closes. Detectives also described being worried that once an arrest is made, people know they are being investigated and might be able to get rid of evidence before the DA can take action. This pre-arrest screening process, though, appears to be a point where cases bleed out of the criminal legal system. One DA who spoke to the researchers estimated that about 80% of cases get rejected at a pre-arrest review, often because the DA says further investigation is required.[16]

Researchers have long observed that both the police and prosecutors orient to what might happen downstream, asking themselves some version of the question: "Will a jury convict?"[17] In principle, police decision-making is supposed to be based on legal factors—that is, the actual evidence that the crime specified in a statute happened or not. In practice, though, researchers have found ample evidence that *extralegal* factors play a role in police decision-making.[18] Extralegal factors are things not spelled out in the criminal statute, such as characteristics of the victim, offender, their relationship, and the incident. For example, how *credible* is the victim? Did she fight back? Does she have mental health problems? Did she drink or do drugs? Is she "uncooperative?" Did she report right away, say, within an hour or a day of the assault? Was she injured?

These kinds of questions reflect and reinforce cultural myths that there is some sort of "real" rape that warrants the legal system's response, with serious consequences for survivors. Consider SANE kits, which can provide critical physical evidence thanks to the women who made the most intimate places of their bodies available for evidence collection. Yet backlogs of untested kits have plagued communities around the country, sometimes because the police never submitted the kits to labs for testing and other times because the labs themselves lacked the staff and funding to keep up with volume of kits. When Rebecca Campbell, a nationally recognized sexual assault researcher, tried to understand what led to a backlog of more than 11,000 untested cases in Detroit alone, she and her collaborators discovered that forensic lab staff prioritized processing kits for cases that seemed "real" or "serious" in the face of budget and personnel shortages.[19]

That notion that there's some sort of "real" rape shows up in the extralegal factors that predict who gets arrested for sexual assault. Arrests are more likely when there was a witness, the assailant used a weapon or caused physical injuries, or when women weren't drinking or doing drugs, fought back, called the police right away, went for a SANE exam (even though the results aren't typically back in time for the arrest), and gave consistent statements to and were perceived as "cooperative" with police.[20] By prioritizing these characteristics, the doors of the criminal legal system end up closed to many victims, regardless of what victims might want.

Myths about "real" rape also affect expectations about how women will respond to sexual assault, which you and I started to consider in terms of credible fear interviews with asylum-seekers in Chapter 4. If rape was "real," women would have fought back, called the police right away, and told the story the same way over and over again. Like listeners in the asylum process, people in the criminal legal system—patrol officers, detectives, prosecutors, and maybe someday you and me as jurors—expect the things that matter to *us* to show up in the stories women tell about the intimate violence. From an investigation perspective, you'd probably expect that someone could tell you the day and time of the assault, what the assailant was wearing, what the room looked like, and so on. If they can't tell you those things, something seems suspicious about their story.

Here we have to go back to what we started to explore about traumatic stress and the brain in thinking about education in Chapter 3. This time, though, we have to think about how sexual assault gets remembered, taking into account how the brain and body respond to traumatic stress. When attacked, the body and brain have to adapt and respond quickly, beginning with assessing the situation. The amygdala gets involved to help figure out if there is danger that needs attention. The amygdala signals other parts of the brain, such as the hippocampus, which tries to compare what is unfolding with expectations of the situation. The body and brain react to the unfolding situation, in part by releasing hormones to help get through this stress and activating intracellular pathways. Stress-related hormones can affect the pre-frontal cortex—that part of the brain responsible for decision-making, planning, and thinking.[21]

If the brain's fast assessment is that there is indeed a threat, a few different things might unfold, sometimes referred to as *fight-flight-or-freeze*.[22] This range of options may seem wildly inconsistent with one another and illogical. After all, wouldn't organisms *always* fight when being attacked? The short answer is that humans (and other animals) have evolved different responses to stress because sometimes fighting back can increase the risk of being killed. Freezing or fleeing might be the ticket to coming out of the stressful situation *alive*.

On top of fight-flight-or-freeze possibilities, psychologist Jim Hopper points out that individuals vary in their habitual responses to stress.[23] When confronted with such serious stressors, humans tend to fall back to habitual responses. For example, women may have learned to respond to aggressive men by trying to placate them to decrease conflict. Women who have already survived other victimizations may have learned to dissociate in response to threat, which might lead to focusing on something other than the assault itself.

This is a recipe for ending up with a story that doesn't necessarily make sense to people who hear the tale later on. To see how that could be, think back to the prefrontal cortex that we considered in terms of traumatic stress, attention, and education, but now we're going to apply that lesson to a crime scene. Stress hormones released by the body during an attack can inhibit some of the functions of the prefrontal cortex. In turn, victims may not be able to plan or take advantage of openings to escape, such as when an offender leaves to go the bathroom for a few minutes. If victims can't plan effectively and their attention systems are working poorly, they may have never even noticed an opportunity to escape, nor been able to organize and initiate a response. Likewise, if people have developed habitual responses to cope with previous violence, such as chronic child abuse, then those habits might kick in during the assault. Victims prone to dissociating may not "see" the opening to flee. In addition, the amygdala, having detected the clear and present danger, may send signals to the brainstem to just stop moving.[24]

At the same time that the rape is unfolding, the brain is also doing things that will have an impact on what is remembered later. Broadly speaking, memory involves three stages: encoding, storage, and retrieval. What gets remembered later depends on what the person's attention focused on because those are the things that get encoded.[25] Attention during highly stressful events shifts to whatever the brain treats as central details. What the brain perceives as central is affected by the emotional salience of the information as well as hormones coursing through the body.[26] Other details of the scene don't get much attention from the brain—those details are peripheral. The catch is that the aspects of the event that the brain treats as central may or may not be what the police or jurors think should be a central detail. For example, a victim's attention might be focused on the furrow of the offender's brows, making those eyebrows a central detail. In the periphery of attention, though, many details about the room and environment may get little attention.

After the event, memory storage will be stronger for central details relative to peripheral ones.[27] Central details are likely to get recalled, and, when they do, they get re-encoded, thus further strengthening their storage. Emotional and sensory aspects of the memories (such as smell) will be especially salient. Peripheral details, however, are less likely to get rehearsed and likely to be forgotten over time.

Taken together, the brain's and body's responses to an attack may not fit with the rape myths to which many listeners ascribe, including law enforcement officers.[28] Some survivors won't have fought back or fled because their bodies and brains took other courses of action, perhaps freezing or ending up unable to plan a way to fight or flee. Habits learned in the course of surviving other victimizations may also contribute to responses that differ from what listeners expect. The victim might pretend to be enjoying herself because that sort of acting helped save her from worse harm with a previous abuser.

When survivors go to tell the story of what happened to police, a day or weeks later, they will often be able to remember central details clearly and vividly. In fact, those memories might be intruding when they're trying to do other things, like grocery shopping, sleeping, or hanging out with friends. But those details might not be what the police expect or wish survivors to remember. A survivor might not be able to say what time the attack happened or what room she was in at a hotel, but she can tell you what his breath smelled like and the shape of his nose, which she stared at as the assault was happening. When the detective interviews her, she might try to piece together what happened beyond the shape of his nose and smell of his breath, but the memory will probably feel fragmented. Like many survivors, she's likely to start doubting herself and unlikely to tell the story in a linear this-then-that fashion. If she doesn't tell a coherent story about fighting back and was drinking at the time or has a history of mental health problems, suddenly lots of stereotypes about "real" rape are violated.

When the legal system operates off stereotypes of "real" rape—either because that's what police and prosecutors believe or because of what they assume jurors will believe—those very stereotypes get reinforced. Is it an accident that drinking and sexual assault go hand-in-hand? Or that sex workers are frequently raped? Or that people with disabilities are likely to be victimized? Perpetrators of sexual violence can select women and situations that play to rape myths and pervert legal systems, thus decreasing the chances that women who disclose will be believed.

That's what seems to have happened when women incarcerated in a correctional facility in Kansas made written reports of harassment and abuse by a dentist who worked in an instructional lab in 2013.[29] At first, their reports went nowhere. In 2017, an auditor recommended the instructor be fired because of abuse allegations, but still nothing happened. In 2018, more disclosures finally led to the investigation and arrest of the instructor. The instructor was convicted in early 2020 on only one of six charges—the most minor of all those filed against him. Why? State law at the time required prosecutors to prove that a corrections employee "engaged in *consensual* sexual intercourse, lewd fondling or touching (or) sodomy" [emphasis added] with the incarcerated individual. The instructor's defense attorney argued that the harassment and abuse were *non*consensual, so the charge of unlawful sexual relations did not apply.[30]

Prosecuting Violence Against Women

If a woman overcomes barriers to police reporting, the decision about whether or not to prosecute her case is the government's to make, not the survivor's. For survivors of sexual assault, the likelihood that their cases will be prosecuted is small. Research funded by the National Institute of Justice found that less than one in five (19%) sexual assault cases reported to the police led to arrests.[31] Only 6.5% of cases resulted in a determination of guilt, most often due to a plea bargain. Guilty verdicts, then, are about as rare as false reports.

Sexual assault cases are different and more difficult to prosecute than other kinds of violence against women, in part because of a straightforward defense: defendants can say the sex was consensual and the prosecution has to prove otherwise. If women aren't willing or able to testify that they did not or could not consent, then there isn't a compelling rebuttal to the defense argument. If women consented to sex previously with the person who later raped them—say a boyfriend, boss, or husband—or continue the relationship with him afterward, then prosecutors worry that juries will believe the "she consented" defense. This is yet another myth—one that got airtime during the Harvey Weinstein trial. The logic went that the women who had come forward were lying because they had either had sex with him before or after the assault or continued their relationships with them. Turns out, though, that if you wanted to work in Hollywood, you had to continue being nice to Harvey Weinstein. Context matters.

Sexual assault is most often committed by someone the victim knows, so of course some women are in relationships before and after sexual assault. One study with more than 250 college women who were sexually assaulted found that three out of four women continued their relationship with the assailant after sexual assault.[32] They were more likely to continue the relationship if the assault involved coercion rather than physical force and if the woman blamed the perpetrator less, hadn't told anyone about the assault, and had higher levels of posttraumatic symptoms. When abusers cajole and coerce women into sex without using physical force, women can struggle to make sense of what happened. I think back to the girls from the Healthy Adolescent Relationship Project who hadn't learned about consent. Coming to understand that they were coerced into sex might be a process, not a moment, because they have to first figure out that they should have had a choice in what happened to their bodies. Even though recognizing and naming intimate violence as such is a process, women are likely to hear some toxic combination of questions that focus on them. "Why did you date that guy/take that job/stay with him?" "Why didn't you cooperate with the police by calling them right away/testifying/doing what they do on *Law and Order*?"

This toxic combination is on display in domestic violence cases as well. As with sexual assault, domestic violence prosecution begins with law enforcement. Incidents have to be reported to be investigated and then prosecuted. Many states have experimented with probable arrest (or similarly named) laws that required law enforcement to make an arrest if there was evidence a crime occurred. This approach was developed to address situations in which women were pressured—by partners, family, or police—not to "press" charges. However, in criminal cases, the decision-maker is the government. The case is theirs, not the victim's. Yet the victim's engagement with prosecution is essential in sexual assault cases as well as in some domestic violence cases.

Thus, women have to make decisions about how much to interact with a system in which they have no formal control of decision-making in the aftermath of a trauma. In both investigation and prosecution, the term "cooperation" gets thrown around a lot when talking about victim's engagement with investigators and prosecutors. The term has a connotation of a willful child or subordinate, a modern-day echo of hysteria. While her non-cooperation gets cited as the reason that a case doesn't move forward, her cooperation doesn't promise that anything in particular will happen in a prosecution.

In her memoir about surviving sexual assault and the subsequent prosecution of the assailant, Chanel Miller described the stress and strain of needing to be the "perfect" victim.[33] To be eternally flexible when court dates were delayed, to tolerate incredible uncertainty as well as the spotlight on her life. Getting through this kind of ambiguity to navigate the complexities of the legal system requires considerable neuropsychological resources, particularly in terms of memory and executive functions. Those same attention skills that came up when we talked about education and housing are required for women to "cooperate" in the criminal legal system. Women have to schedule, attend, and prepare for appointments over time, which involves planning and initiating skills. Appointments are often in locations that are complicated to access, often involving security checkpoints; navigating these locations requires holding information in working memory to follow directions while ignoring distractions. Victims are also expected to interact with multiple representatives from the criminal legal system, which might range from the officer to whom the initial report is made, a system-based victim advocate, a detective, and, ultimately, a prosecutor. These interactions require memory as well as the ability to ignore distracting information. Victims have to repeatedly recall and describe the intimate violence, from initial reporting through preparation for trial if they are asked to testify. When testifying, victims must be able to respond to questions in an environment where the legal discussions between attorneys and judges as well as presence of a jury, the offender, and/or courtroom observers may be distracting.

Not surprisingly given the complexities involved in navigating legal processes, community-based agencies end up playing a critical role in women's engagement. Back in the Triage Project, my team along with criminologists Joanne Belknap and Angela Gover set out to look at just what kind of impact community agencies could have. At the time, there were growing calls for community-coordinated responses to domestic (and other forms of) violence. Community-coordinated responses are characterized by collaboration between criminal legal and community-based agencies. The criminal legal system partners in such collaborations might include police, prosecutors, and/or probation and pre-trial services. Community-based partners might include domestic violence shelters, legal advocacy organizations, hospitals, and/or other victim service agencies from outside the legal system. The goals of coordinated responses can vary from trying to contain the offender to supporting the victim.

Part of the logic of coordinated responses is to share information—at least that information which can be shared. Sexual assault cases are different, but in domestic violence cases, much of what the police learn is a matter of public record. Police reports, court filings, arrest records are all public records; however, agencies working with victims can't quickly access such information. The agency (and the victim) may not know that the partner was arrested for a domestic violence incident using a weapon with a different victim. Knowing that can be key to assessing risk and helping women make safety plans.

In her book *No Visible Bruises*, award-winning journalist Rachel Louise Snyder investigated the murder of Michelle Monson and her two children. In painstaking detail, Snyder identified information that different people and agencies had—each a piece of the puzzle, but none able to see from their single perspective that the risk he was going to kill Monson was going up day by day. Reckoning with the murders, Monson's community established a coordinated approach so that agencies could build relationships to share information (that they were legally allowed to share) in the hopes of saving lives.[34]

My community developed coordinated responses more than fifteen years ago. The Triage Team brought together representatives from the police department, DA's office, probation, and several key community agencies. The Team met every weekday morning to review new domestic violence cases. In general, someone from the criminal legal system who had information that could be shared because it was publicly available would summarize the case: what had happened, what was known about the partner, what the victim said to the police or a system-based advocate. Rarely could community-based agencies share anything that they might know about cases because of client confidentiality; however, those agencies played a key role in the coordinated response. Based on what was known about the case, the Team would identify a community-based agency to make a phone call to the victim to offer services. The idea behind this phone outreach was that victims wouldn't have to piece together where to get the help they needed in the aftermath of the trauma of domestic violence. Other communities have implemented similar kinds of outreach and care, including after sex trafficking, for example.[35]

Our research team got involved to answer the question of whether the outreach made a difference in the outcome of the legal case and in women's lives. Back then, no rigorous tests of coordinated responses to domestic violence existed. Prosecutors wondered whether having community-based agencies involved in cases would cause problems or help at trials. Community-based agencies wondered if women would find it intrusive to have someone call them out of the blue. As a social scientist, I wanted to know if a community intervention could really make a difference in women's lives.

We balanced all of our questions and concerns in developing a random-ized control design to test Denver's relatively new coordinated response. As researchers, my team stepped into the process at a unique time. Denver had established their review process, but doing outreach was still new and staff capacity was limited. This meant that only some victims were getting the community outreach. It was ethically reasonable, then, during this window of time to randomize women to get outreach calls or treatment as usual. At the time, treatment as usual typically involved a victim advocate from the po-lice department mailing a list of local resources to victims.

We rolled out a study procedure in which the Team reviewed their cases and shared information. During the review, they identified cases that had warning signs for lethal risk and took action immediately; those cases did not become part of the research. After the safety review, cases were randomly selected to get the community outreach or treatment as usual. With outreach, a community agency took the lead to contact the survivor to offer services. In the meantime, I carried police reports back to our research offices, where we invited any woman who was identified as a victim of domestic violence by a man to a study on women's health. We sent letters and made phone calls, never mentioning domestic violence out of concern that an abusive partner might overhear or read her mail. When women came to our offices, we told them that we had gotten their names from police reports and that the study was about domestic violence. Knowing the full purpose of the study then, 236 of 237 women stayed to be interviewed. After that initial interview, we followed up six months and one year later to ask women how they were and hear what happened in their cases.

We learned a few key things.[36] First, the coordinated responses did not get in the way of the prosecution's work. Verdicts did not differ across cases with and without outreach, which meant having more people be in contact with survivors to offer services didn't upset trials.

We also discovered that the intervention did not make women safer. Women were equally likely to be revictimized over the subsequent year whether they got the community outreach or not. At the start of the study, my team and our collaborators had hoped that the coordinated response would support women's safety. In hindsight, we realized how naïve that hope was. Interventions focused on women do not make men change their behaviors.

The intervention did improve women's well-being, though, in some important ways. A year later, women who got outreach reported less psychological distress. Compared to other women, those who got the outreach reported less severe PTSD and depression symptoms and less fear. Women who got the coordinated responses were also more likely to have left or be making plans to leave their abusive partners than women in the treatment-as-usual condition.

The positive impacts from the Triage Team's work on women's well-being were particularly exciting, although we found ourselves puzzling over just why the intervention had worked. After all, it was just a phone call, and we learned throughout the course of the study that not all women had picked up the phone. Women told us, though, that it mattered that someone out there in the world cared what happened to them. I recall the women who described that she had tucked the number away and liked knowing that there was somewhere she could turn later, if and when she wanted to reach out for help.

Looking Beyond the Criminal Legal System

Even if a survivor decides not to engage with the criminal legal system, she is not free of the burden of a host of legal issues. For example, survivors might need to take action to make their addresses confidential; file for divorce, child custody, child support, or civil protection orders; or seek resolution of landlord–tenant, immigration, identity theft, or employment issues. All of these legal needs connect to the *civil* legal system. The civil system has laws and judges, just like in the criminal system; however, there is no prosecutor or DA, no arrest or jail time. Instead, a survivor is a party in a civil case, such as when she takes action to amend a custody agreement with an abusive partner or fight a landlord's eviction after the police showed up for a domestic violence incident.[37]

An upside of the civil system is that survivors are in the driver's seat, unlike the criminal system where the government is the decision-maker. The downside is that survivors have to figure out how to navigate laws, legal forms, and courtrooms themselves and/or hire attorneys to represent them. For instance, a survivor might want to pursue a *civil protection order* as part of a safety plan. These orders, sometimes known as *restraining* or *no-contact orders*, tell the *other* person what they can and cannot do. For example, the order might indicate that the other person cannot be physically near the victim, enter a shared home, or have access to children and pets.

The process for getting a protection order varies from state to state and even across counties.[38] In Colorado, a mandatory protection order might be issued as part of a criminal case if there was enough evidence for an arrest and the defendant has appeared before the judge. Those orders have a life as long as the criminal case. When the case ends, such as when charges are dropped, so does the protection order. To have a protection order in place after the criminal case requires a separate civil process.

Regardless of involvement in the criminal legal system, victims of domestic violence, sexual assault, stalking, and trafficking in Colorado who fear for their safety can take steps to request a civil protection order. The process involves filing paperwork to request a temporary protection order. If the paperwork and the victim's testimony show that she is in imminent danger, a judge or magistrate can enter a temporary protection order against the abusive person, which lasts for two weeks. The order goes into effect when the abusive person is "served"—that is, handed a copy of the order. Once in effect, violations of the civil protection order can be treated as a criminal matter. For example, the victim can call the police to say that the abuser went somewhere or did something they weren't supposed to do and law enforcement can act.

After the two-week temporary protection order runs its course, victims can appear before the Court to request that the order be made permanent. Their abusive partners, referred to as the *Respondent* in the civil case, can also appear in Court to argue against the order. If the judge decides, based on a preponderance of evidence, that the abuse happened and would continue without a protection, the protection order can be made permanent.

Getting to the courthouse, filling out the paperwork, and presenting evidence to get the temporary or permanent protection order is one thing; notifying the abuser in person of the Court's order can be another. The law requires that someone deliver the order in person to the Respondent. Typically, this would be a law enforcement officer, such as a Sheriff in Colorado; however, life sometimes gets complicated. An abuser might get tipped off—perhaps by the notification of a temporary protection order hearing or by a family member—and refuse to answer the door, hide, or otherwise avoid getting served.

Law enforcement officers only do so much to locate the abuser, which means that Respondents may go unserved. Legal scholar Jane Stoever at the University of California Irvine School of Law noted that an estimated one-third of protection order cases across are impacted by the fact that the order was never served to the Respondent.[39] Stoever also observed that alternate service that does not require in-person delivery is permitted for all manner of notifications, from business, eviction, bankruptcy, and criminal cases to divorce and child custody—but not for protection orders.[40]

Rebecca Jane Griego was so afraid of a former romantic partner who started stalking her that she moved, changed her phone number, and even tried working from home for a month. According to *Seattle Times* reporting, she got a protection order, but the authorities could not find him and therefore did not serve him. They ultimately left the protection order with her in case he came to her office. Rebecca and her sister tried to track him down themselves to serve him. Though they risked their safety to do so, they were not successful. One day in April, he came to her workplace with a gun and murdered her.[41]

When I was trying to learn more about protection orders years ago, a long-time victim services colleague told me, "I've never seen a piece of paper stop a bullet, but it's still a tool worth trying." Protections orders do seem to help, to a degree. A meta-analysis of sixty-three studies from the US and other countries found a small but statistically significant effect of protection orders, such that women who had them were less likely to be revictimized, particularly in terms of physical violence.[42] For some women, the data suggested that physical violence went down, but not other forms of aggression and abuse.

The authors speculated that protection orders might help for a few different reasons. For example, orders may make abuse more difficult to carry out—either because of lack of physical proximity to the victim or because behaviors are clearly laid out limiting the kinds of excuses or gaslighting that abusers can make for their behavior. The order may also put offenders on notice that they can be arrested and punished for violating the order while also empowering victims to call the police.[43]

In the Triage Project, we learned that it's not always clear to women if and when to call the police—even among women who had called the police before. We asked women who were revictimized six months or a year after the original incident if they had called the police and, if not, why not. As discussed when exploring challenges facing immigrant women in Chapter 4, some of the Triage participants had learned that the criminal legal system didn't offer solutions they wanted; others thought the system took too long. But some told us that they just weren't sure if the new incident warranted calling the police. They weren't sure if the incident was "severe enough."

I found myself on the phone to a colleague at the DA's office asking, "So, what kind of incident warrants calling the police? A certain severity of incident? Is there advice that advocates give to survivors about when to call the police?" The short answer was that there's no one answer for if-this-happens-but-not-that or if-it's-this-severe-but-not-that, then call the police. This is because what looks not terribly concerning to you, me, or a victim advocate might actually be a situation in which imminent danger is around the corner given the particular abusive partner's patterns. But a protection order makes some things clear at least: when the lines detailed in the protection order are crossed, call the police—if women want to do so.

Protection orders also offer a window into the larger web of civil legal needs and remedies that become relevant after intimate violence because getting a protection order isn't necessarily as straightforward as a woman going to a courthouse to fill out an application on her own. When a research team observed court proceedings for about 300 protection order cases, they discovered that orders were granted in 65% of those cases.[44] Women who had their own lawyer, a victim advocate, or an informal support person with them were more likely than other women to have the order granted. While the civil protection order is touted as a tool for which women can advocate for themselves, having professionals—an advocate or lawyer—makes a difference in whether women leave the courthouse with a protection order. Given this reality, legal advocacy organizations across the country have developed protection order programs that often have some of their victim advocacy staff situated in courthouses. These advocates are typically not lawyers offering legal advice. Rather, they provide information, such as about forms and what to expect in the courtroom. By situating advocates in the courthouse, victims don't have to have sign up for services with an agency ahead of time—they can learn about and use the advocacy services at the courthouse.

This kind of legal advocacy, as well as representation by attorneys, can be critical for a host of issues that extend well beyond protection orders. For example, victims might need to seek a divorce. After leaving the relationship, though, harassment and stalking may continue, particularly if there are children in common.[45] In the face of ongoing abuse post-divorce, women might need to amend child custody agreements. Or they might need to fight evictions or figure out how to access benefits to which they are entitled. Sometimes a lawyer is needed, sometimes an advocate. And as we learned in the Legal Information Network of Colorado project, sometimes survivors really need accurate information—stat.

The What Systems?

In 2012, I sat at a conference table with a group of victim service leaders from across Denver. The federal government had put out a call for communities to apply to work together to build wraparound legal services for crime victims. The project required a research partner who would conduct a need assessment to guide the design of the program developed with the grant funds, which is how I got invited to the table. By the end of the meeting, we agreed to do a grant proposal together, led by Rocky Mountain Victim Law Center. When the news arrived months later that Denver was one of six cites nationally selected to build wraparound legal services, we ended up back at a conference table to talk about the needs assessment.

Initially, the conversation turned to the possibility of using the funds to hire lawyers who could be embedded in organizations serving victims. Hiring lawyers to deal with legal issues seems like a pretty obvious direction to go, but there were a couple of problems. The grant money was time-limited, which meant that hiring lawyers would be only as good as the time we had the grant funding. And while hiring lawyers made sense to meet legal needs, we hadn't yet gone through the paces of doing the needs assessment, which was required by the grant.

My team worked with the project's Steering Committee to design and carry out a needs assessment that would unfold in three phases.[46] The goal was to take into account what we were learning in each phase in the next phase of assessment. In the first phase, we interviewed twenty-five individuals working in organizations that provided services to crime victims. These agencies were diverse—some were in the criminal legal system, many were community-based agencies; they served diverse communities after all kinds of crimes, from domestic violence to identity theft and elder abuse; they worked with clients across the life span, from childhood to older adulthood.

After we wrapped up interviews with twenty-five victim service professionals, we took a step back with the Steering Committee to try to make sense of the data. We had all expected the interviews would point to a few key legal service needs or barriers to getting needs met that the group could home in on. In hindsight, that was probably quite naïve.

Victims service professionals did identify strengths in our community for meeting crime victims legal service needs; however, they more frequently identified gaps. Not just a gap or two, but gaps across *all* the areas asked about in the interviews. Strengths and gaps were not mutually exclusive. Instead, the picture was more complex. For example, interagency collaboration was cited as a strength in some instances, but the lack of it was a limitation in other instances. Surrounded with piles of data, we realized we had likely captured the complex reality of legal services in a larger metropolitan area where there had been considerable effort invested in collaboration, particularly among key agencies, and there was need for ongoing maintenance as well as a deepening and broadening of those collaborative links.

Next we invited victims and survivors to participate in focus groups during which we asked them to share their perspectives on legal needs after domestic violence, sexual assault, child abuse/neglect, elder abuse, and human sex trafficking. Like the providers we interviewed, survivors told us about a range and diversity of legal needs, gaps, and barriers while offering specific examples of the day-to-day challenges they faced in seeking services and justice following crime.

Two things especially stood out. First, focus group participants described an *urgent* need for access to information about legal issues and services. One woman captured this in a way I'll never forget. After surviving intimate violence, she had many legal questions. Initially, she assumed that she could call a victim service agency, ask her questions, and get accurate answers. She quickly discovered, however, that she often got wrong information. The whole experience was maddening and exhausting, so she changed strategies. She decided to treat each of her legal questions like an opinion poll. She would identify agencies that might have answers, call each, and then go with the most common answer, hoping it was the correct answer.

Other women told different versions of this same story. We heard time and again that, even if survivors could get legal questions answered, professionals often talked in legal jargon. Survivors needed to decipher legal information to figure out what the answer meant and what their next question was. To translate the jargon, they were left to guess or rely on defense attorneys' websites. As it turned out, defense attorneys were explaining things in plain language for potential clients, but victim service agencies weren't.

The other thing that stood out was the degree to which the particular details and challenges in women's lives affected their efforts to deal with legal issues. In essence, legal services were never divorced from the complexity and richness of survivors' lives. Poverty, houselessness, discrimination—all of these things affected what information survivors had access to and the steps they could take to address their legal problems.

My research team went on to do more surveying of both survivors and professionals to double check that what we learned with smaller groups of people rang true when we asked bigger groups of people. We heard the same things over and over again. After months of data collection, we had to scrap our initial hope that the needs assessment would point to one or two things that the Steering Committee could target. Instead, we spent hours with the Steering Committee combing through data to figure out how to synthesize all the shards of information. It felt like trying to put pieces of colored glass in place to get to the best kaleidoscope image. In the end, our kaleidoscope had four sections that made up the whole.

First, victims and survivors were living in an information desert. Sometimes information just wasn't available. Even if available, information often came in at the wrong time, say in the immediate aftermath of the crime when it was likely to be lost or forgotten. Sometimes information seemed to be out there, but it was written in a way that was hard to make sense of without a law degree or from a defense perspective.

Second, a lack of resources and funding got in the way of survivors being able to get help with legal issues. Sometimes this came up in terms of high caseloads that left providers little time to work with individual clients. Other times, there just weren't enough people to call, such as low-cost attorneys. Long waitlists and problems such as lack of technology or transportation made accessing legal services difficult.

Third, survivors wanted trauma-informed, victim-centered approaches to legal issues. They were weary of legal professionals who didn't know enough about trauma and its consequences and victim service providers who didn't know enough about legal issues.

Fourth, survivors wanted systems to work better together. Victims could not neatly divide the world into legal versus non-legal services because getting needs met in one arena affected the other. Even within the criminal and civil legal systems barriers emerged. Victims worried about their safety while engaging with the legal system, say, during prosecution or civil protection order proceedings or when seeking enforcement of protections orders. They were worried about their loved ones, concerned that they would lose their children or have their legal status in the US challenged as a result of engaging with the legal systems. On top of all these challenges, the legal systems were complex, took too long, and no one seemed to talk to anyone else. From a survivor's perspective, it was mind-boggling that judges weren't talking to one another when the same abusive person was involved in multiple cases. From the court's perspective, judges don't talk to each other across jurisdictions and cases.

So there we were with four major issues and a clock running. The grant would only provide a few years of limited funding to solve the interconnected, complicated problems identified in the needs assessment. We needed a plan, and it turned out that the plan was going to start with changing us.

Changing Systems Starts with Changing Us

Every few months, I present on the needs assessment to victim service professionals as part of a larger Legal Information Network of Colorado training on how to spot and respond to legal issues when working with crime victims. I share the feedback from survivors about the all-too-many ways that the legal systems don't work. Court processes take too long. Judges don't talk to one another. An accident of geography can mean that cases fall into two different jurisdictions if crimes happened at the victim's house in one town and the partner's in another town. In describing survivors' views of system problems, the potential for giving up seems palpable. After all, these providers understand just what survivors are up against in trying to navigate any number of systems, from social services to child protection and the courts.

Yet, in the face of this overwhelming problem is exactly where we can begin to discover our own individual power—that capacity to act that community organizers talk about. While none of us in those training rooms is in the position to change how the courts work or what judges do, we can change how *we* respond to victims. We are in the position to get candid, accurate, digestible information to survivors so that they can make decisions about engaging with legal systems, understand what to expect, and begin get answers to the questions most important to them.

Figuring out where we had the collective power to act for sustainable change is just what the Steering Committee did in response to the needs assessment. Together, this multidisciplinary group outlined a multistep approach. Step one was to get accurate legal information to survivors about criminal and civil legal matters that could be understood by non-lawyers. They designed an interactive website with tools *for* survivors. The second step was to provide training and networks for staff who were already embedded in diverse organizations across Denver—and now the state. Staff from across diverse agencies would become Navigators, provided training to help them spot legal issues regardless of what kind of agency they worked in. This meant that they could connect victims with accurate information, resources, and referrals no matter where survivors' first contact with the victim service world was. Navigators would expand the entire community's capacity to respond effectively to survivors, including as they got to know one another so that they could help clients get myriad needs met. There would be fewer wrong doors, say, where providers missed connections between housing or other basic needs and legal issues.

There's a lot to be excited about in this networked approach, which focuses on helping people who already have expertise do their jobs better. The approach also democratizes knowledge so that survivors and providers alike have access to information that is necessary for understanding options. Readily accessible information can prepare communities to coordinate services across criminal legal, civil legal, community-based, social service, and school organizations in ways that better serve intervention and prevention goals. For example, with clear information, a community might be able to better spot resources that are missing and survivors may realize choices that they didn't know they had. Coordinating and leveraging expertise, access to information, and resources has the potential to help everyone do their jobs better in ways that best serve survivors and our communities.

We can change ourselves in other ways too that have the potential to open doors to justice, safety, and choice. How we do business, how we respond to survivors—one phone call at a time. After all, a phone call made a difference in the Triage Project. All these years later, I've come to think of that phone call as a first step to restoring dignity and humanity after violence. That small step can become the first crack in the alienation that so often follows intimate violence. As social creatures, humans are meant to be connected to and in relationships with others. Violence can shatter that, and feelings of alienation go hand-in-hand with many different forms of psychological distress. My colleagues and I have found time and again that greater alienation predicts worse PTSD, depression, *and* dissociation symptoms in adolescents and adults, after child abuse and domestic violence alike.[47]

If one of the most damning consequences of violence is to leave a person feeling disconnected from themselves and others, then maybe one of the most powerful interventions is to reignite connection. In the aftermath of this very private violation, women may or may not disclose what happened. If they tell anyone, they are more likely to tell friends, family, romantic partners—the people in our lives whom researchers call *informal* supports. They sometimes, though less often, tell *formal* supports what happened—police, medical providers, counselors, and advocates.

Women who disclose intimate violence can be on the receiving end of both positive and negative social reactions from informal and formal supports. Psychologist Sarah Ullman has led the field in trying to understand the kinds of reactions women get when they disclose.[48] She and research teams like mine have documented both positive and negative reactions. Positive social reactions can include emotional support and tangible aid, such as helping women obtain information about coping, helping them access healthcare or the police, and providing information and options. Negative social reactions can include blaming women, taking away their control to make decisions, and treating them differently because of the assault.

When my team interviewed 225 women who were sexually assaulted in the past year about what it was like to disclose the assault as part of the Sexual Assault Support Services Project, we compared the kinds of reactions that women got when they disclosed to two different kinds of formal supports—those based in the community, such as medical providers and counselors, and those in the criminal legal system, such as police and prosecutors.[49] We also asked about reactions from friends and family. Community-based service providers offered the most positive social reactions while friends and family the most negative social reactions. In fact, negative social reactions from friends and family were significantly worse than from people in the criminal legal system or at community-based agencies.

Negative reactions predict negative things. Researchers Emily Dworkin and Sarah Ullman along with their colleagues proposed that negative reactions are harmful because they represent a violated assumption. When women disclose sexual assault or other violence, they expect support and help. When women are instead blamed, treated differently, or controlled, then the damage is that much worse. Across a meta-analysis of fifty-one studies, the researchers found evidence that negative social reactions are linked with negative psychological outcomes, such as PTSD symptoms; however, positive reactions didn't necessarily predict good outcomes.[50] That pattern, they argued, showed that violating assumptions of help and support causes harms.

Back when we were doing interviews for the Triage Project, I spoke with a woman whose story showed how easily expectations of help can get violated very early in the criminal legal process. This woman's abuser kept showing up at her house. The Court had entered a protection order against him, which clearly told him that he was supposed to stay away from her and her property.

Nevertheless, he showed up at her house regularly with some sad story about something he needed. Sometimes he'd wear her down and she would let him in. Some of those times, he would end up yelling at her, insulting her, and hitting her. She called the police during one incident because she wanted the abuse to stop and him to leave. The police showed up and removed him, but not before telling her that she was responsible to stop letting him in. They told her that *she* was causing these problems by violating the protection order. She had had enough of being blamed, though. She told us that she stood up a bit taller as she told the officers: "I know you're not supposed to say that to me. He's the one who violated the protection order, not me. I'm in a study and I'm going to tell the researchers what you've said."

Her story reminds me that we face systems that don't work and are unjust, and yet, we do have power to act. My team had listened to her and promised we would take action based on what we learned from her and other women. No longer did she have to face the system alone. We became witness to the private trauma and indignities she faced. Together, she saw an opening for the long journey to restore dignity, fairness, opportunity, and safety. We all share a stake in that journey.

Our Common Cause

After intimate violence, survivors make all kinds of decisions about disclosure, help-seeking, and service use—including which door they move through first, if any door at all. What happens through those doors can be the difference between abuse-to-prison pipelines and further injustices or healing.

The entrance to the criminal and civil legal systems may actually be through a rape crisis center where a community-based advocate listens and explains choices to a survivor and meets her at the hospital for a SANE exam. Advocates working both inside and outside the criminal system may provide direct services to victims. These can include emotional support, information, referrals, and/or resources. Referrals might be for help to access housing, employment, legal assistance, transportation, education, childcare, healthcare, food, services for children, or social support. Advocates might also help with safety planning and accompaniment to important appointments or in getting crime victim compensation, emergency shelter, and emergency financial assistance. Many of those kinds of services start on the phone, others in waiting rooms.

My team and I have spent a lot of time in waiting rooms. Waiting to meet with community and criminal legal system partners, to give presentations, to pitch research ideas. Lots of those meetings require that we make our way through security before the waiting even starts. Ahead of one presentation to a police sexual assault unit, I jokingly warned the graduate students on my team: "You'll have to go through security, so no weapons!" I said this because, first of all, the sign on the door to the police department actually says that. And second, because I had recently been pulled out of a security line when a dirty fork from some homemade lunch at the bottom of my bag set off the scanner as I tried to enter a courthouse. I had to surrender the offending fork, though I learned I could fill out a property form to reclaim it upon leaving the courtroom. I declined the form and abandoned the fork.

On that presentation day, one of the grad students on my team was uncharacteristically late. Word made its way up to the secure floor where the presentation was set to begin that she was stuck in security because she had weapons on her. An emergency bicycle tire repair kit to be precise. The repair kit *looked* weapon-like enough that she had to go through a long process of surrendering anything metallic on her person and in her bag.

Getting your dirty fork and tire repair tools confiscated makes a funny story later but is embarrassing in the moment. It feels like the whole waiting room turns to look at you. You feel self-conscious of just who might be staring at you as you peel off clothing and unpack bags to find the offending objects. That's how it feels on a good day, when you're the expert coming to give a presentation. Imagine a bad day when waiting to be interviewed about sexual assault or testify on the stand or ask for a rape kit.

Many of the women whom we interviewed for the Sexual Assault Support Services Project told us that they spent time in public waiting rooms to seek health and police services after a sexual assault.[51] One thing was clear: what may seem to be small indignities begin the process of curtailing survivors' choices. Women told us about feeling intimated in police stations, as if they had done something wrong. Some found themselves nervous that their assailant might walk in. Sitting on metal chairs in a cavernous room exacerbated women's feelings of stress. When things went better, there was a welcoming, more private space for them. Better yet, victim advocates and detectives sometimes met women at side doors, separate from entrances that perpetrators walk through, and walked them immediately to a private room.

The situation often wasn't much better at hospitals than police departments. Women described waiting to be seen by medical staff in full or busy public waiting areas. Some described that the general commotion in the waiting area made them feel unsafe, isolated, and scared. "No one was there for me," described one woman. Other women told us about feeling embarrassed, self-conscious, and even claustrophobic in these spaces in the moments after intimate violence. One woman described the shame she felt when she had to go up to a desk to tell someone why she was there. She felt that the whole room could hear her say she had been raped and needed a SANE exam. Despite the shame and embarrassment she felt, she persevered. Yet modest changes had the potential to make things a lot better. Some hospitals made sure a sexual assault specialist immediately came out to meet the woman or moved her to a private room away from the public waiting area.

I'm belaboring waiting rooms because they are both real and metaphorical. Women's observations of the waiting areas align with other things women have told us about factors—big and small—that can affect their paths toward justice. Quick interactions in hospital or police station waiting rooms set the tone for interactions with that agency and influence whether women will leave with real options. Similarly, our brief interactions in living rooms and classrooms set the stage for how whole communities respond to violence against women.

The dogged reality we face is this: violence against women harms individuals *and* communities. The harms come in many forms—to an individual's education and entire schools, to a patient's health and the well-being of our hospitals, to a woman's career opportunity and our local businesses. Our neighbor's and our neighborhood's ability to thrive are tangled up and affected by violence against women. The successful prosecution of a case here or a protection order served there can be powerful but will not restore choice and safety to the millions of individual women and the scores of communities around the country harmed by violence.

So we're all left to sit in this waiting room together. Maybe you're sitting here worried about schools. The person next to you is fretting about the healthcare system. The person across from me is thinking about immigration. And the person who just walked in is focused on injustices in legal systems. All the while, we have the pieces between us to imagine a future none of us has known—the shared interest, passion, and creativity. And we're just here waiting, so we might as well get to it.

7

From Hysteria to Justice

Transforming Awareness into Action

A century and a half ago, doctors averted their collective gaze from the intimate violence in women's lives to blame hysteria on women themselves. Meanwhile, violence against women continued to be wielded as a weapon of social control, tearing at the fabric of Indigenous and Black communities in the US. In the 1970s, the women's movement ushered in an age of awareness that promised change. Awareness-building led us down interconnected paths of criminalization and medicalization. Along those paths, gun laws have saved lives but focusing on criminal legal responses hasn't deterred violence against women overall. Effective treatments for PTSD relieved suffering even as the root causes of violence against women persist.

One step forward, two steps back. This has been our dance for decades.

Today, stopping violence against women falls to few. The criminal legal system is charged with enforcing laws. A school delivers prevention programming to the children in attendance that day. A doctor privately addresses a survivor's pain.

And still, every ninety seconds a woman is sexually assaulted. Another is abused by an intimate partner.

We are not fated to this pattern, though. A world without intimate violence is possible, as much as that sounds like science fiction. After all, social change *is* science fiction, according to organizer adrienne maree brown. To end violence against women would be to imagine into existence a world that none of us has known and to persuade people that the actions they believe impossible are actually the only and best way forward.[1]

To realize that transformation, we're going to need a vision that is more compelling than the status quo.[2]

A Compelling Reason

Our compelling vision starts with finding an irresistible reason for change.[3]

In recent history, we've had no shortage of reasons proffered to end vio- lence against women. Protect women. Law and order. Reasons like these get bandied about when intimate violence makes the headlines. Inevitably, some politician—usually a man—stands up to tell us that they care about ending violence against women because they have a daughter, sister, mother, and/ or wife.

If stopping violence against women simply required having a daughter, sister, mother, and/or wife, though, we'd have ended it already. Since we haven't, let's assume knowing or being related to a woman isn't a compelling reason for social change.

Personally, I'd prefer we end violence against women and address its many impacts because it's the right thing to do. Because girls and women, like all human beings, deserve to live lives free of violence and abuse. Because there's no dignity in being abused, abusing others, or being the person who does nothing despite the knowledge that a woman is harmed every ninety seconds in *our* communities.

However, we're not going to stop violence against women because it's the right thing to do, because we know the facts, or because we're altruistic. We know this from nineteenth-century France and the many #MeToo moments that have passed us by. We know this from watching interrelated movements to end racism and other forms of oppression where facts and altruism don't change systems.

What, then, is *our* compelling reason to move from awareness to action?

Our reason is right there in the interconnections between the issues we each care about: violence against women is inextricably linked to the is- sues that stoke our greatest passions and affect our communities. Each trip to the emergency room for an injury from intimate violence adds an en- tirely preventable cost to overburdened healthcare systems. Gun violence in public spaces is often rooted in violence against women. Traumatic stress from witnessing and enduring violence against women disrupts learning in schools, from kindergarten to college. Women fleeing intimate violence in home countries thousands of miles away risk sexual assault during migration only to find a perilous political and legal landscape when they seek asylum in the US. Violence against women costs billions of dollars each year, con- tributing to widespread poverty even as economic uncertainty makes inti- mate partner abuse more likely. All the while, justice remains out of reach in today's legal systems.

This complicated picture means that each of *our* paths to reshaping the world must pass directly through violence against women. Whether our passion is to improve healthcare access, end school-to-prison pipelines, increase the GDP, build an immigration system that respects the dignity of human beings, or create pathways to justice—all of that work requires ending and responding effectively to violence against women.

Ending violence against women, then, is in each of *our* self-interests, in *our* collective interest. Ending violence against women is the only and best way forward to create transformative change on the most pressing problems of our time.

An Invitation

This, then, is your invitation to imagine and build together a world without intimate violence. House by house, block by block, city by city. Even bench by bench.

The bench part is something that I learned years ago, working closely with Denver's sexual assault prevention and response agency. When I first started working with them, their name was the Rape Assistance and Awareness Program (RAAP). I was quite fond of the name because it reminded me of the history of the traumatic stress studies field, in which Vietnam veteran rap groups played such an important role. Eventually, the agency revisited their name as part of a strategic planning process. I still recall the meeting at which the Executive Director, Karmen Carter, revealed a new name: The Blue Bench.

I admit, I didn't get it—at first. What did a blue bench have to do with anything? Karmen patiently explained the name choice (clearly not for the first time) to a sea of skeptically curious expressions. Two things have stayed with me. First, she told us that making that first call to The Blue Bench would no longer require people to use or identify with the word "rape." Second, the metaphor of the bench mattered. There's always room to sit down and talk about sexual assault on the blue bench—no judging, no stigma, no conference rooms. Just the image of a bench where we can meet up to talk about this issue that matters so much in our communities.

And that's what we need now. A persistently open door (or warm bench) to bring people into the conversation and invite them to action. We need a way to make it easy for people to join us in imaging into existence the end of violence because we're going to need all of our collective creativity, passion, knowledge, and skill to build this new world.

We also need a way to help people see that there is room for them in a movement to end violence against women. Organizer Daniel Hunter offers a useful shorthand to illustrate that there's room for people to take different kinds of action in social change. He talks about helpers, advocates, organizers, and rebels. *Helpers* are the people in our lives who recognize an individual in need and bring what resources they can to bear. Maybe they work in direct service agencies or rally friends to respond when someone in their peer group is struggling. *Advocates* also help people, but with more of a focus on navigating systems. These would be like the Legal Information Network of Colorado Navigators in Chapter 6—people who try to help victims get their needs met despite problems and challenges in legal systems. *Organizers* focus their work on building solidarity across groups of people to make progress on addressing the root causes of problems. These are the folks who use the parable of the river to inspire and guide people toward action that will stop the babies from going into the river in the first place. *Rebels* bring a deep-seated passion to visible, public actions, such as marches and civil disobedience, to demand fundamental change.[4]

Across these different kinds of roles, Hunter describes that people bring both strengths and limitations to social movement work. For example, helpers might make powerful emotional connections when helping people address immediate issues but miss the overall picture of how larger systems contribute to the circumstances in which those individual people are entrenched. Advocates bring deep knowledge of systems. Being immersed in systems, though, can mean that they tend to focus on incremental reform instead of fundamental change. Organizers bring people together to address root causes of problems and offer a strategic approach to change. That said, they can get overly focused on taking actions that they're sure will be winnable. They may tend to take leadership roles instead of elevating others to lead. Rebels are willing to be bold, to sacrifice, to speak truth-to-power. Their hardline commitment to change can be at the expense of strategy and teamwork, according to Hunter.[5]

Of course, people generally don't fit neatly into categories. You may see parts of yourself in more than one role. The point is not to fit a category, but to see that there's room for each of us. And to recognize that we're going to need each other to collectively maximize our strengths and minimize our limitations.

We're also going to need to think about how we show up to work together. Consider, for example, what sociologist Hava Gordon discovered when looking at education reform in one community. Reformers who advocated for changes to local education policy tended to value community nonprofits while devaluing parents and community members directly affected by those policies, such as decisions to close a neighborhood school. A fierce urgency to *do something* fed the belief that professional organizations were better prepared to work faster and more efficiently for change than community members themselves. Gordon found that when organizing focused on non-profit organizations and power brokers outside the communities affected, arguments became reductionistic; for example, economic rationales were used to make the case for narrow change instead of simultaneously recognizing the impact of racial and other injustices and going for something bigger. This had many costs, including limiting how much change was possible. Building connections to people with shared interests, though, can shift dynamics in powerful ways. Taking an intersectional approach can expand the scope and type of change communities can demand and win. That's what teachers in Los Angeles showed when they bargained for the common good in 2019.[6]

The same pattern of professionalization and marginalization that Gordon observed happens in the movement to end violence against women, too. When survivors are marginalized, the movement is diminished in many ways—and so are survivors themselves. Fortunately, you and I have already started to think about trauma-informed principles that can guide us here. The same principles that have the potential to contribute to healthy schools and institutions are also critical to this invitation to collaborate: we know that our work together must be built on a bedrock of trustworthiness and transparency, empowerment and equity.

An Approach to Change

The goal to end violence against women may seem overwhelming, even audacious. The invitation to be part of such transformation can be even more daunting if we tell ourselves that there is only one path to change—that we each have to become rebels, even if we're not; that only big actions matter, like rallying millions of people to march on Washington or launching a new non-profit with national reach.

Yes, social change can arise out of big and bold action. However, we'll also need to approach change in small, everyday ways, according to adrienne maree brown. In fact, brown urges us to look for opportunities for change in the everyday patterns of our lives, trusting that changes in those patterns will create openings for large-scale social change.[7]

Practically speaking, what might this look like for you and me? Instead of starting with a march on Washington, imagine we each begin by fleshing out how our self-interests connect to ending violence against women. We'll also want to think a bit about the kind of role we want to play in change. Are you more of a helper or more of a rebel?

Next, we'll each have to do some homework to learn about violence against women in our communities. What resources exist and what needs are unmet? Is local news covering intimate violence? Who is already organizing around intimate violence and interconnected issues? Are there initiatives under way that are led by People of Color, women, or community groups?

With this foundation, we will probably notice that we're starting to connect with people in new ways. For example, we might see changes in *how* we talk about violence against women over dinner tables with family, during coffee breaks with co-workers, or in driveways with neighbors. Instead of avoiding the topic or talking in superficial ways about the latest headlines, we're ready to describe our self-interests in ending violence against women and encourage others to explore theirs. As we discover new ways to talk with loved ones and strangers about our collective interest in ending violence against women, we'll shake up old patterns. We'll show that talking about violence isn't taboo; that intimate violence matters to all of us.

Now comes the part where we transform the awareness we've built into action. Depending on what you've learned about your community, you might join an organizing effort already under way. You might contact your local newspaper to encourage them to cover domestic violence stories differently—or at all. You might begin to connect people in your neighborhood, faith community, or workplace who share interests in preventing violence against women. Perhaps that network grows to bring in a friend of a friend who is working on healthcare access in your city, someone else who is a school administrator, and the person down the street who works on housing and food insecurity problems in your community.

Now you've started to open doors to explore collaborating at the intersections of violence against women and other pressing public problems. At those intersections, we will discover compelling solutions to move ourselves and our communities from awareness to action. Solutions that mobilize ordinary people to work together to stop violence against women, collaborating and creating change in a way we never have before.

A Framework

We already know that restoring and ensuring dignity, fairness, opportunity, and safety is going to require many intersecting actions and approaches. The actions needed to prevent intimate violence in the first place will differ from those required to respond effectively when violence does happens. To prevent violence, we have to target the root causes. To respond effectively, we'll need survivor-centered, trauma-informed programs and policies that address the negative impacts of violence against women. Of course, responding effectively to intimate violence when it occurs becomes a way to prevent new violence. It's all connected.

We'll want a way to organize our thinking about different kinds of interconnected actions. Here we can draw on prevention science for a useful framework to think about primary, secondary, and tertiary prevention work.[8]

Primary prevention strategies focus on stopping violence against women before it ever happens. Thinking back to our parable of the babies in the river, primary prevention is when we go upstream to take action so that babies don't end up in the river at all. This means addressing the factors that make intimate violence likely to happen in the first place. You and I know a lot about root causes now—the ways that economic uncertainty, rigid views of gender, childhood adversity, and a host of factors contribute to the circumstances that make intimate violence possible. Primary prevention targets those tangled roots.

Secondary prevention focuses on responding effectively to violence when it occurs to mitigate negative impacts. In our river parable, this means working together to get babies out of the river to safety as soon as possible and promptly addressing the harm already caused. Secondary prevention strategies, then, focus on identifying people who have been victimized (or who have victimized others) as soon as possible to take action to stop harm and promote healing. For example, when doctor's offices and emergency rooms screen for violence against women to connect patients to counseling or other needed services, they're doing secondary prevention.

Tertiary prevention focuses on responding to long-term impacts of intimate violence. In the river parable, babies thrown in the river face long-term health, educational, and other consequences of that stress, and our community needs ways to address those impacts. Tertiary approaches, then, focus on supporting survivors to address the long-term effects of violence, which we know are many—from PTSD and physical health problems, to economic insecurity and career loss, and even school-to-prison pipelines.

Of course, this overall approach to thinking about primary, secondary, and tertiary prevention strategies shouldn't sound new. Across the chapters of this book, we've seen examples of primary prevention strategies in terms of school-based programs to prevent adolescent dating violence, secondary prevention strategies to identify intimate violence in the lives of pregnant women, and tertiary strategies to treat the long-term mental and physical health consequences of intimate violence.

What *is* new, however, is how we can apply this framework to make sure we're working at multiple levels in ways that reveal new synergies to bring an ever-expanding network of ordinary people together to end violence against women.

Building a Roadmap

You and I have started piecing together what actions to end violence against women could look like: partnerships with libraries to address root causes of violence, people working together to identify solutions that make sense for their neighborhoods, educating future professionals—from medicine to property management—to recognize and respond to intimate violence.

Now we have to up that game because every ninety seconds, violence takes away dignity, fairness, opportunity, and safety from women and our communities. To move from that awareness to action, we'll need a plan—a roadmap to set us on a path toward collaboration with people who share a collective interest to end violence against women.

Here I invite you to consider a few ideas for our roadmap. These are simply illustrations to inspire you to think about the kinds of connections you might explore in light of your passions and the role you'd like to play in building a world without intimate violence. Ultimately, though, the kind of change we need will have to arise out of ideas we develop *together*.

Promote healthy relationships, early and often. Promoting healthy adolescent dating relationships is an obvious primary prevention strategy to stop intimate violence before it starts. To do so, dating violence prevention programs typically involve some combination of exploring values and gender roles, building knowledge, and practicing skills for healthy relationships free of intimate violence. These programs are *also* a way to work toward other kinds of change, from education reform and prison abolition to civic participation and men's health.

After all, preventing relationship violence promises to help young people of all genders to stay engaged in their education, thus thwarting school-to-prison pipelines. Preventing relationship violence also supports educational success by decreasing the trauma-related impacts of violence on learning as well as curtailing a source of school absenteeism and attrition from colleges. Knowing about consent and communication promises to decrease perpetration of sexual violence, helping to keep young people out of juvenile justice and eventually adult criminal legal systems. Furthermore, teaching young people the skills necessary for healthy relationships—such as how to communicate and resolve conflict effectively—are life lessons, critical, too, to civic participation and the work of democracy.

A growing body of research on different prevention programs gives communities room to select approaches that fit their needs. With resources and community support, prevention programming can be delivered in physical locations and during developmental periods that make sense, too. For example, prevention lessons can be integrated into school and community athletic programs as well as faith-based and after-school programs. Communities can organize together to make this content available by middle school, when youth are exploring their developing views of gender roles. Disrupting the development of rigid views of gender has the potential to go a long way in preventing relationship violence as well as in engaging boys and men as leaders in redefining healthy masculinity for their health and well-being.

Of course, promoting healthy relationships in adolescence is critical to preventing intimate violence *in adulthood*. Preventing intimate partner violence will *also* help prevent child abuse and other adverse childhood experiences. Here we have an opportunity to leverage connections with people passionate about preventing child abuse and to expand resources such as visiting nurse programs and Early Head Start.[9] Visiting nurse and similar programs have many potential benefits for children's and families' well-being. For example, these programs can help families get set up with health insurance so that they can access care when the nursing visits end; support children's cognitive development, which will be essential for education attainment; and connect parents with information and resources related to education and employment.[10] In so doing, these programs can move the needle on a host of pressing problems that are the passion of people dedicated to ending violence as well as improving healthcare and education access or economic justice.

Advance antipoverty actions. No matter whether we think of violence against women as a cause or consequence, it's tangled up with economic uncertainty and poverty. Economic uncertainty and poverty create conditions where violence against women is more likely, and intimate violence has serious and long-term economic consequences for survivors. Thus, pursuing anti-poverty policies has the potential for both primary and tertiary prevention—stopping violence at its tangled roots before it starts or ameliorating its lifetime economic impacts.

This means that you and I have the potential to build collaborations with people working on a host of initiatives that fight poverty, such as paid leave. As my University of Denver colleagues, led by Dr. Jennifer Greenfield, have pointed out, the lack of a national paid leave policy costs the US an estimated $500 billion each year in economic activity. Paid leave policies have the potential to benefit workers, who have more economic security in the face of health and caregiving crises, as well as businesses, who will face less absenteeism and turnover.[11]

Policies that promote economic stability while giving workers flexibility to address health and caregiving needs are sorely needed in *our* work to end violence against women. Thus, you and I are well positioned to collaborate to urge local, state, and federal policymakers to advance paid leave policies in ways that *also* meet the needs of women victimized by their intimate partners, for example.

We also share self-interests in collaborating with those working to address the national housing affordability crisis, which has hurt many of our local economies and increased houselessness in our communities.[12] High housing prices can make it harder for women to leave homes that they share with their abusive partners. Those high prices can also add to a family's economic insecurity and make intimate partner abuse more likely to occur. Indeed, domestic violence has long been recognized as a major driver of housing instability and houselessness, though the domestic violence and housing services have historically operated separate from one another.[13] You and I have the potential to make the case that working together to design and advocate for policies that decrease housing insecurity while also meeting the needs of women and children in the aftermath of intimate partner violence is a win-win.

If we don't collaborate, there's more at stake than just missed opportunities. Without collaboration, there can be many unintended negative consequences for women's safety. Consider, for example, the innovative use of microfinance initiatives to expand women's economic opportunity and health. Expanding economic opportunity and health should be good for preventing or escaping violence against women. Indeed, there is encouraging evidence around the globe that microfinance strategies can reduce poverty; however, there are also dangers if these economic interventions aren't informed by what we know about violence against women. When economic interventions directed at women happen separate from also addressing men's economic certainty or traditional beliefs about gender, interventions can go awry to create environments that increase gender violence risk. We need voices at the table with knowledge about the policy and practical work of implementing economic interventions along with those who are knowledgeable about the dynamics of violence against women. Both movements—to end poverty and to end violence against women—have the potential to benefit from working together.[14]

Pursue education reform that is trauma-informed. We have a chance to team up with advocates for education access, those working to end school-to-prison pipelines, and parents to make progress on the issues that they care about—particularly if we work together to expand trauma-informed schools as a key component of education reform.

As you and I considered in Chapter 3, trauma-informed schools lay out a vision that values administrators, teachers, and staff who understand the ways that trauma and its consequences impede learning and who recognize that traditional disciplinary practices punish the kinds of behaviors that are common after trauma. Trauma-informed schools are committed, then, to developing policies and practices that address students' trauma symptoms, which requires attending to students holistically. When schools do so, they are better positioned to consider *each* child's unique needs, which offers a path to improve education for *all* children by tackling other kinds of inequities that impede learning. Parents advocating for their children with neurodiversity or to overcome technological barriers, like slow internet speeds at home, will find partners for education reform in those of us concerned about the impact of violence against women on education.

The kinds of changes that trauma-informed reform can bring about would benefit teachers, too, at a time when the organizing power of teachers has been increasing coast-to-coast. Teachers and anti-violence advocates alike share an interest in primary prevention of school shootings driven by gender violence as well as secondary and tertiary prevention of learning problems arising from witnessing or experiencing intimate violence. These are movements with natural alliances that are, as yet, relatively untapped. Teachers' unions have the potential to be partners in demanding action to stop and respond more effectively to violence against women because such trauma impacts young people's education and teachers' effectiveness. And those of us working to end intimate violence have the potential to be partners in demanding fair compensation and workplace security for teachers.

We also share a stake here with civic leaders who are worried about declines in civic participation. After all, schools are about the very foundation of a democratic society as much as they are about ABCs and 123s. As more and more people across the US realize the crises facing democracy on many fronts, we can find allies among people who want to do something about our collective civic health—those who care about teaching young people what it means to be connected to communities in terms of the benefits and responsibilities of active participation. Trauma-informed schools embrace teamwork, collaboration, and community connection. To engage in teamwork and collaboration requires knowing something about oneself and others. That knowledge of values, identity, and perspective is nothing short of essential to a functioning democracy where we live and work across difference, driving toward solutions that are in the service of the common good.

Expect good business practice to include prevention. There's a perfect storm brewing in terms of the potential to bring businesses to collaborations to end violence against women in new ways. When #MeToo exploded onto social media, the movement brought attention to the persistent and awful problem of sexual harassment and intimate violence in workplaces. Since then, colleges, government offices, and private businesses alike have continued to make headlines for covering up or ignoring sexual harassment and assault in their workplaces. There's growing awareness that such institutional betrayal exacerbates the impacts of intimate violence on individuals while also hurting the institutions themselves.[15]

Meanwhile, other forces have been pushing businesses toward related kinds of change. For instance, activists and unions have been organizing for living wages, worker protections, and paid leave. Shareholders and customers have agitated companies, small and large, to demonstrate that they're socially or environmentally conscious and deserve their investment dollars and business.

In this mix, you and I can find many collaborators to end violence against women. When businesses recognize that intimate violence can disrupt their employees' well-being and productivity as well as their reputations, we have a chance to invite them to prevention work. Primary prevention can take many forms, including implementing policies that promote economic security for their employees.

There's also room for businesses to do the work of secondary and tertiary prevention. They can show institutional courage by acknowledging and responding to sexual harassment in the workplace, which promises to support employees' well-being and commitment to the company as well as enhance their reputations.[16] They can design and implement policies that support survivors, encouraging cultures in which victims can safely disclose what's happening and get help. They can focus on building respect up and down the organizational chart to ensure employees feel safe and empowered to speak out against harassment.

To build prevention strategies into their business practices, the business sector need not recreate the wheel. Here we find potential for collaborations between schools and health professions, which have already started building trauma-informed systems. After all, schools and health professionals share a stake in what happens to their graduates and patients in workplaces.

You and I can be part of helping businesses apply trauma-informed principles that contribute to workplaces that are rooted in safety and transparency, support and collaboration, as well as empowerment and equity. This might be work you can embark on sooner than later. Maybe you're a company executive or a team leader, in which case you have room to create immediate change in how you work with colleagues and advocate for change in your company's policies and practices.[17]

Of course, we also have room to agitate for change as customers, too, in big and small ways. The small ways came to mind recently when I took a tour of a historic hotel rumored to be haunted by ghosts. Between questions and answers from other tour guests about ghost sightings and renovations, I asked if the hotel gave panic buttons to staff to prevent and respond to sexual harassment. They didn't, but the owner explained a series of other prevention strategies used by their team. The owner learned that potential customers care about sexual harassment in their workplace, and people on the tour who hadn't thought about the need for such protections had a new way to evaluate where they spend their hotel dollars. And then we all got back to the business of ghosts.

Work for racial justice. The story of violence against women is in so many ways a story of racial violence and injustice. Sexual violence has long been a tool of colonization and enforcement of racial hierarchies. The sexual assault, kidnapping, and murder of Indigenous women was a means of destroying communities and taking land as Europeans pushed across what is now the US.[18] Black women were routinely assaulted by White men to enforce enslavement, and later, Jim Crow laws; meanwhile, sexual assault harassment and assault allegations were wielded against Black men as an excuse to lynch, maim, and imprison them.[19]

This history lives on. Today, we can measure the connections between intimate violence and racial injustice in many ways—from the number of deaths of Black trans women and Indigenous women to the ways that racial inequities perpetuate the economic circumstances that make intimate violence more likely to happen and harder to escape.

In these connections, we find more than an invitation to see efforts to end violence against women as related to racial justice work—there's an imperative to work for both at the same time. Our approach to collaboration and collective action should follow the lead of Women of Color across history, from civil rights organizers and the Combahee River Collective to the current Black Lives Matter movement, who have shown that the struggle to end racial injustice is fundamentally the struggle for the restoration of dignity, fairness, opportunity, and safety across all aspects of a human life.

This means we have a chance to show up to engage the wide range of people who share an interest in racial justice to simultaneously work to end violence against women. That recognition is built into the Black Lives Movement platform, for example, in the commitment to "build a space that affirms Black women and is free from sexism, misogyny, and environments in which men are centered."[20]

However, *how* we show up to racial justice work matters. The Black Lives Matter and other movements for racial justice have revealed much about the importance of leadership and accountability, particularly the serious problem of well-intentioned actions by White people and people who bring power and privilege because of other identities who are not accountable to affected communities. In the action plan that we're building, we have to keep asking over and over again where each of us should lead and where we should listen; where we should act and where we should advance and amplify someone else's actions. This mirrors the complicated dance that ending violence against women is not women's responsibility and yet we need to support women survivors and leaders, to be accountable to women in moving forward.

Advocate for community responses to social problems. Across the country, communities are grappling with the consequences of long-standing dependence on criminal legal responses to circumstances that arise from a host of social problems, from mental illness and addiction to poverty. This dependence is on display, for example, when communities turn to 911 because there are unhoused individuals in their neighborhoods or politicians promote the criminalization of overnight camping to stop those experiencing homelessness from sleeping in tents in public spaces.[21] Criminalizing mental illness, addiction, and poverty puts more people in contact with the criminal legal system, a system that is ill-equipped to prevent those social problems, while simultaneously perpetuating racial and economic inequities.

Here, you and I share self-interests with people across the country focused on decreasing reliance on the criminal legal system. You and I have already seen pitfalls when our collective ability to imagine answers is constrained by what we've been doing. For example, focusing attention on incremental changes to criminal statutes or funding that prioritizes collaboration with law enforcement has reinforced calling 911 *after* violence occurs instead of *preventing* the interrelated problems that make intimate violence likely to occur or difficult to address when it does happen.

You and I have a chance to be part of collaborative efforts to radically re-imagine a shift from reliance on criminal policies after the fact to economic, public health, community, and human rights policies that prevent intimate violence and related social problems.[22] This includes, for example, investing in mental and behavioral health responses to prevent violence long before ambulances and police investigators get called to turn up at the scenes of shootings.

Of course, policy shifts to public health or economic strategies to prevent intimate violence and related problems will take time to have an impact, but there are steps we can take in the meantime to test new ways of imagining responses to violence. In my corner of Colorado, for example, Denver has been piloting a co-responder program, which pairs police officers with mental health professionals to respond to calls for service where there seems to be a mental health component.[23] They're going one step further in the Support Team Assisted Response (STAR) program to send response teams that include medical technicians and behavioral health clinicians, but not police, to address mental health, substance abuse, and housing-related crises.[24]

Broaden options for justice and accountability. Across the country, there's palpable concern over the state of the US criminal legal system and broad agreement that long-standing racial and economic inequities must be remedied. Whether people want to abolish or reform the modern penal system, you and I share the awareness of fundamental problems in the criminal legal system. That shared awareness can be leveraged for action, including actions that expand notions of justice and accountability to emphasize healing for survivors.

Consider, for example, what survivors say they want after intimate violence. They tend to talk about wanting a mix of things, such as material and practical support, safety, recognition of the harm from the community, accountability for the offender, prevention, and to be valued and heard.[25] Few of these survivor goals can be met through the criminal legal system, an adversarial system focused on punishment.

By elevating and amplifying survivors' perspectives, we can move toward a more expansive view of justice that focuses on restoring and ensuring dignity, fairness, opportunity, and safety for individuals and communities. By prioritizing what victims and communities want and need to restore dignity or opportunity, we'll likely find ourselves looking outside the constraints of the criminal legal system. Individual and community needs and desires are likely to be varied, which is where our collective action comes in. Survivors may need medical care or financial help to address myriad costs related to the violence; communities may need resources to build community-driven programs to promote safety. Taking this broader view, we see that accountability from offenders is one piece of a larger constellation of issues to be addressed after intimate violence. Once we're able to look at the breadth of what survivors and communities want and need, the limitations of the criminal legal system come into sharper relief. Solutions beyond the criminal legal system become clearer priorities.

Some of those priorities can be thought about in terms of the concepts of restorative and transformative justice. Programs designed around restorative justice goals shift from a focus on punishment to what the victim and community need. Through facilitated, intentional, victim-centered work, the people who perpetrated harm can better understand the impact of their actions, and survivors and the community can get what they need in the healing process.[26]

Transformative justice approaches also emphasize acknowledging harm, though the focus is on community-created strategies to stop and address the harm. The development of transformative justice work has been led by marginalized communities who recognize that restoring often isn't enough. Instead, transformative justice work includes a call to go upstream to make changes in the root causes that created the circumstances where harm was possible in the first place.[27]

Here we find potential for collaboration and connection with community organizers working on diverse kinds of harm, from environmental issues where harm to communities affects livelihoods and health to racial injustices. Together, we have the potential to reimagine community solution-building, which has enormous implications for democracy and a vast array of public problems, not least of which is violence against women.

Don't decide where it ends. I'm hard pressed to think of a public problem that doesn't connect in one way or another to violence against women. You've probably identified issues you care about that we haven't addressed in these pages or that warrant a deeper diver. For example, we spent little space exploring links between climate change and intimate violence. Yet, as climate change drives increases in migration around the world, we'll share interests in preventing the dangers girls and women face during migration. This means we have potential collaborators in environmental sustainability movements around the world *and* locally who are trying to prevent the climate disasters that force people to flee their homes and undertake dangerous journeys.

When connecting with neighbors and policy-makers who care about environmental sustainability, we may be surprised at points of connection. Consider, for example, our shared interest in making green spaces available. Our environmental colleagues might support actions that will sequester carbon, create tree canopies to provide protection from dangerous summer temperatures, educate residents about being stewards of the natural world, and impart a lifelong love of nature in children. Our friends committed to antipoverty strategies will find opportunities for building community gardens in green spaces, through which families can access nutritious foods and learn valuable skills related to raising and even marketing what they grow.

Businesses will discover a way to publicly demonstrate their corporate so-cial responsibility through their involvement in building or maintaining the spaces. Neighbors can access outdoor space to benefit from the natural world.

For me, I see a place for that blue bench. For neighbors to meet one an-other and maybe talk about intimate violence but, as importantly, to be-come invested in each other's lives. When we're invested, we're going to help each other solve problems, we're going to check in on each other. We have the potential to create organically what nurse visitor programs structure for-mally—social support, helping people connect to resources, knowing when neighbors are stressed and strained to help them solve problems in ways that preserve everyone's dignity and opportunity—that is, without intimate violence.

Reimagining a Just World

Across centuries, we have called women who speak about violence "hyster-ical." We have medicalized and sometimes criminalized their reactions to in-justice. We have responded to those who perpetrate violence with a dizzying combination of criminalizing, ignoring, condoning, and rewarding their behaviors. Individually, we have had strong motivation to avert our gaze be-cause the threat to our own sense of self can be overwhelming; the threat that it could be me who is victimized, who victimizes someone, who is accused of victimizing someone. We have fooled ourselves into thinking that violence against women is best addressed by someone else. To be sure, there's an im-portant place for professional responses, for ensuring access to services and expanding survivor-centered, trauma-informed options that give survivors real choices. But *relying* solely on someone else or on the state—whether to fund agencies in our communities or lock people up—is neither effective, nor humane, nor compelling. It's also too late. Once a woman has no choice but to pick up the phone to call 911 or an emergency shelter, we've missed too many opportunities. First responders arrive on scenes long after our first chance to prevent violence has passed by.

Now we are called to create something new because violence against women affects us all by diminishing individuals and communities; it's tan-gled up with myriad other public problems. Awareness of that tangle isn't enough. Instead, we have a chance to build a world where solutions arise out of *our* homes and neighborhoods, *our* creativity and wisdom, *our* humility born of life experiences, knowledge, and passion. With creativity, we can imagine into existence new structures. With wisdom, we can distill the best of research and policy into the building blocks to a new future. With humility, we can center survivors' expertise and experiences while drawing on research and policy evidence to guide our collective action.

In organizing, there's a saying: "We're the ones we've been waiting for." We've been waiting for *you*—your passions, your knowledge, your commitment to working on the issues you care about. Together, we have an interest in ending violence against women, and the path we forge together promises a better world for *all* of us.

Notes

Introduction

1. The estimate for every ninety seconds was derived using multiple sources, including Desmarais, Sarah L., Kim A. Reeves, Tonia L. Nicholls, Robin P. Telford, and Martin S. Fiebert. 2012. "Prevalence of Physical Violence in Intimate Relationships, Part 1: Rates of Male and Female Victimization." *Partner Abuse* 3 (2): 140–69. doi:10.1891/1946-6560.3.2.140; Elliott, Diana M., Doris S. Mok, and John Briere. 2004. "Adult Sexual Assault: Prevalence, Symptomatology, and Sex Differences in the General Population." *Journal of Traumatic Stress* 17 (3): 203–11; Morgan, Rachel E., and Barbara A. Oudekerk. 2018. *Criminal Victimization, 2018.* US Department of Justice; Morgan, Rachel E. & Jennifer L. Truman 2020. "Criminal Victimization, 2019." Washington DC: U.S. Department of Justice. Other statistics in this paragraph drawn from Smith, S.G., X. Zhang, K. C. Basile, M. T. Merrick, J. Wang, M. Kresnow, and J. Chen. 2018. "The National Intimate Partner and Sexual Violence Survey (NISVS): 2015 Data Brief—Updated Release." Atlanta, GA: National Center for Injury Prevention and Control, Centers for Disease Control and Prevention; Hawks, Laura, Steffie Woolhandler, David U. Himmelstein, David H. Bor, Adam Gaffney, and Danny McCormick. 2019. "Association Between Forced Sexual Initiation and Health Outcomes Among US Women." *JAMA Internal Medicine* 179 (11): 1551–58. https://doi.org/10.1001/jamainternmed.2019.3500; Muehlenhard, Charlene L., Zoë D. Peterson, Terry P. Humphreys, and Kristen N. Jozkowski. 2017. "Evaluating the One-in-Five Statistic: Women's Risk of Sexual Assault While in College." *Journal of Sex Research* 54 (4–5): 549–76. https://doi.org/10.1080/00224499.2017.1295014

2. Relevant to this paragraph, see, for example, Bachman, Ronet, Rachel Kallmyer, Margarita Poteyeva, and Christina Lanier. 2008. *Violence Against American Indian and Alaska Native Women and the Criminal Justice Response: What Is Known.* Research report submitted to the US Department of Justice. https://www.ojp.gov/pdffiles1/nij/grants/223691.pdf; Deer, Sarah. *Beginning and End of Rape Confronting Sexual Violence in Native America.* Minneapolis: University of Minnesota Press, 2016; Dinno, Alexis. September 2017. "Homicide Rates of Transgender Individuals in the United States: 2010–2014." *American Journal of Public Health* 107 (9): 1441–47; McGuire, Danielle L. 2010. *At the Dark End of the Street: Black Women, Rape, and Resistance: A New History of the Civil Rights Movement, from Rosa Parks to the Rise of Black Power.* New York: Alfred A. Knopf.

3. For example, Menakem, Resmaa. 2017. *My Grandmother's Hands: Racialized Trauma and the Pathway to Mending Our Hearts and Bodies.* Illustrated edition. Las Vegas, NV: Central Recovery Press.

4. For example, Muehlenhard et al., 2017, "Evaluating the One-in-Five Statistic."

5. Xie, Min, and James P. Lynch. 2017. "The Effects of Arrest, Reporting to the Police, and Victim Services on Intimate Partner Violence." *Journal of Research in Crime and Delinquency* 54 (3): 338–78. https://doi.org/10.1177/0022427816678035

6. Broadwater, Luke, and Catie Edmondson. 2020. "A.O.C. Unleashes a Viral Condemnation of Sexism in Congress." *The New York Times.* July 23. https://www.nytimes.com/2020/07/23/us/alexandria-ocasio-cortez-sexism-congress.html

7. Bowley, G., and Jacobs, J. 2021. "Bill Cosby Freed as Court Overturns His Sex Assault Conviction." *The New York Times.* June 30. https://www.nytimes.com/2021/06/30/arts/television/bill-cosby-release-conviction.html

8. For example, Persson, Sofia, and Katie Dhingra. 2020. "Attributions of Blame in Stranger and Acquaintance Rape: A Multilevel Meta-Analysis and Systematic Review." *Trauma, Violence, and Abuse* December: 1524838020977146. https://doi.org/10.1177/1524838020977146

9. Roiphe, Katie. 1993. "Date Rape's Other Victim" *The New York Times.* June 13. https://www.nytimes.com/1993/06/13/magazine/date-rape-s-other-victim.html

10. Whittier, Nancy. 2009. *The Politics of Child Sexual Abuse Emotion, Social Movements, and the State/Nancy Whittier.* New York: Oxford University Press.

11. A version of this story appears in DePrince, A. P. 2009. *Public Good and the Nexus of Social Justice, Feminism, and Rock 'n' Roll. Journal of Higher Education Outreach and Engagement* 13(1): 69–83.

12. Torres, Jesús. 2013. Keynote Presentation at the Center for Community Engagement and Service Learning Community Organizing Institute, University of Denver. Denver, Colorado.

13. Whittier, Nancy. 2018. *Frenemies: Feminists, Conservatives, and Sexual Violence.* New York: Oxford University Press.

14. As cited in Pearce, Kimber Charles. 1999. "The Radical Feminist Manifesto as Generic Appropriation: Gender, Genre, and Second Wave Resistance." *Southern Communication Journal* 64 (4): 307–15, at 311. https://doi.org/10.1080/10417949909373145

15. Rosenthal, Naomi Braun. 2016. "Consciousness Raising: From Revolution to Re-Evaluation." *Psychology of Women Quarterly* 8 (4): 309–26. doi:10.1111/j.1471-6402.1984.tb00639.x

16. Burgess, Ann Wolbert, and Lynda Lytle Homstrom. 1974. "Rape Trauma Syndrome." *American Journal of Psychiatry* 131 (9): 981–986, at 985.

17. "ISTSS – History." n.d. Accessed August 5, 2021. https://istss.org/about-istss/history. See also Bloom, Sandra. 2000. "Our Hearts and Our Hopes Are Turned to Peace: Origins of the International Society for Traumatic Stress Studies," in *The International Handbook of Human Response to Trauma*, edited by Arieh Y. Shalev, Rachel Yehuda, and Alexander C. McFarlane. New York: Kluwer Academic/Plenum Publishers, 27–50..

18. Shatan, Chaim F. 1972. "Post-Vietnam Syndrome." *The New York Times.* May 6, at 35. https://www.nytimes.com/1972/05/06/archives/postvietnam-syndrome.html

19. Thuma, Emily L. 2019. *All Our Trials: Prisons, Policing, and the Feminist Fight to End Violence*. Champaign: University of Illinois Press.

20. Whittier, 2018, *Frenemies*.

21. See, for example, Valente, Roberta L., Barbara J. Hart, Seema Zeya, and Mary Malefyt. 2001. "The Violence Against Women Act of 1994: The Federal Commitment to Ending Domestic Violence, Sexual Assault, Stalking, and Gender-Based Crimes of Violence," in *Sourcebook on Violence Against Women*, edited by Claire M. Renzetti, Jeffrey L. Edleson, and Reaquel Kennedy Bergen, 279–301. Thousand Oaks CA: Sage Publications.

22. Kennedy, Pagan. 2020. "Opinion | There Are Many Man-Made Objects. The Rape Kit Is Not One of Them." *The New York Times*, June 17. https://www.nytimes.com/interactive/2020/06/17/opinion/rape-kit-history.html

23. Whittier, 2018, *Frenemies*.

24. Ibid.

25. The Combahee River Collective. 1978. "The Combahee River Collective Statement," Zillah Eisenstein.

26. Biden, Joseph R. 1993. "Violence Against Women: The Congressional Response." *American Psychologist* 48 (10): 1059–61.

27. Schmidt, Caroline. 2014. "What Killed the Violence Against Women Act's Civil Rights Remedy Before the Supreme Court Did?" University of Virginia. https://doi.org/10.18130/V3N956

28. Whittier, 2018, *Frenemies*.

29. Ibid.

30. Ibid.

31. Ibid.

32. Goodmark, Leigh. 2020. "Reimagining VAWA: Why Criminalization Is a Failed Policy and What a Non-Carceral VAWA Could Look Like." *Violence Against Women*. 107780122094968. doi:10.1177/1077801220949686.

33. For example, Calton, Jenna M., Lauren Bennett Cattaneo, and Kris T. Gebhard. 2016. "Barriers to Help Seeking for Lesbian, Gay, Bisexual, Transgender, and Queer Survivors of Intimate Partner Violence." *Trauma, Violence, and Abuse* 17 (5): 585–600. https://doi.org/10.1177/1524838015585318

34. Whittier, 2018, *Frenemies*.

35. See, for example, Zhou, Li. 2019. "The NRA Tried to Block an Updated Violence Against Women Act in the House—and Failed." Vox. April 4. https://www.vox.com/2019/4/4/18294057/violence-against-women-act-house-democrats-national-rifle-association

36. Cimons, Marlene. 2019. "Women Are More than Twice as Likely as Men to Suffer from PTSD: Studies Are Underway to Find Out Why." *The Washington Post*. https://www.washingtonpost.com/health/women-are-more-than-twice-as-likely-as-men-to-suffer-from-ptsd-studies-are-underway-to-find-out-why/2019/10/18/0a8da112-e5f7-11e9-b403-f738899982d2_story.html

37. Herman, Judith Lewis. 1997. *Trauma and Recovery*, revised ed. New York: Basic Books, at 240.

38. Becker-Blease, Kathryn. 2017. "As the World Becomes Trauma-Informed, Work to Do." *Journal of Trauma and Dissociation* 18 (2): 131–38. doi:10.1080/15299732.2017.1253401

39. For example, Johnson, K. C., and Stuart Taylor. 2017. "Opinion | The Path to Obama's 'Dear Colleague' Letter." *The Washington Post.* January 31. https://www.washingtonpost.com/news/volokh-conspiracy/wp/2017/01/31/the-path-to-obamas-dear-colleague-letter/; McCaughey, Betsy. 2017. "The Beginning of the End for Campus Kangaroo Courts." *New York Post* blog. September 25. https://nypost.com/2017/09/25/the-beginning-of-the-end-for-campus-kangaroo-courts/

40. Retrieved from https://www.thenation.com/article/politics/betsy-devos-title-ix-mens-rights/

41. INCITE! Women of Color Against Violence. 2016. *Color of Violence: The INCITE! Anthology.* North Carolina: Duke University Press.

42. See for example Fridel, Emma E., and James Alan Fox. 2019. "Gender Differences in Patterns and Trends in US Homicide, 1976–2017." *Violence and Gender* 6 (1): 27–36. doi:10.1089/vio.2019.0005. The Marshall Project. "New FBI Data Shows Violent Crime Still Falling, Except Rapes," September 30, 2019. https://www.themarshallproject.org/2019/09/30/new-fbi-data-violent-crime-still-falling

43. For example, Grundy, Saida. 2020. "The False Promise of Anti-Racism Books." *The Atlantic.* July 21. https://www.theatlantic.com/culture/archive/2020/07/your-anti-racism-books-are-means-not-end/614281/

44. For example, Mennicke, Annelise, Heather M. Bush, Candace J. Brancato, and Ann L. Coker. 2021. "Bystander Intervention Efficacy to Reduce Teen Dating Violence Among High School Youth Who Did and Did Not Witness Parental Partner Violence: A Path Analysis of a Cluster RCT." *Journal of Family Violence.* https://doi.org/10.1007/s10896-021-00297-y

45. Janoff-Bulman, Ronnie. 1992. *Shattered Assumptions: Towards a New Psychology of Trauma.* New York: The Free Press.

46. See, for example, Luders, Joseph E. 2010. *The Civil Rights Movement and the Logic of Social Change.* New York: Cambridge University Press; McAlevey, Jane F. 2016. *No Shortcuts: Organizing for Power.* New York: Oxford University Press.

47. McAlevey, Jane. 2020. *A Collective Bargain: Unions, Organizing, and the Fight for Democracy.* New York: Ecco-Harper Collins.

48. See Gordon, Hava Rachel. 2021. *This Is Our School! Race and Community Resistance to School Reform.* New York: New York University Press; Jaffe, Sarah. 2019. "The Radical Organizing That Paved the Way for LA's Teachers' Strike," January 19. https://www.thenation.com/article/archive/los-angeles-teachers-strike-utla-organizing-solidarity/

49. McAlevey, 2020, *A Collective Bargain.*

Chapter 1

1. See for example, Hustvedt, Asti. 2011. *Medical Muses: Hysteria in Nineteenth-Century Paris.* New York: W.W. Norton; Walusinski, Olivier. 2014. In J. Bogousslavsky (Ed.),

"The Girls of La Salpêtrière." In *Hysteria: The Rise of an Enigma*. Vol. 35, 65–77. Basel, Switzerland: S. Karger AG. doi:10.1159/000359993; Walusinski, Olivier, Jacques Poirier, and Hubert Déchy. 2013. "Augustine." *European Neurology* 69 (4): 226–28. doi:10.1159/000346032.

2. For reprinted photos, see Didi-Humberman, 2003, and Walusinski, Olivier. 2014. "The Girls of La Salpêtrière." *Frontiers of Neurology and Neuroscience* 35 (October): 65–77. https://doi.org/10.1159/000359993. See also Bogousslavsky, Julien, and Thierry Moulin. 2011. "Birth of Modern Psychiatry and the Death of Alienism: The Legacy of Jean-Martin Charcot." In J. Bogousslavsky (Ed.), *Following Charcot: A Forgotten History of Neurology and Psychiatry*. Frontiers of Neurology and Neuroscience, Vol. 29, 1–8. New York: Karger.

3. Didi-Huberman, Georges. 2003. *The Invention of Hysteria: Charcot and the Photographic Iconography of the Salpêtrière*. Cambridge, MA: MIT Press.

4. Walusinki, 2014, "The Girls of La Salpêtrière."

5. See, for example, Hustvedt, 2011, *Medical Muses*.

6. See, for example, Harris, James C. 2005. "A Clinical Lesson at the Salpêtrière." *Archives of General Psychiatry* 62 (5): 470–72. https://doi.org/10.1001/archpsyc.62.5.470.

7. As cited in Herman, Judith Lewis. 1997. *Trauma and Recovery*. Rev. ed. New York: Basic Books.

8. In 1893, just before his death, Charcot wrote that he had grown to believe that the origins of hysteria lay in psychological factors, particularly trauma. See Walusinski, Olivier, and Julien Bogousslavsky. 2020. "Charcot, Janet, and French Models of Psychopathology." *European Neurology* 83 (3): 333–40. https://doi.org/10.1159/000508267.

9. Herman, 1997, *Trauma and Recovery*.

10. As cited in Herman, 1997, *Trauma and Recovery*.

11. Herman, 1997, *Trauma and Recovery*.

12. For example, see Herman, 1997, *Trauma and Recovery*. Loewenstein, Richard J. 2018. "Dissociation Debates: Everything You Know Is Wrong." *Dialogues in Clinical Neuroscience* 20 (3): 229–42; Masson, J. M. 1984. *The Assault on Truth: Freud's Suppression of the Seduction Theory by Jeffrey Mous[s]Aieff Masson*. New York: New York: Farrar, Straus, and Giroux.

13. Herman, 1997, *Trauma and Recovery*.

14. Masson, 1984, *Assault on Truth*, 9.

15. As cited in Herman, 1997, *Trauma and Recovery*; Masson, *Assault on Truth*, 1984.

16. Herman, *Trauma and Recovery*, 1997, 7.

17. See, for example, Herman, 1997, *Trauma and Recovery*.

18. See, for example, Loewenstein, 2018, "Dissociation Debates." .

19. Samulowitz, Anke, Ida Gremyr, Erik Eriksson, and Gunnel Hensing. 2018. "'Brave Men' and 'Emotional Women': A Theory-Guided Literature Review on Gender Bias in Health Care and Gendered Norms towards Patients with Chronic Pain." *Pain Research and Management*. https://doi.org/10.1155/2018/6358624.

20. For example, Hoffman, Kelly M., Sophie Trawalter, Jordan R. Axt, and M. Norman Oliver. 2016. "Racial Bias in Pain Assessment and Treatment Recommendations, and False Beliefs About Biological Differences Between Blacks and Whites." *Proceedings*

of the National Academy of Sciences 113 (16): 4296–4301, https://doi.org/10.1073/pnas.1516047113; Lee, Paulyne, Maxine Le Saux, Rebecca Siegel, Monika Goyal, Chen Chen, Yan Ma, and Andrew C. Meltzer. 2019. "Racial and Ethnic Disparities in the Management of Acute Pain in US Emergency Departments: Meta-Analysis and Systematic Review." *The American Journal of Emergency Medicine* 37 (9): 1770–77. https://doi.org/10.1016/j.ajem.2019.06.014.

21. Chinn, Juanita J., Iman K. Martin, and Nicole Redmond. 2020. "Health Equity Among Black Women in the United States." *Journal of Women's Health*, November. https://doi.org/10.1089/jwh.2020.8868.

22. Centers for Disease Control and Prevention, USA. 2008. "Adverse Health Conditions and Health Risk Behaviors Associated with Intimate Partner Violence—United States, 2005." *MMWR: Morbidity and Mortality Weekly Report* 57 (5): 113–17.

23. For example, Loxton, Deborah, Xenia Dolja-Gore, E. Anderson Amy, and Natalie Townsend. 2017. "Intimate Partner Violence Adversely Impacts Health Over 16 Years and Across Generations: A Longitudinal Cohort Study." *PLoS ONE* 12 (6): e0178138. doi:10.1371/journal.pone.0178138.

24. Golding, Jacqueline M. 1996. "Sexual Assault History and Women's Reproductive and Sexual Health." *Psychology of Women Quarterly* 20 (1): 101–21. doi:10.1111/j.1471-6402.1996.tb00667.x.

25. Gibson, Carolyn J., Shira Maguen, Feng Xia, Deborah E. Barnes, Carrie B. Peltz, and Kristine Yaffe. 2019. "Military Sexual Trauma in Older Women Veterans: Prevalence and Comorbidities." *Journal of General Internal Medicine.* doi:10.1007/s11606-019-05342-7.

26. Chandan Joht Singh, Thomas Tom, Bradbury-Jones Caroline, Taylor Julie, Bandyopadhyay Siddhartha, and Nirantharakumar Krishnarajah. 2020. "Risk of Cardiometabolic Disease and All-Cause Mortality in Female Survivors of Domestic Abuse." *Journal of the American Heart Association* 9 (4): e014580. https://doi.org/10.1161/JAHA.119.014580.

27. For example, DePrince, Anne P., Srinivas, Tejaswinhi, and Gagnon, Kerry. October, 2013. "Human Trafficking and Trauma-Related Needs." Presentation at the 25th Annual Colorado Organization for Victim Assistance (COVA) Annual Conference. Keystone, CO.

28. For example, Golding, Jacqueline M. 1996. "Sexual Assault History and Women's Reproductive and Sexual Health." *Psychology of Women Quarterly* 20 (1): 101–21. doi:10.1111/j.1471-6402.1996.tb00667.x; Kapur, Nitin, and Donna Windish. 2011. "Health Care Utilization and Unhealthy Behaviors Among Victims of Sexual Assault in Connecticut: Results from a Population-Based Sample." *Journal of General Internal Medicine* 26 (5): 524–30. doi:10.1007/s11606-010-1614-4; Plichta, Stacey B., and Marilyn Falik. 2001. "Prevalence of Violence and Its Implications for Women's Health." *Women's Health Issues* 11 (3): 244–58. doi:10.1016/S1049-3867(01)00085-8; Sadler, Anne G., Brenda M. Booth, Michelle A. Mengeling, and Bradley N. Doebbeling. 2004. "Life Span and Repeated Violence Against Women During Military Service: Effects on Health Status and Outpatient Utilization." *Journal of Women's Health (2002)* 13 (7): 799–811. doi:10.1089/jwh.2004.13.799.

29. Hustvedt, 2011, *Medical Muses*.
30. Eghigian, Greg. 2010. *From Madness to Mental Health Psychiatric Disorder and Its Treatment in Western Civilization*, edited by Greg Eghigian. New Brunswick, NJ: Rutgers University Press.
31. Campbell, Jacquelyn C., Linda C. Pugh, Doris Campbell, and Marie Visscher. 1995. "The Influence of Abuse on Pregnancy Intention." *Women's Health Issues* 5 (4): 214–23. doi:10.1016/1049-3867(95)00058-5; Neighbors, C. J., A. O'Leary, and E. Labouvie. 1999. "Domestically Violent and Nonviolent Male Inmates' Responses to Their Partners' Requests for Condom Use: Testing a Social-Information Processing Model." *Health Psychology: Official Journal of the Division of Health Psychology, American Psychological Association* 18 (4): 427–31.
32. Heather McCauley, email message to author, June 26, 2021.
33. Silverman, Jay G., Heather L. McCauley, Michele R. Decker, Elizabeth Miller, Elizabeth Reed, and Anita Raj. 2011. "Coercive Forms of Sexual Risk and Associated Violence Perpetrated by Male Partners of Female Adolescents." *Perspectives on Sexual and Reproductive Health* 43 (1): 60–65. https://doi.org/10.1363/4306011.
34. Hill, Amber L., Kelley A. Jones, Heather L. McCauley, Daniel J. Tancredi, Jay G. Silverman, and Elizabeth Miller. 2019. "Reproductive Coercion and Relationship Abuse Among Adolescents and Young Women Seeking Care at School Health Centers." *Obstetrics & Gynecology* 134 (2): 351–59. https://doi.org/10.1097/AOG.0000000000003374.
35. Holliday, Charvonne N., Heather L. McCauley, Jay G. Silverman, Edmund Ricci, Michele R. Decker, Daniel J. Tancredi, Jessica G. Burke, Patricia Documét, Sonya Borrero, and Elizabeth Miller. 2017. "Racial/Ethnic Differences in Women's Experiences of Reproductive Coercion, Intimate Partner Violence, and Unintended Pregnancy." *Journal of Women's Health* 26 (8): 828–35. https://doi.org/10.1089/jwh.2016.5996.
36. Grace, Karen Trister, and Jocelyn C. Anderson. 2018. "Reproductive Coercion: A Systematic Review." *Trauma, Violence, & Abuse* 19 (4): 371–90. doi:10.1177/1524838016663935.
37. Brodsky, Alexandra. 2017. "'Rape-Adjacent': Imagining Legal Responses to Nonconsensual Condom Removal." *Columbia Journal of Gender and Law*, 28.
38. Brodsky, 2017, "'Rape-Adjacent.'"
39. Davis, Kelly Cue. 2019. "'Stealthing': Factors Associated with Young Men's Nonconsensual Condom Removal." *Health Psychology* 38 (11): 997–1000. https://doi.org/10.1037/hea0000779.
40. Elmquist, JoAnna, Ryan C. Shorey, Lindsay Labrecque, Andrew Ninnemann, Heather Zapor, Jeniimarie Febres, Caitlin Wolford-Clevenger, Maribel Plasencia, Jeff R. Temple, and Gregory L. Stuart. 2016. "The Relationship Between Family-of-Origin Violence, Hostility, and Intimate Partner Violence in Men Arrested for Domestic Violence: Testing a Mediational Model." *Violence Against Women* 22 (10): 1243–58. https://doi.org/10.1177/1077801215621177.
41. For example, McCauley, Heather L., Kathryn L. Falb, Tara Streich-Tilles, Denise Kpebo, and Jhumka Gupta. 2014. "Mental Health Impacts of Reproductive Coercion

Among Women in Côte d'Ivoire." *International Journal of Gynecology & Obstetrics* 127 (1): 55–59. https://doi.org/10.1016/j.ijgo.2014.04.011.

42. Gortzak-Uzan, L., M. Hallak, F. Press, M. Katz, and I. Shoham-Vardi. 2001. "Teenage Pregnancy: Risk Factors for Adverse Perinatal Outcome." *Journal of Maternal-Fetal Medicine* 10 (6): 393–97. doi:10.1080/jmf.10.6.393.397.

43. For example, see Bianchi, Ann L., Judith McFarlane, Sandra Cesario, Lene Symes, and John Maddoux. 2016. "Continued Intimate Partner Violence During Pregnancy and After Birth and Its Effect on Child Functioning." *Journal of Obstetric, Gynecologic, & Neonatal Nursing: Clinical Scholarship for the Care of Women, Childbearing Families, & Newborns* 45 (4): 601–09. https://doi.org/10.1016/j.jogn.2016.02.013. Gazmararian, Julie, Ruth Petersen, Alison Spitz, Mary Goodwin, Linda Saltzman, and James Marks. 2000. "Violence and Reproductive Health: Current Knowledge and Future Research Directions." *Maternal and Child Health Journal* 4 (2): 79–84. doi:10.1023/A:1009514119423.

44. Saltzman, Linda, Christopher Johnson, Brenda Gilbert, and Mary Goodwin. 2003. "Physical Abuse Around the Time of Pregnancy: An Examination of Prevalence and Risk Factors in 16 States." *Maternal and Child Health Journal* 7 (1): 31–43. doi:10.1023/A:1022589501039.

45. Goodwin, Mary, Julie Gazmararian, Christopher Johnson, Brenda Gilbert, Linda Saltzman, and Linda PRAMS Working Group. 2000. "Pregnancy Intendedness and Physical Abuse Around the Time of Pregnancy: Findings from the Pregnancy Risk Assessment Monitoring System, 1996–1997." *Maternal and Child Health Journal* 4 (2): 85–92. doi:10.1023/A:1009566103493.

46. Lipsky, Sherry, Victoria Holt, Thomas Easterling, and Cathy Critchlow. 2004. "Police-Reported Intimate Partner Violence During Pregnancy and the Risk of Antenatal Hospitalization." *Maternal and Child Health Journal* 8 (2): 55–63. doi:10.1023/B:MACI.0000025727.68281.aa.

47. Dietz, Patricia M., Julie A. Gazmararian, Mary M. Goodwin, F. Carol Bruce, Christopher H. Johnson, and Roger W. Rochat. 1997. "Delayed Entry into Prenatal Care: Effect of Physical Violence." *Obstetrics & Gynecology* 90 (2): 221–24. doi:10.1016/S0029-7844(97)00252-4.

48. Jamieson, Brittany. 2018. "Exposure to Interpersonal Violence During Pregnancy and Its Association with Women's Prenatal Care Utilization: A Meta-Analytic Review." *Trauma, Violence & Abuse*: 904–21. doi:10.1177/1524838018806511.

49. Babcock Fenerci, Rebecca L., and Anne P. DePrince. 2018. "Shame and Alienation Related to Child Maltreatment: Links to Symptoms Across Generations." *Psychological Trauma: Theory, Research, Practice, and Policy* 10 (4): 419–26. doi:10.1037/tra0000332.

50. See, for example, Duran, Eduardo. 2006. *Healing the Soul Wound: Counseling with American Indians and Other Native People.* New York: Teachers College Press.

51. PettyJohn, Morgan E., Taylor A. Reid, Elizabeth Miller, Katherine W. Bogen, and Heather L. McCauley. 2021. "Reproductive Coercion, Intimate Partner Violence, and Pregnancy Risk Among Adolescent Women with a History of Foster Care Involvement." *Children and Youth Services Review* 120 (January): 105731. https://doi.org/10.1016/j.childyouth.2020.105731.

52. DePrince, Anne P., Eileen L. Zurbriggen, Ann T. Chu, and Lindsay Smart. 2010. "Development of the Trauma Appraisal Questionnaire." *Journal of Aggression, Maltreatment & Trauma* 19 (3): 275–99. https://doi.org/10.1080/1092677100 3705072.

53. Sparrow, Katherine, Jamie Kwan, Louise Howard, Nicola Fear, and Deirdre MacManus. 2017. "Systematic Review of Mental Health Disorders and Intimate Partner Violence Victimisation Among Military Populations." *Social Psychiatry and Psychiatric Epidemiology* 52 (9): 1059–80. https://doi.org/10.1007/s00127-017-1423-8. Trevillion, Kylee, Siân Oram, Gene Feder, and Louise M. Howard. 2012. "Experiences of Domestic Violence and Mental Disorders: A Systematic Review and Meta-Analysis." *PLOS ONE* 7 (12): e51740. https://doi.org/10.1371/journal.pone.0051740.

54. DePrince, Anne P., Joanne Belknap, Jennifer S. Labus, Susan E. Buckingham, and Angela R. Gover. 2012. "The Impact of Victim-Focused Outreach on Criminal Legal System Outcomes Following Police-Reported Intimate Partner Abuse." *Violence Against Women* 18 (8): 861–81. doi:10.1177/1077801212456523.

55. DePrince, Anne P., Ann T. Chu, and Annarheen S. Pineda. 2011. "Links Between Specific Posttrauma Appraisals and Three Forms of Trauma-Related Distress." *Psychological Trauma: Theory, Research, Practice, and Policy* 3 (4): 430–41. https://doi.org/10.1037/a0021576.

56. See, for example: DePrince, Anne P., Rafaële J. C. Huntjens, and Martin J. Dorahy. 2015. "Alienation Appraisals Distinguish Adults Diagnosed with DID from PTSD." *Psychological Trauma: Theory, Research, Practice, and Policy* 7 (6): 578–82. https://doi.org/10.1037/tra0000069; McIlveen, Rachel, Ryan Mitchell, David Curran, Kevin Dyer, Mary Corry, Anne P. DePrince, Martin Dorahy, and Donncha Hanna. 2019. "Exploring the Relationship Between Alienation Appraisals, Trauma, Posttraumatic Stress, and Depression." *Psychological Trauma: Theory, Research, Practice, and Policy,* https://doi.org/10.1037/tra0000523.

57. Freyd, Jennifer J. 1996. *Betrayal Trauma: The Logic of Forgetting Childhood Abuse.* Cambridge, MA: Harvard University Press.

58. For example, Goldsmith, Rachel E., Jennifer J. Freyd, and Anne P. DePrince. 2012. "Betrayal Trauma: Associations with Psychological and Physical Symptoms in Young Adults." *Journal of Interpersonal Violence* 27 (3): 547–67. https://doi.org/10.1177/0886260511421672.

59. For example, Dworkin, Emily R., Heidi Ojalehto, Michele A. Bedard-Gilligan, Jennifer M. Cadigan, and Debra Kaysen. 2018. "Social Support Predicts Reductions in PTSD Symptoms When Substances Are Not Used to Cope: A Longitudinal Study of Sexual Assault Survivors." *Journal of Affective Disorders* 229 (March): 135–40. https://doi.org/10.1016/j.jad.2017.12.042.

60. Tirone, Vanessa, Daria Orlowska, Ashton M. Lofgreen, Rebecca K. Blais, Natalie R. Stevens, Brian Klassen, Philip Held, and Alyson K. Zalta. 2021. "The Association Between Social Support and Posttraumatic Stress Symptoms among Survivors of Betrayal Trauma: A Meta-Analysis." *European Journal of Psychotraumatology* 12 (1): 1883925. https://doi.org/10.1080/20008198.2021.1883925.

61. For example, DePrince, Anne P., Susan E. Buckingham, and Joanne Belknap. 2014. "The Geography of Intimate Partner Abuse Experiences and Clinical Responses." *Clinical Psychological Science* 2 (3): 258–71. https://doi.org/10.1177/2167702613507556.

62. Menon, David K., Karen Schwab, David W. Wright, and Andrew I. Maas. 2010. "Position Statement: Definition of Traumatic Brain Injury." *Archives of Physical Medicine and Rehabilitation* 91 (11): 1637–40. doi:10.1016/j.apmr.2010.05.017.

63. For example, Cnossen, Maryse C., Annemieke C. Scholten, Hester F. Lingsma, Anneliese Synnot, Juanita Haagsma, Prof. Ewout W. Steyerberg, and Suzanne Polinder. 2017. "Predictors of Major Depression and Posttraumatic Stress Disorder Following Traumatic Brain Injury: A Systematic Review and Meta-Analysis." *The Journal of Neuropsychiatry and Clinical Neurosciences* 29 (3): 206–24. https://doi.org/10.1176/appi.neuropsych.16090165; Mollayeva, Tatyana, Shirin Mollayeva, Nicole Pacheco, Andrea D'Souza, and Angela Colantonio. 2019. "The Course and Prognostic Factors of Cognitive Outcomes After Traumatic Brain Injury: A Systematic Review and Meta-Analysis." *Neuroscience & Biobehavioral Reviews* 99 (April): 198–250. https://doi.org/10.1016/j.neubiorev.2019.01.011.

64. DePrince, Anne P., Joanne Belknap, Jennifer S. Labus, Susan E. Buckingham, and Angela R. Gover. 2012. "The Impact of Victim-Focused Outreach on Criminal Legal System Outcomes Following Police-Reported Intimate Partner Abuse." *Violence Against Women* 18 (8): 861–81. doi:10.1177/1077801212456523; DePrince, Anne P., Jennifer Labus, Joanne Belknap, Susan Buckingham, and Angela Gover. 2012. "The Impact of Community-Based Outreach on Psychological Distress and Victim Safety in Women Exposed to Intimate Partner Abuse." *Journal of Consulting and Clinical Psychology* 80 (2): 211–21. doi:10.1037/a0027224.

65. Gagnon, Kerry L., and Anne P. Deprince. 2017. "Head Injury Screening and Intimate Partner Violence: A Brief Report." *Journal of Trauma & Dissociation* 18 (4): 635–44. doi:10.1080/15299732.2016.1252001.

66. DePrince, Anne P., Srinivas, Tejaswinhi, and Gagnon, Kerry. October, 2013. "Human Trafficking and Trauma-Related Needs." Presentation at the 25th Annual Colorado Organization for Victim Assistance (COVA) Annual Conference. Keystone, CO.

67. DePrince, Anne P. 2020. "Check-In + Check Out: Traumatic Brain Injury and Intimate Partner Abuse." *Trauma Research Notes* (blog). June 15, 2020. https://traumaresearchnotes.blog/2020/06/15/tbiupdate/.

68. Haag, Halina Lin, Dayna Jones, Tracey Joseph, and Angela Colantonio. 2019. "Battered and Brain Injured: Traumatic Brain Injury Among Women Survivors of Intimate Partner Violence: A Scoping Review." *Trauma, Violence & Abuse*: 1–18. doi:10.1177/1524838019850623.

69. Pritchard, Adam J., Amy Reckdenwald, and Chelsea Nordham. 2017. "Nonfatal Strangulation as Part of Domestic Violence: A Review of Research." *Trauma, Violence & Abuse* 18 (4): 407–24. doi:10.1177/1524838015622439.

70. Spencer, Chelsea M., and Sandra M. Stith. 2020. "Risk Factors for Male Perpetration and Female Victimization of Intimate Partner Homicide: A Meta-Analysis." *Trauma, Violence, & Abuse* 21 (3): 527–40. https://doi.org/10.1177/1524838018781101.

71. World Health Organization. 2013. *Responding to Intimate Partner Violence and Sexual Violence Against Women: WHO Clinical and Policy Guidelines*. Geneva: World Health Organization.

72. Waalen, Jill, Mary M. Goodwin, Alison M. Spitz, Ruth Petersen, and Linda E. Saltzman. 2000. "Screening for Intimate Partner Violence by Health Care Providers: Barriers and Interventions." *American Journal of Preventive Medicine* 19 (4): 230–37. https://doi.org/10.1016/S0749-3797(00)00229-4.

73. Miller, Elizabeth, Brigid McCaw, Betsy L. Humphreys, and Connie Mitchell. 2015. "Integrating Intimate Partner Violence Assessment and Intervention into Healthcare in the United States: A Systems Approach." *Journal of Women's Health (2015)* 24 (1): 92–99. https://doi.org/10.1089/jwh.2014.4870.

74. Miller, Chanel. 2019. *Know My Name: A Memoir*. New York: Viking at 14

75. See, for example, "Sexual Assault Information and Resources | Division of Criminal Justice." n.d. Accessed August 6, 2021. https://dcj.colorado.gov/sexual-assault-info rmation-and-resources.

76. NBC News. "After a Sexual Assault, Where Can You Get a Medical and Forensic Exam?" Accessed February 5, 2021. https://www.nbcnews.com/health/sexual-hea lth/after-sexual-assault-where-can-you-get-medical-forensic-exam-n1240035.

77. García-Moreno, Claudia, Kelsey Hegarty, Ana D'Oliveira Flavia Lucas, Jane Koziol-Mclain, Manuela Colombini, and Gene Feder. 2015. "The Health-Systems Response to Violence Against Women." *The Lancet* 385 (9977): 1567–79. doi:10.1016/S0140-6736(14)61837-7.

78. "Intimate Partner Violence." 2012. Committee Opinion No. 518. American College of Obstetricians and Gynecologists. *Obstetrics and Gynecology* 119 (2012): 412–17. Miller, Elizabeth, Brigid McCaw, Betsy L. Humphreys, and Connie Mitchell. 2015. "Integrating Intimate Partner Violence Assessment and Intervention into Healthcare in the United States: A Systems Approach." *Journal of Women's Health* 24 (1): 92–99. https://doi.org/10.1089/jwh.2014.4870.

79. Sharps, Phyllis W., Linda F. Bullock, Jacquelyn C. Campbell, Jeanne L. Alhusen, Sharon R. Ghazarian, Shreya S. Bhandari, and Donna L. Schminkey. 2016. "Domestic Violence Enhanced Perinatal Home Visits: The DOVE Randomized Clinical Trial." *Journal of Women's Health* 25 (11): 1129–38.

80. For a review, see Danese, Andrea, and Bruce S. McEwen. 2011. "Adverse Childhood Experiences, Allostasis, Allostatic Load, and Age-Related Disease." *Physiology & Behavior* 106 (1): 29–39.

81. National Center for Injury Prevention and Control. Costs of Intimate Partner Violence Against Women in the United States. Atlanta, GA: Centers for Disease Control and Prevention; 2003.

82. Brown, Derek S., Eric A. Finkelstein, and James A. Mercy. 2008. "Methods for Estimating Medical Expenditures Attributable to Intimate Partner Violence." *Journal of Interpersonal Violence* 23 (12): 1747–66. doi:10.1177/0886260508314338.

83. Peterson, Cora, Megan C. Kearns, Wendy LiKamWa McIntosh, Lianne Fuino Estefan, Christina Nicolaidis, Kathryn E. McCollister, Amy Gordon, and Curtis Florence. 2018. "Lifetime Economic Burden of Intimate Partner Violence Among U.S. Adults."

American Journal of Preventive Medicine 55 (4): 433–44. https://doi.org/10.1016/j.amepre.2018.04.049.

84. Bonomi, Amy E., Melissa L. Anderson, Frederick P. Rivara, and Robert S. Thompson. 2009. "Health Care Utilization and Costs Associated with Physical and Nonphysical-Only Intimate Partner Violence." *Health Services Research* 44 (3): 1052–67. doi:10.1111/j.1475-6773.2009.00955.x.

85. Snow Jones, Alison, Jacqueline Dienemann, Janet Schollenberger, Joan Kub, Patricia O'campo, Andrea Carlson Gielen, and Jacquelyn C. Campbell. 2006. "Long-Term Costs of Intimate Partner Violence in a Sample of Female HMO Enrollees." *Women's Health Issues* 16 (5): 252–61. doi:10.1016/j.whi.2006.06.007.

Chapter 2

1. Zeoli, April M., and Jennifer K. Paruk. 2020. "Potential to Prevent Mass Shootings Through Domestic Violence Firearm Restrictions." *Criminology & Public Policy* 19 (1): 129–45. https://doi.org/10.1111/1745-9133.12475

2. Follman, Mark. 2019. "Armed and Misogynist: A Mother Jones Investigation Uncovers How Toxic Masculinity Fuels Mass Shootings." *Mother Jones*. May/June. https://www.motherjones.com/crime-justice/2019/06/domestic-violence-misogyny-incels-mass-shootings/

3. Byerly, Carolyn M. 2020. "Incels Online Reframing Sexual Violence." *The Communication Review* 23 (4/October 1): 290–308. https://doi.org/10.1080/10714421.2020.1829305

4. Rojas, Rick, and Kristin Hussey. 2018. "Newly Released Documents Detail Sandy Hook Shooter's Troubled State of Mind." *The New York Times*. December 11, , sec. New York. https://www.nytimes.com/2018/12/10/nyregion/documents-sandy-hook-shooter.html

5. Grady, Constance. 2019. "The Dayton, Ohio, Shooter Reportedly Kept a 'Rape List' of Potential Victims." Vox. August 5. https://www.vox.com/identities/2019/8/5/20754918/dayton-ohio-shooter-rape-list-mass-shootings-misogyny-link

6. Fonrouge, Gabrielle, and Ruth Brown. 2018. "Alleged School Shooter Was Abusive to Ex-Girlfriend: Classmate." *New York Post* blog. February 15. https://nypost.com/2018/02/15/alleged-school-shooter-was-abusive-to-ex-girlfriend-classmate/

7. "Girl Who Was Harassed by Gunman Among the Victims of Texas Shooting." 2018. Think Progress. May 20. https://archive.thinkprogress.org/girl-who-was-harassed-by-gunman-among-the-victims-of-texas-shooting-5b01999c52bc/

8. United Nations. 2019. "Amid Rising Femicide, Proportion of Women Killed Grows as Overall Murder Rates Fall, Deputy Secretary-General Tells Spotlight Initiative Event | Meetings Coverage and Press Releases." September 26. https://www.un.org/press/en/2019/dsgsm1349.doc.htm

9. Goldstick, Jason E., April Zeoli, Christina Mair, and Rebecca M. Cunningham. 2019. "US Firearm-Related Mortality: National, State, and Population Trends, 1999–2017." *Health Affairs (Project Hope)* 38 (10): 1646–52. doi:10.1377/hlthaff.2019.00258

10. Siegel, Michael B., and Emily F. Rothman. 2016. "Firearm Ownership and the Murder of Women in the United States: Evidence That the State-Level Firearm Ownership Rate Is Associated with the Nonstranger Femicide Rate." *Violence and Gender* 3 (1): 2–26. doi:10.1089/vio.2015.0047

11. Stansfield, Richard, Daniel Semenza, and Trent Steidley. 2021. "Public Guns, Private Violence: The Association of City-Level Firearm Availability and Intimate Partner Homicide in the United States." *Preventive Medicine* 148 (July): 106599. https://doi.org/10.1016/j.ypmed.2021.106599

12. Campbell, Jacquelyn C., Daniel Webster, Jane Koziol-McLain, Carolyn Block, et al. 2003. "Risk Factors for Femicide in Abusive Relationships: Results from a Multisite Case Control Study." *American Journal of Public Health* 93 (7): 1089–97.

13. Sorenson, Susan B. 2017. "Guns in Intimate Partner Violence: Comparing Incidents by Type of Weapon." *Journal of Women's Health* 26 (3): 249–58. doi:10.1089/jwh.2016.5832.

14. Lynch, Kellie R., and T. K. Logan. 2018. "'You Better Say Your Prayers and Get Ready': Guns Within the Context of Partner Abuse." *Journal of Interpersonal Violence* 33 (4): 686–711, at 693. doi:10.1177/0886260515613344

15. Lynch and Logan, 2018, "You Better Say Your Prayers," at 696.

16. Sorenson, 2017, "Guns in Intimate Partner Violence."

17. Zeoli, April M., and Daniel W. Webster. 2010. "Effects of Domestic Violence Policies, Alcohol Taxes and Police Staffing Levels on Intimate Partner Homicide in Large US Cities." *Injury Prevention* 16 (2): 90. http://dx.doi.org.du.idm.oclc.org/10.1136/ip.2009.024620

18. Small, Dylan, Susan Sorenson, and Richard Berk. 2019. "After the Gun: Examining Police Visits and Intimate Partner Violence Following Incidents Involving a Firearm." *Journal of Behavioral Medicine* 42 (4): 591–602. doi:10.1007/s10865-019-00013-8

19. Ibid. Lynch and Logan, 2018, "You Better Say Your Prayers"

20. "Domestic Violence & Firearms." n.d. *Giffords* blog. Accessed June 17, 2021. https://giffords.org/lawcenter/gun-laws/policy-areas/who-can-have-a-gun/domestic-violence-firearms/

21. Diez, Carolina, Rachel P. Kurland, Emily F. Rothbaum, Megan Bair-Merritt, Eric Fleeger, Ziming Xuan, et al. 2017. "State Intimate Partner Violence-Related Firearm Laws and Intimate Partner Homicide Rates in the United States, 1995 to 2015." *Annals of Internal Medicine* 167: 536–43.

22. Wintemute, Garen J. 2018. "How to Stop Mass Shootings." *New England Journal of Medicine* 379 (13): 1193–96. https://doi.org/10.1056/NEJMp1807277

23. See, for example, Zhou, Li. 2019. "The NRA Tried to Block an Updated Violence Against Women Act in the House—and Failed." *Vox.* April 4. https://www.vox.com/2019/4/4/18294057/violence-against-women-act-house-democrats-national-rifle-association

24. Sorenson, Susan B., and Devan Spear. 2018. "New Data on Intimate Partner Violence and Intimate Relationships: Implications for Gun Laws and Federal Data Collection." *Preventive Medicine* 107: 103–108. https://doi.org/10.1016/j.ypmed.2018.01.005

25. See, for example, Zhou, 2019, "The NRA Tried."

26. Diez et al., 2017, "State Intimate Partner Violence-Related Firearm Laws."

27. Ibid.

28. Swanson, Jeffrey, Michael Norko, Hsiu-Ju Lin, Kelly Alanis-Hirsch, Linda Frisman, Madelon Baranoski, Michele Easter, Allison Robertson, Marvin Swartz, and Richard Bonnie. 2017. "Implementation and Effectiveness of Connecticut's Risk-Based Gun Removal Law: Does It Prevent Suicides?" *Law and Contemporary Problems* 80: 179–208. (2).

29. Zeppegno, Patrizia, Carla Gramaglia, Sarah di Marco, Chiara Guerriero, Cristiana Consol, Lucia Loreti, Maria Martelli, Debora Marangon, Vladimir Carli, and Marco Sarchiapone. 2019. "Intimate Partner Homicide Suicide: A Mini-Review of the Literature (2012–2018)." *Current Psychiatry Reports* 21 (2): 13. https://doi.org/10.1007/s11920-019-0995-2

30. Snyder, Rachel Louise. 2019. *No Visible Bruises: What We Don't Know About Domestic Violence Can Kill Us.* New York: Bloomsbury.

31. Eliason, Scott. 2009. "Murder-Suicide: A Review of the Recent Literature." *Journal of the American Academy of Psychiatry and the Law* 37 (3): 371–76.

32. Salari, Sonia, and Carrie Lefevre Sillito. 2016. "Intimate Partner Homicide–Suicide: Perpetrator Primary Intent Across Young, Middle, and Elder Adult Age Categories." *Aggression and Violent Behavior* 26: 26–34. doi:10.1016/j.avb.2015.11.004

33. For example, Zeppegno et al., 2019. "Intimate Partner Homicide Suicide."

34. "Colorado Domestic Violence Fatality Review Board: Annual Report 2019." https://coag.gov/app/uploads/2019/12/2019-Colorado-Domestic-Violence-Fatality-Review-Board-Annual-Report-1.pdf

35. National Public Radio. 2020. "2 Big Teachers Unions Call for Rethinking Student Involvement in Lockdown Drills." NPR.Org. February 11. https://www.npr.org/2020/02/11/804468827/2-big-teachers-unions-call-for-rethinking-student-involvement-in-lockdown-drills

36. Eisler, Richard M., and Jay R. Skidmore. 1987. "Masculine Gender Role Stress: Scale Development and Component Factors in the Appraisal of Stressful Situations." *Behavior Modification* 11 (2): 123–36. doi:10.1177/01454455870112001

37. For example, Mcdermott, Ryon C., and Frederick G. Lopez. 2013. "College Men's Intimate Partner Violence Attitudes: Contributions of Adult Attachment and Gender Role Stress." *Journal of Counseling Psychology* 60 (1): 127–36. doi:10.1037/a0030353

38. For example, Jakupcak, Matthew, David Lisak, and Lizabeth Roemer. 2002. "The Role of Masculine Ideology and Masculine Gender Role Stress in Men's Perpetration of Relationship Violence." *Psychology of Men & Masculinity* 3 (2): 97–106. doi:10.1037/1524-9220.3.2.97. See also Baugher, Amy R., and Julie A. Gazmararian. 2015. "Masculine Gender Role Stress and Violence: A Literature Review and Future Directions." *Aggression and Violent Behavior* 24 (September): 107–12. https://doi.org/10.1016/j.avb.2015.04.002

39. Moore, Todd M., Gregory L. Stuart, James K. McNulty, Michael E. Addis, James V. Cordova, and Jeff R. Temple. 2010. "Domains of Masculine Gender Role Stress and Intimate Partner Violence in a Clinical Sample of Violent Men." *Psychology of Violence* 1: 68–75. doi:10.1037/2152-0828.1.S.68

40. McCauley, Heather L., Daniel J. Tancredi, Jay G. Silverman, Michele R. Decker, S. B. Austin, Marie C. Mccormick, Maria Catrina Virata, and Elizabeth Miller. 2013. "Gender-Equitable Attitudes, Bystander Behavior, and Recent Abuse Perpetration Against Heterosexual Dating Partners of Male High School Athletes," edited by Heather L. McCauley. *American Journal of Public Health* 103 (10): 1882–87. https://doi.org/10.2105/AJPH.2013.301443

41. Foshee, Vangie A., G. Fletcher Linder, Karl E. Bauman, Stacey A. Langwick, Ximena B. Arriaga, Janet L. Heath, Pamela M. Mcmahon, and Shrikant Bangdiwala. 1996. "The Safe Dates Project: Theoretical Basis, Evaluation Design, and Selected Baseline Findings." *American Journal of Preventive Medicine* 12 (5): 39–47. doi:10.1016/S0749-3797(18)30235-6

42. Miller, E., K. A. Jones, L. Ripper, T. Paglisotti, P. Mulbah, and K. Z. Abebe. 2020. "An Athletic Coach–Delivered Middle School Gender Violence Prevention Program: A Cluster Randomized Clinical Trial." *JAMA Pediatrics* 174 (3): 241–249. doi:10.1001/jamapediatrics.2019.5217

43. For a review, see Temple, Jeff R., Vi D. Le, Alexandra Muir, Laurie Goforth, and Amy L. Mcelhany. 2013. "The Need for School-Based Teen Dating Violence Prevention." *Journal of Applied Research on Children: Informing Policy on Children at Risk.* 4 (1)..

44. Banyard, Victoria L., Katie M. Edwards, Andrew J. Rizzo, Matt Theodores, Ryan Tardiff, Katherine Lee, and Patricia Greenberg. 2019. "Evaluating a Gender Transformative Violence Prevention Program for Middle School Boys: A Pilot Study." *Children and Youth Services Review* 101: 165–73. doi:10.1016/j.childyouth.2019.03.052

45. Temple et al. 2013. *The Need for School-Based Teen Dating Violence Prevention.*

46. Moms Demand Action. "Everytown, Moms Demand Action Statement as House Prepares to Vote on the Violence Against Women Reauthorization Act of 2019." 2019. Moms Demand Action. April 2. https://momsdemandaction.org/everytown-moms-demand-action-statement-as-house-prepares-to-vote-on-the-violence-against-women-reauthorization-act-of-2019/

47. "Denver DA Hires Investigator to Make Sure Domestic Violence Offenders Turn over Guns." 2020. *The Denver Post* blog. January 7. https://www.denverpost.com/2020/01/07/denver-domestic-violence-gun-investigator-red-flag/

48. Cabral, Marika, Bokyung Kim, Maya Rossin-Slater, Molly Schnell, and Hannes Schwandt. 2021. "Trauma at School: The Impacts of Shootings on Students' Human Capital and Economic Outcomes." w28311. National Bureau of Economic Research. https://doi.org /10.3386/w28311

Chapter 3

1. American Civil Liberties Union. 2021. "Cops and No Counselors." Accessed February 5. https://www.aclu.org/report/cops-and-no-counselors.

2. "School Nurses in U.S. Public Schools." April 2020. *Data Point*: A Publication of the National Center for Education Statistics at IES. https://nces.ed.gov/pubs2020/2020 086.pdf.

3. Moylan, Carrie A., McKenzie Javorka, Megan K. Maas, Elizabeth Meier, and Heather L. McCauley. 2021. "Campus Sexual Assault Climate: Toward an Expanded Definition and Improved Assessment." *Psychology of Violence* 11 (3): 296–306. https://doi.org/10.1037/vio0000382/

4. KHOU.com. "School Principal Was Victim in Apparent Murder-Suicide at League City Home, Texas City ISD Confirms." 2021. May 13. https://www.khou.com/article/news/local/league-city-double-fatal-shooting-murder-suicide-on-westwood-late-wednesday/285-040ea650-0760-4c2a-8d58-51a61b44fca9

5. Jobe-Shields, Lisa, Angela D. Moreland, Rochelle F. Hanson, Ananda Amstadter, Benjamin E. Saunders, and Dean G. Kilpatrick. 2018. "Co-Occurrence of Witnessed Parental Violence and Child Physical Abuse from a National Sample of Adolescents." *Journal of Child & Adolescent Trauma* 11 (2): 129–39. https://doi.org/10.1007/s40653-015-0057-9

6. Caldwell, Jennifer E., Suzanne C. Swan, and V. Diane Woodbrown. 2012. "Gender Differences in Intimate Partner Violence Outcomes." *Psychology of Violence* 2 (1): 42–57. https://doi.org/10.1037/a0026296

7. Hamby, Sherry, David Finkelhor, Heather Turner, and Richard Ormrod. 2010. "The Overlap of Witnessing Partner Violence with Child Maltreatment and Other Victimizations in a Nationally Representative Survey of Youth." *Child Abuse & Neglect* 34 (10): 734–41. https://doi.org/10.1016/j.chiabu.2010.03.001

8. Holmes, Megan R., Francisca G. C. Richter, Mark E. Votruba, Kristen A. Berg, and Anna E. Bender. 2018. "Economic Burden of Child Exposure to Intimate Partner Violence in the United States." *Journal of Family Violence* 33 (4): 239–49. doi:10.1007/s10896-018-9954-7

9. For a review, see Thomason, Moriah E., and Hilary A. Marusak. 2017. "Toward Understanding the Impact of Trauma on the Early Developing Human Brain." *Neuroscience; Neuroscience* 342: 55–67. doi:10.1016/j.neuroscience.2016.02.022.

10. Milani, Ana Carolina C., Elis V. Hoffmann, Victor Fossaluza, Andrea P. Jackowski, and Marcelo F. Mello. 2017. "Does Pediatric Post-Traumatic Stress Disorder Alter the Brain? Systematic Review and Meta-Analysis of Structural and Functional Magnetic Resonance Imaging Studies." *Psychiatry and Clinical Neurosciences* 71 (3): 154–69. https://doi.org/10.1111/pcn.12473.

11. See, for example, Fong, Vanessa C., David Hawes, and Jennifer L. Allen. 2019. "A Systematic Review of Risk and Protective Factors for Externalizing Problems in Children Exposed to Intimate Partner Violence." *Trauma, Violence, & Abuse* 20 (2): 149–67. https://doi.org/10.1177/1524838017692383; McLaughlin, Katie A., Natalie L. Colich, Alexandra M. Rodman, and David G. Weissman. 2020.

"Mechanisms Linking Childhood Trauma Exposure and Psychopathology: A Transdiagnostic Model of Risk and Resilience." *BMC Medicine* 18 (1): 96. https://doi. org/10.1186/s12916-020-01561-6

12. DePrince, Anne P., Kristin M. Weinzierl, and Melody D. Combs. 2009. "Executive Function Performance and Trauma Exposure in a Community Sample of Children." *Child Abuse & Neglect* 33 (6): 353–61. https://doi.org/10.1016/j.chiabu.2008.08.002.

13. For example, Biedermann, Sarah V., Stefanie Meliss, Candice Simmons, Jani Nöthling, Sharain Suliman, and Soraya Seedat. 2018. "Sexual Abuse but Not Posttraumatic Stress Disorder Is Associated with Neurocognitive Deficits in South African Traumatized Adolescents." *Child Abuse and Neglect* 80: 257–67. doi:10.1016/ j.chiabu.2018.04.003; De Bellis, Michael D., Donald P. Woolley, and Stephen R. Hooper. 2013. "Neuropsychological Findings in Pediatric Maltreatment: Relationship of PTSD, Dissociative Symptoms, and Abuse/Neglect Indices to Neurocognitive Outcomes." *Child Maltreatment* 18 (3): 171–83. doi:10.1177/1077559513497420

14. DeCarlo Santiago, Catherine, Tali Raviv, and Lisa H. Jaycox. 2018. *Creating Healing School Communities: School-Based Interventions for Students Exposed to Trauma.* Washington DC: American Psychological Association Books.

15. For discussion, see Ibid.

16. De Bellis et al., 2013, "Neuropsychological Findings in Pediatric Maltreatment."

17. Kiesel, Lisa R., Kristine N. Piescher, and Jeffrey L. Edleson. 2016. "The Relationship Between Child Maltreatment, Intimate Partner Violence Exposure, and Academic Performance." *Journal of Public Child Welfare* 10 (4): 434–56. doi:10.1080/ 15548732.2016.1209150

18. Fong et al., 2017, "A Systematic Review of Risk and Protective Factors" ; Hunt, Tenah K. A., Kristen S. Slack, and Lawrence M. Berger. 2017. "Adverse Childhood Experiences and Behavioral Problems in Middle Childhood." *Child Abuse and Neglect* 67: 391–402. doi:10.1016/j.chiabu.2016.11.005

19. See, for example, Schiff, Mara. 2018. "Can Restorative Justice Disrupt the 'School-to-Prison Pipeline?'" *Contemporary Justice Review* 21 (2): 121–39. doi:10.1080/ 10282580.2018.1455509

20. For example, Hunt et al., 2017, "Adverse Childhood Experiences."

21. For example, Dutil, Stacey. 2020. "Dismantling the School-to-Prison Pipeline: A Trauma-Informed, Critical Race Perspective on School Discipline." *Children & Schools.* doi:10.1093/cs/cdaa016; Hunt et al., 2017, "Adverse Childhood Experiences" ; Owens, Jayanti, and Sara S McLanahan. 2020. "Unpacking the Drivers of Racial Disparities in School Suspension and Expulsion." *Social Forces* 98 (4/June 12): 1548–77. https://doi.org/10.1093/sf/soz095

22. Prior, Karen. 2002. *Don't Shoot the Dog! The New Art of Teaching and Training.* Surrey, UK: Ringpress Books.

23. For example, Fenerci, Rebecca L. Babcock, and Anne P. DePrince. 2018. "Intergenerational Transmission of Trauma: Maternal Trauma-Related Cognitions and Toddler Symptoms." *Child Maltreatment* 23 (2): 126–36. https://doi.org/10.1177/ 1077559517737376

24. "Taking Risks: Implementing Grassroots Community Accountability Strategies." 2016. Communities Against Rape and Abuse. https://doi.org/10.1215/9780822373445-030

25. See, for example, CBS News. 2020. "Hundreds of Stories of Sexual Assault at Colleges Around the World Shared on Anonymous Instagram Accounts." September 29. https://www.cbsnews.com/news/st-andrews-survivors-instagram-scottish-university-sexual-assault/

26. For example, NBC. 2021. "Los Gatos High School Hit by Student Sex Assault Accusations." April 29. NBC Bay Area blog. https://www.nbcbayarea.com/investigations/los-gatos-high-school-hit-by-student-sex-assault-accusations/2522557/

27. Hawks, Laura, Steffie Woolhandler, David U. Himmelstein, David H. Bor, Adam Gaffney, and Danny McCormick. 2019. "Association Between Forced Sexual Initiation and Health Outcomes Among US Women." *JAMA Internal Medicine* 179 (11): 1551–58. https://doi.org/10.1001/jamainternmed.2019.3500

28. Wincentak, Katherine, Jennifer Connolly, and Noel Card. 2017. "Teen Dating Violence: A Meta-Analytic Review of Prevalence Rates." *Psychology of Violence* 7 (2): 224–41. https://doi.org/10.1037/a0040194

29. White, Jacquelyn W. 2009. "A Gendered Approach to Adolescent Dating Violence: Conceptual and Methodological Issues." *Psychology of Women Quarterly* 33 (1): 1–15. doi:10.1111/j.1471-6402.2008.01467.x

30. For example, Foshee, Vangie A., Karl E. Bauman, Fletcher Linder, Jennifer Rice, and Rose Wilcher. 2007. "Typologies of Adolescent Dating Violence: Identifying Typologies of Adolescent Dating Violence Perpetration." *Journal of Interpersonal Violence* 22 (5): 498–519. doi:10.1177/0886260506298829

31. Zurbriggen, Eileen L. 2000. "Social Motives and Cognitive Power–Sex Associations: Predictors of Aggressive Sexual Behavior." *Journal of Personality and Social Psychology* 78 (3): 559–81. https://doi.org/10.1037/0022-3514.78.3.559

32. Reuter, Tyson R., and Sarah W. Whitton. 2018. "Adolescent Dating Violence Among Lesbian, Gay, Bisexual, Transgender, and Questioning Youth." In *Adolescent Dating Violence: Theory, Research, and Prevention*, edited by David Wolfe and Jeff R. Temple, 215–31. San Diego: Elsevier Science and Technology.

33. Ibid.

34. Wincentak et al., 2017, "Teen Dating Violence."

35. Ybarra, Michele L., Dorothy L. Espelage, Jennifer Langhinrichsen-Rohling, Josephine D. Korchmaros, and Danah Boyd. 2016. "Lifetime Prevalence Rates and Overlap of Physical, Psychological, and Sexual Dating Abuse Perpetration and Victimization in a National Sample of Youth." *Archives of Sexual Behavior* 45 (5): 1083–99. doi:10.1007/s10508-016-0748-9

36. For example, Ouytsel, Joris Van, Ellen Van Gool, Michel Walrave, Koen Ponnet, and Emilie Peeters. 2017. "Sexting: Adolescents' Perceptions of the Applications Used for, Motives for, and Consequences of Sexting." *Journal of Youth Studies* 20, 4 (April 21): 446–70. https://doi.org/10.1080/13676261.2016.1241865

37. Reed, Lauren A., Richard M. Tolman, and L. M. Ward. 2017. "Gender Matters: Experiences and Consequences of Digital Dating Abuse Victimization in Adolescent Dating Relationships." *Journal of Adolescence (London, England)*: 79–89. doi:10.1016/j.adolescence.2017.05.015

38. For example, Muñoz-Rivas, Marina J., Jose Luis Graña, K. Daniel O'Leary, and M. Pilar González. "Aggression in Adolescent Dating Relationships: Prevalence, Justification, and Health Consequences." *Journal of Adolescent Health* 40, no. 4 (April 1, 2007): 298–304. https://doi.org/10.1016/j.jadohealth.2006.11.137. Tharp, Andra Teten, H. Luz McNaughton Reyes, Vangie Foshee, Monica H. Swahn, Jeffrey E. Hall, and Joseph Logan. "Examining the Prevalence and Predictors of Injury From Adolescent Dating Violence." *Journal of Aggression, Maltreatment & Trauma* 26, no. 5 (May 28, 2017): 445–61. https://doi.org/10.1080/10926771.2017.1287145. See also Wincentak, Katherine, Jennifer Connolly, and Noel Card. "Teen Dating Violence: A Meta-Analytic Review of Prevalence Rates." *Psychology of Violence* 7, no. 2 (2017): 224–41. https://doi.org/10.1037/a0040194.

39. Adhia, Avanti, Mary A. Kernic, David Hemenway, Moncia S. Vavilala, Frederick P. Rivara. 2019. "Intimate Partner Homicide of Adolescents." *JAMA Pediatrics* 173 (6): 571–77.

40. Fix, Rebecca L., Nancy Nava, and Rebecca Rodriguez. 2021. "Disparities in Adolescent Dating Violence and Associated Internalizing and Externalizing Mental Health Symptoms by Gender, Race/Ethnicity, and Sexual Orientation." *Journal of Interpersonal Violence* March: 0886260521997944. https://doi.org/10.1177/0886260521997944

41. For example, Banyard, Victoria L., and Charlotte Cross. 2008. "Consequences of Teen Dating Violence: Understanding Intervening Variables in Ecological Context." *Violence Against Women* 14 (9): 998–1013. doi:10.1177/1077801208322058; Jouriles, Ernest N., Hye Jeong Choi, Caitlin Rancher, and Jeff R. Temple. 2017. "Teen Dating Violence Victimization, Trauma Symptoms, and Revictimization in Early Adulthood." *Journal of Adolescent Health* 61 (1): 115–19. https://doi.org/10.1016/j.jadohealth.2017.01.020

42. Mulford, Carrie, and Peggy C. Giordano. 2008. "Teen Dating Relationships: A Closer Look at Adolescent Romantic Relationships." *National Institute of Justice Journal*, 261, 34–40.

43. Ellsberg, Mary, Chelsea Ullman, Alexandra Blackwell, Amber Hill, and Manuel Contreras. 2018. "What Works to Prevent Adolescent Intimate Partner and Sexual Violence? A Global Review of Best Practices." In *Adolescent Dating Violence: Theory, Research, and Prevention*, edited by David Wolfe and Jeff R. Temple, 381–414. San Diego: Elsevier Science and Technology.

44. Jouriles et al., 2017. "Teen Dating Violence."

45. Jordan, Carol E., Jessica L. Combs, and Gregory T. Smith. 2014. "An Exploration of Sexual Victimization and Academic Performance Among College Women." *Trauma, Violence, & Abuse* 15 (3/July 1): 191–200. https://doi.org/10.1177/1524838014520637

46. For example, Carey, Kate B., Sarah E. Durney, Robyn L. Shepardson, and Michael P. Carey. 2015. "Incapacitated and Forcible Rape of College Women: Prevalence Across

the First Year." *Journal of Adolescent Health* 56 (6): 678–80. https://doi.org/10.1016/j.jadohealth.2015.02.018

47. Banyard, Victoria L., Jennifer M. Demers, Ellen S. Cohn, Katie M. Edwards, Mary M. Moynihan, Wendy A. Walsh, and Sally K. Ward. 2020. "Academic Correlates of Unwanted Sexual Contact, Intercourse, Stalking, and Intimate Partner Violence: An Understudied but Important Consequence for College Students." *Journal of Interpersonal Violence* 35 (21–22/November 1): 4375–92. https://doi.org/10.1177/0886260517715022

48. Boyraz, Güler, Sharon G. Horne, Archandria C. Owens, and Aisha P. Armstrong. 2013. "Academic Achievement and College Persistence of African American Students with Trauma Exposure." *Journal of Counseling Psychology* 60 (4): 582–92. https://doi.org/10.1037/a0033672

49. For a review, see Muehlenhard, Charlene L., Zoë D. Peterson, Terry P. Humphreys, and Kristen N. Jozkowski. 2017. "Evaluating the One-in-Five Statistic: Women's Risk of Sexual Assault While in College." *Journal of Sex Research* 54 (4–5): 549–76. https://doi.org/10.1080/00224499.2017.1295014

50. For example, Campe, Margaret I. 2019. "College Campus Sexual Assault and Female Students with Disabilities." *Journal of Interpersonal Violence.* April: 0886260519840405. https://doi.org/10.1177/0886260519840405; Carey et al., 2015, "Incapacitated and Forcible Rape"; Muehlenhard et al., 2017, "Evaluating the One-in-Five Statistic.".

51. Smith, Carly Parnitzke, and Jennifer J. Freyd. 2013. "Dangerous Safe Havens: Institutional Betrayal Exacerbates Sexual Trauma: Institutional Betrayal Exacerbates Sexual Trauma." *Journal of Traumatic Stress* 26 (1): 119–24. https://doi.org/10.1002/jts.21778

52. For example, USA Today. 2020. "LSU Mishandled Sexual Misconduct Complaints Against Students, Including Top Athletes." Accessed December 13. https://www.usatoday.com/in-depth/sports/ncaaf/2020/11/16/lsu-ignored-campus-sexual-assault-allegations-against-derrius-guice-drake-davis-other-students/6056388002/

53. For example, see Matthews, Dylan. 2014. "What Obama Can Do Next to Stop Sexual Assault." Vox. May 7. https://www.vox.com/2014/5/7/5690682/student-activists-pushed-obama-to-act-on-sexual-assault-this-is-where

54. "Dear Colleague Letter from Assistant Secretary for Civil Rights Russlynn Ali. Pg 1." 2021. Policy Guidance. US Department of Education (ED). January 5. https://www2.ed.gov/about/offices/list/ocr/letters/colleague-201104.html

55. "Title IX and Sex Discrimination." 2021. Policy Guidance. US Department of Education (ED). May 5. https://www2.ed.gov/about/offices/list/ocr/docs/tix_dis.html

56. See, for example, "How a 20-Page Letter Changed the Way Higher Education Handles Sexual Assault." 2017. *The Chronicle of Higher Education.* February 8. https://www.chronicle.com/article/how-a-20-page-letter-changed-the-way-higher-education-handles-sexual-assault/

57. Holland, Kathryn J., Lilia M. Cortina, and Jennifer J. Freyd. 2018. "Compelled Disclosure of College Sexual Assault." *American Psychologist* 73 (3): 256–68. https://doi.org/10.1037/amp0000186

58. Olomi, Julie M., Anne P. DePrince, and Kerry L. Gagnon. 2019. "Institutional Responses to Campus Sexual Assault: Examining the Development and Work of a Multidisciplinary Team." *Journal of Trauma & Dissociation* 20 (3): 324–39. https://doi.org/10.1080/15299732.2019.1571886

59. "Life Inside the Title IX Pressure Cooker." 2019. *The Chronicle of Higher Education.* September 5. https://www-chronicle-com.du.idm.oclc.org/article/life-inside-the-title-ix-pressure-cooker/

60. Javorka, McKenzie, and Rebecca Campbell. (2021). "'This Isn't Just a Police Issue': Tensions Between Criminal Justice and University Responses to Sexual Assault among College Students." *American Journal of Community Psychology, 67*: 152–65. doi:10.1002/ajcp.12448

61. For example, *Washington Post.* 2017. "Opinion | The Path to Obama's 'Dear Colleague' Letter." January 31. https://www.washingtonpost.com/news/volokh-conspiracy/wp/2017/01/31/the-path-to-obamas-dear-colleague-letter/.   ; McCaughey, Betsy. 2017. "The Beginning of the End for Campus Kangaroo Courts." *New York Post* blog. September 25. https://nypost.com/2017/09/25/the-beginning-of-the-end-for-campus-kangaroo-courts/

62. Bedera, Nicole, Seth Galanter, and Sage Carson. 2020. "A New Title IX Rule Essentially Allows Accused Sexual Assailants to Hide Evidence Against Them." *Time.* August 14. https://time.com/5879262/devos-title-ix-rule/

63. In August 2021, the Biden Department of Education published a memo indicating that they would cease enforcing this rule; see U.S. Department of Education. August 24, 2021. "Update on Court Ruling about the Department of Education's Title IX Regulations." https://content.govdelivery.com/accounts/USED/bulletins/2ee0a5d.

    "How 20 Years of Education Reform Has Created Greater Inequality (SSIR)." 2020. Accessed December 8, 2020. https://ssir.org/articles/entry/how_20_years_of_education_reform_has_created_greater_inequality

64. "How 20 Years of Education Reform Has Created Greater Inequality (SSIR)."

65. For example, Cole, Susan F., Anne Eisner, Michael Gregory, and Joel Ristuccia. 2013. *Creating and Advocating for Trauma Sensitive Schools.* Trauma and Learning Policy Initiative. www.traumasensitiveschools.org; DeCarlo Santiago, Catherine, Tali Raviv, and Lisa H. Jaycox. 2018. *Creating Healing School Communities: School-Based Interventions for Students Exposed to Trauma.* Washington DC: American Psychological Association Books.

66. Substance Abuse and Mental Health Services Administration. 2014. *SAMHSA's Concept of Trauma and Guidance for a Trauma-Informed Approach.* Health and Human Services Publication No. 14-4884. Rockville, MD: SAMHSA.

67. Khan, Jennifer S. Hirsch, and Shamus. 2020. "How College Dorm Rooms Facilitate Sexual Assault." *Medium.* January 13. https://gen.medium.com/how-college-dorm-rooms-facilitate-sexual-assault-fec10b9626ed

68. Taylor, Bruce G., Nan D. Stein, Elizabeth A. Mumford, and Daniel Woods. 2013. "Shifting Boundaries: An Experimental Evaluation of a Dating Violence Prevention Program in Middle Schools." *Prevention Science* 14 (1): 64–76. https://doi.org/10.1007/s11121-012-0293-2

69. Canzano, John. 2014. "16 Years After Oregon State Football Gang-Rape Allegation, Brenda Tracy Steps from the Shadows." *Oregonian*. November 14. https://www.oregonlive.com/sports/oregonian/john_canzano/2014/11/canzano_her_name_is_brenda_tra.html

70. Becker-Blease, Kathryn, and Anne P. DePrince. 2021. "Opinion: When Allegations of Sexual Assault and Harassment Emerge, Institutions Need to Take Action." *The Colorado Sun*. March 15. https://coloradosun.com/2021/03/15/sexual-harassment-opinion/

71. For example, "LSU Mishandled Sexual Misconduct Complaints."

72. Olomi et al., 2019, "Institutional Responses."

73. For example, Cole et al., 2013, *Creating and Advocating for Trauma Sensitive Schools*; DeCarlo Santiago et al., 2018, *Creating Healing School Communities*; Venet, Alex Shevrin. 2021. *Equity-Centered Trauma-Informed Education*. New York: Norton Professional Books.

74. Venet, 2021, *Equity-Centered Trauma-Informed Education*.

75. Gordon, Hava Rachel. 2021. *This Is Our School! Race and Community Resistance to School Reform*. New York: New York University Press.

Chapter 4

1. "'Feminist Emergency' Declared in Spain After Summer of Violence." 2019. *The Guardian*. September 20. http://www.theguardian.com/world/2019/sep/20/mass-protests-in-spain-after-19-women-murdered-by-partners

2. "16 Days of Activism Against Gender-Based Violence." n.d. UN Women. Accessed August 3, 2021. https://www.unwomen.org/en/news/in-focus/end-violence-against-women

3. "'The Rapist Is You!': Why a Chilean Protest Chant Is Being Sung Around the World." 2020. *The Guardian*. February 3. http://www.theguardian.com/society/2020/feb/03/the-rapist-is-you-chilean-protest-song-chanted-around-the-world-un-iolador-en-tu-camino

4. "France Is Putting Domestic Abuse Victims in Hotels During Coronavirus Lockdown." 2020. *Vice News*. March 31. https://www.vice.com/en/article/y3mj4g/france-is-putting-domestic-abuse-victims-in-hotels-during-coronavirus-lockdown?utm_campaign=sharebutton&fbclid=IwAR3P-b9hCvlyFmyhrBlLRqmegnAYIuY64YZfDt2hfxp_SZFmMgEUP7TCx2I

5. "Lockdowns Around the World Bring Rise in Domestic Violence." 2020. *The Guardian*. March 28. http://www.theguardian.com/society/2020/mar/28/lockdowns-world-rise-domestic-violence

6. "Guidelines for Mobile and Remote Gender-Based Violence (GBV) Service Delivery [EN/MY]—World." 2018. International Rescue Committee. https://reliefweb.int/report/world/guidelines-mobile-and-remote-gender-based-violence-gbv-service-delivery-enmy

7. For example, Maruo, Mirai, Alicia Hammond, and Diana J. Arango. 2021. "Thinking About Using Technology to Address Gender-Based Violence? Five Recommendations from Experts." World Bank Blogs. https://blogs.worldbank.org/voices/thinking-about-using-technology-address-gender-based-violence-five-recommendations-experts

8. "Global and Regional Estimates of Violence Against Women: Prevalence and Health Effects of Intimate Partner Violence and Non-Partner Sexual Violence. 2013. World Health Organization. https://apps.who.int/iris/bitstream/handle/10665/85239/9789241564625_eng.pdf;jsessionid=EF05385AA67763ACE35FFAD22495F04D?sequence=1

9. Fiorella, Kathryn J., Pooja Desai, Joshua D. Miller, Nicky O. Okeyo, and Sera L. Young. 2019. "A Review of Transactional Sex for Natural Resources: Under-Researched, Overstated, or Unique to Fishing Economies?" *Global Public Health* 14 (12): 1803–14. doi:10.1080/17441692.2019.1625941

10. Nathenson, Pamela, Samantha Slater, Patrick Higdon, Carmen Aldinger, and Erin Ostheimer. 2017. "No Sex for Fish: Empowering Women to Promote Health and Economic Opportunity in a Localized Place in Kenya." *Health Promotion International* 32 (5): 800–807. doi:10.1093/heapro/daw012

11. *Promoting Gender Equality to Prevent Violence Against Women.* 2009. Geneva: World Health Organization (WHO).

12. "Women Are Fleeing Death at Home. The U.S. Wants to Keep Them Out." 2019. *New York Times.* August 18. https://www.nytimes.com/2019/08/18/world/americas/guatemala-violence-women-asylum.html.

13. Ibid.

14. For discussion, see Briddick, Catherine. 2021. "Rethinking Refuge from Gender-Based Violence: Persecution for Which Convention Reason?" Rethinking Refuge. https://www.rethinkingrefuge.org/articles/rethinking-refuge-from-gender-based-violence-persecution-for-which-conventi

15. See Weis, Anne. 2020. "Fleeing for Their Lives: Domestic Violence Asylum and Matter of A-B." *California Law Review* 108 (4): 1319–55. https://doi.org/10.15779/Z384F1MJ96

16. For example, Araujo, Juliana de Oliveira, Fernanda Mattos de Souza, Raquel Proença, Mayara Lisboa Bastos, Anete Trajman, and Eduardo Faerstein. 2019. "Prevalence of Sexual Violence Among Refugees: A Systematic Review." *Revista de Saúde Pública* 53: 78. https://doi.org/10.11606/s1518-8787.2019053001081 https://www.ncbi.nlm.nih.gov/pmc/articles/PMC6752644/

17. Fernandez, Manny. 2019. "'You Have to Pay with Your Body': The Hidden Nightmare of Sexual Violence on the Border." *New York Times.* March 3, sec. U.S. https://www.nytimes.com/2019/03/03/us/border-rapes-migrant-women.html

18. Delara, Mahin. 2016. "Social Determinants of Immigrant Women's Mental Health." *Advances in Public Health*. doi:10.1155/2016/9730162

19. Hernández, César Cuauhtémoc García. 2019. *Migrating to Prison: America's Obsession with Locking up Immigrants*. New York: New Press.

20. See, for example, "New Proposed Asylum Regulations Would Endanger Women's Lives." 2020. Lawfare. July 7. https://www.lawfareblog.com/new-proposed-asylum-regulations-would-endanger-womens-lives

21. See, for example, Weis, 2020, "Fleeing for Their Lives."

22. Mosley, Alana. 2018. "Re-Victimization and the Asylum Process: Jimenez Ferreira v. Lynch: Re-Assessing the Weight Placed on Credible Fear Interviews in Determining Credibility." *Law & Inequality: A Journal of Theory and Practice* 36 (2): 314–34.

23. For discussion, see Briddick, 2021, "Rethinking Refuge."

24. Mosley, 2018, "Re-Victimization and the Asylum Process." For related discussion, see "Credibility Assessment in Asylum Procedures." 2015. United Nations High Commission for Refugees Roundtable on Credibility Assessment in Asylum Procedures. https://www.refworld.org/pdfid/554c9aba4.pdf

25. For example, Garza, Alondra D., and Cortney A. Franklin. 2021. "The Effect of Rape Myth Endorsement on Police Response to Sexual Assault Survivors." *Violence Against Women* 27 (3–4): 552–73. https://doi.org/10.1177/1077801220911460; Shaw, Jessica, Rebecca Campbell, Debi Cain, and Hannah Feeney. 2017. "Beyond Surveys and Scales: How Rape Myths Manifest in Sexual Assault Police Records." *Psychology of Violence* 7 (4): 602–14. https://doi.org/10.1037/vio0000072

26. See, for example, Ibid.

27. Mosley, 2018, "Re-Victimization and the Asylum Process."

28. Ibid.

29. Miller, Chanel. 2019. *Know My Name: A Memoir*. New York: Viking, at 149.

30. Mosley, 2018, "Re-Victimization and the Asylum Process."

31. Vari, Elsa, and Richard A. Boswell. 2019. "Grace v. Whitaker: Advancing Refugee Rights Beyond the Credible Fear Interview." *Bender's Immigration Bulletin* 24: 685–92; Weis, 2020, "Fleeing for Their Lives." Note that beyond the issues discussed here, legal scholars have detailed a host of problematic issues in Sessions's denial of the Ecuadorian woman's asylum. The American Civil Liberties Union and the University of California's Center for Gender and Refugee Studies filed a lawsuit challenging Sessions's decision. The District Court that heard the case issued a permanent injunction to stop the implementation of the new rules that Sessions had set in motion. As of this writing, the District Court ruling is awaiting an appeal though the injunction has been allowed to stand for the time being.

32. Weis, 2020, "Fleeing for Their Lives," at 1344.

33. Vari, Elsa, and Richard A. Boswell. 2019. "Grace v. Whitaker: Advancing Refugee Rights Beyond the Credible Fear Interview."

34. For example, "Every Day I Live in Fear." 2020. Human Rights Watch. October 7. https://www.hrw.org/report/2020/10/07/every-day-i-live-fear/violence-and-discrimination-against-lgbt-people-el-salvador

35. For example, "Ten Harmful Beliefs That Perpetuate Violence Against Women and Girls." 2019. Oxfam International. November 26. https://www.oxfam.org/en/ten-harmful-beliefs-perpetuate-violence-against-women-and-girls

36. Vari and Boswell, 2019, "Grace v. Whitaker."

37. For related discussion, see Ellison, Charles Shane, and Anjum Gupta. 2021. "Unwilling or Unable?: The Failure to Conform the Nonstate Actor Standard in Asylum Claims to the 'Refugee Act.'" *Columbia Human Rights Law Review* 52 (2): 441–522. doi/10.3316/agispt.20210419044757

38. See, for example, Gonçalves, Mariana, and Marlene Matos. 2016. "Prevalence of Violence Against Immigrant Women: A Systematic Review of the Literature." *Journal of Family Violence* 31 (6): 697–710. doi:10.1007/s10896-016-9820-4

39. Sabri, Bushra, Jacquelyn C. Campbell, and Jill T. Messing. 2018. "Intimate Partner Homicides in the United States, 2003–2013: A Comparison of Immigrants and Nonimmigrant Victims," edited by Bushra Sabri. *Journal of Interpersonal Violence*, article no.: 886260518792249. https://doi.org/10.1177/0886260518792249

40. Critelli, Filomena, and Asli Cennet Yalim. 2019. "Improving Access to Domestic Violence Services for Women of Immigrant and Refugee Status: A Trauma-Informed Perspective." *Journal of Ethnic & Cultural Diversity in Social Work*: 1–19. doi:10.1080/15313204.2019.1700863

41. Erez, Edna, Madelaine Adelman, and Carol Gregory. 2009. "Intersections of Immigration and Domestic Violence: Voices of Battered Immigrant Women." *Feminist Criminology* 4 (1): 32–56. doi:10.1177/1557085108325413

42. Erez et al. 2009, "Intersections of Immigration and Domestic Violence," at 46.

43. Gover, Angela R., Courtney Welton-Mitchell, Joanne Belknap, and Anne P. Deprince. 2013. "When Abuse Happens Again: Women's Reasons for Not Reporting New Incidents of Intimate Partner Abuse to Law Enforcement." *Women & Criminal Justice* 23 (2): 99–120. doi:10.1080/08974454.2013.759069

44. Erez et al., 2009, "Intersections of Immigration and Domestic Violence," at 46.

45. Critelli and Yalim, 2019, "Improving Access," at 9.

46. " 'He Was Masturbating . . . I Felt Like Crying': What Housekeepers Endure to Clean Hotel Rooms." 2017. Huffington Post. November 18. https://www.huffpost.com/entry/housekeeper-hotel-sexual-harassment_n_5a0f438ce4b0e97dffed3443

47. See McAlevey, Jane. 2020. *A Collective Bargain: Unions, Organizing, and the Fight for Democracy.* New York: Ecco-Harper Collins.

48. Wright, Naomi M., Julie M. Olomi, and Anne P. DePrince. 2020. "Community-Engaged Research: Exploring a Tool for Action and Advocacy." *Journal of Trauma & Dissociation* 21 (4): 452–67. https://doi.org/10.1080/15299732.2020.1770150

49. Ibid.

50. Bixby, Scott. 2019. "ICE Courthouse Arrests Up 1700% in NY Since Trump's Inauguration: Report." *The Daily Beast.* January 28, sec. politics. https://www.thedailybeast.com/report-ice-arrests-at-courthouses-up-1700-since-trumps-inauguration

51. Lopez, Mark Hugo, Ana Gonzalez-Barrera, and Jens Manuel Krogstad. 2018. "More Latinos Have Serious Concerns About Their Place in America Under Trump." Pew

Research Center. https://www.pewresearch.org/hispanic/wp-content/uploads/sites/5/2018/10/Pew-Research-Center_Latinos-have-Serious-Concerns-About-Their-Place-in-America_2018-10-25.pdf

52. Erez et al., 2009, "Intersections of Immigration and Domestic Violence," at 46.

53. "Colorado Advocates See Rise in Immigrant Domestic Violence Victims Reporting Deportation Threats by Their Abusers." 2019. *The Colorado Sun.* July 29. https://coloradosun.com/2019/07/29/colorado-domestic-violence-immigration-threats/

54. DePrince, Anne P., Emily Tofte Nestaval, and Naomi Wright. "Opinion: For Domestic Violence Victims, the Price of Immigration-Related Fears May Be Nothing Short of Death." 2019. *The Colorado Sun.* August 18. https://coloradosun.com/2019/08/18/domestic-violence-immigration-police-ice-opinion/

55. Snyder, Rachel Louise. 2019. *No Visible Bruises: What We Don't Know About Domestic Violence Can Kill Us.* New York: Bloomsbury.

56. "Some El Paso Shooting Victims 'Too Scared to Get Medical Help for Fear over Immigration Status.'" 2019. *The Independent.* August 4. https://www.independent.co.uk/news/world/americas/el-paso-shooting-victims-walmart-immigration-ice-raids-trump-mexico-a9038671.html

57. "DU Grand Challenges | DU Grand Challenges." n.d. Accessed August 9, 2021. https://grandchallenges.du.edu/.

Chapter 5

1. Ellingrud, Kweilin, Anu Madgavkar, James Manyika, Jonathan Woetzel, Vivian Riefberg, Mekala Krishnan, and Mili Seoni. 2016. "The Power of Parity: Advancing Women's Equality in the United States." McKinsey and Company. https://www.mckinsey.com/featured-insights/employment-and-growth/the-power-of-parity-advancing-womens-equality-in-the-united-states

2. Pitofsky, Marina. "Barr Calls for Investigations into Landlords Demanding Sexual Favors in Place of Rent." 2020. *The Hill.* April 23. https://thehill.com/homenews/administration/494381-barr-calls-on-us-attorneys-to-investigate-reports-of-landlords

3. DePrince, Anne P., and Joan Cook. 2020. "Downturn in the Economy, Uptick in Exploitation." *The Hill.* May 19. https://thehill.com/opinion/finance/498588-downturn-in-the-economy-uptick-in-exploitation

4. Baker, Charlene K., Kris A. Billhardt, Joseph Warren, Chiquita Rollins, and Nancy E. Glass. 2010. "Domestic Violence, Housing Instability, and Homelessness: A Review of Housing Policies and Program Practices for Meeting the Needs of Survivors." *Aggression and Violent Behavior* 15 (6): 430–39. doi:10.1016/j.avb.2010.07.005

5. Smith Story by Leora. "When the Police Call Your Landlord." *The Atlantic.* Accessed December 18, 2020. https://www.theatlantic.com/politics/archive/2020/03/crime-free-housing-lets-police-influence-landlords/605728/. See also Sullivan, Cris, Gabriela López-Zerón, Heather Bomsta, and Anne Menard. 2019. "'There's Just All

These Moving Parts:' Helping Domestic Violence Survivors Obtain Housing." *Clinical Social Work Journal* 47 (2): 198–206. https://doi.org/10.1007/s10615-018-0654-9

6. "Sex Assault and Stalking Victims May Break Leases | Colorado General Assembly." Accessed December 18, 2020. https://leg.colorado.gov/bills/hb17-1035.

7. https://thehill.com/opinion/finance/498588-downturn-in-the-economy-uptick-in-exploitation

8. For example, "'It's a Time Bomb': 23 Die as Virus Hits Packed Homeless Shelters – The New York Times." Accessed December 18, 2020. https://www.nytimes.com/2020/04/13/nyregion/new-york-coronavirus-homeless.html

9. Piquero, Alex R., Wesley G. Jennings, Erin Jemison, Catherine Kaukinen, and Felicia Marie Knaul. 2021. "Domestic Violence During Covid-19: Evidence from a Systematic Review and Meta-Analysis." Report presented to the National Commission on COVID-19 and Criminal Justice. Retrieved March 1, 2021. https://cdn.ymaws.com/counciloncj.org/resource/resmgr/covid_commission/Domestic_Violence_During_COV.pdf; Wood, Leila, Elizabeth Baumler, Rachel Voth Schrag, Shannon Guillot-Wright, Dixie Hairston, Jeff Temple, and Elizabeth Torres. 2021. "'Don't Know Where to Go for Help': Safety and Economic Needs among Violence Survivors During the COVID-19 Pandemic." *Journal of Family Violence* (2021) 1–9. https://doi.org/10.1007/s10896-020-00240-7

10. For example, Baker et al., 2010, "Domestic Violence, Housing Instability, and Homelessness."

11. Sullivan, Cris M. October 2012. *Domestic Violence Shelter Services: A Review of the Empirical Evidence.* Harrisburg, PA: National Resource Center on Domestic Violence.

12. Sullivan, Cris M., and Tyler Virden. 2017. "Interrelationships Among Length of Stay in a Domestic Violence Shelter, Help Received, and Outcomes Achieved." *American Journal of Orthopsychiatry* 87 (4): 434–42. doi:10.1037/ort0000267

13. Ibid.

14. https://www.theguardian.com/lifeandstyle/2019/sep/19/disabled-victim-of-domestic-violence-on-her-struggle-to-survive

15. Baker et al., 2010, "Domestic Violence, Housing Instability, and Homelessness."

16. Clark, Dessie Lee, Leila Wood, and Cris Sullivan. 2019. "Examining the Needs and Experiences of Domestic Violence Survivors in Transitional Housing." *Journal of Family Violence* (34), 275–286. doi:10.1007/s10896-018-0010-4.

17. Baker et al., 2010, "Domestic Violence, Housing Instability, and Homelessness.".

18. https://nnedv.org/wp-content/uploads/2020/03/Library_Census_2019_national_summary.pdf

19. Clark et al., 2019, *Examining the Needs.*

20. Baker et al., 2010, "Domestic Violence, Housing Instability, and Homelessness."

21. See for example, Ibid.

22. Sullivan et al., 2019, "'There's Just All These Moving Parts.'"

23. Lee, M. S., and A. P. Deprince. 2017. "Impact of Executive Function on Efficacy Obtaining Resources Following Intimate Partner Violence." *Journal of Community Psychology*, 45 (6): 704–14. doi:10.1002/jcop.21887

24. Shoener, Sara Jane. 2016. *The Price of Safety: Hidden Costs and Unintended Consequences for Women in the Domestic Violence Service System.* Nashville, TN: Vanderbilt University Press.

25. Sullivan et al., 2019, "'There's Just All These Moving Parts.'"

26. For example, Fowler, Patrick J., Peter S. Hovmand, Katherine E. Marcal, and Sanmay Das. 2019. "Solving Homelessness from a Complex Systems Perspective: Insights for Prevention Responses." *Annual Review of Public Health* 40 (1): 465–86. https://doi.org/10.1146/annurev-publhealth-040617-013553

27. "Crime Victim Compensation | Division of Criminal Justice." n.d. Accessed June 29, 2021. https://dcj.colorado.gov/dcj-offices/victims-programs/crime-victim-compensation

28. Goodman, Shaina. "The Difference Between Surviving and Not Surviving: Public Benefits Programs and Domestic and Sexual Violence Victims' Economic Security." 2018. A Joint Report of National Resource Center on Domestic Violence, Center on Poverty and Inequality, and Economic Security and Opportunity Initiative. https://vawnet.org/sites/default/files/assets/files/2018-10/NRCDV-TheDifferenceBetweenSurvivingandNotSurviving-UpdatedOct2018_0.pdf, at 5.

29. For discussion, see Holcomb, Stephanie, Laura Johnson, Andrea Hetling, Judy L. Postmus, Jordan Steiner, Larry Braasch, and Annette Riordan. 2017. "Implementation of the Family Violence Option 20 Years Later: A Review of State Welfare Rules for Domestic Violence Survivors." *Journal of Policy Practice* 16 (4): 415–31. doi:10.1080/15588742.2017.1311820

30. Holcomb et al., 2017, "Implementation of the Family Violence Option."

31. Goodman, 2018, "The Difference Between Surviving and Not Surviving," at 8.

32. Ibid.

33. McCauley, Heather L., and Taylor Reid. 2020. "Assessing Vulnerability, Prioritizing Risk: The Limitations of the VI-SPDAT for Survivors of Domestic & Sexual Violence." Special Series: Coordinated Entry & Domestic/Sexual Violence from Safe Housing Partnerships and National Resource Center on Domestic Violence. https://safehousingpartnerships.org/sites/default/files/2020-08/CoordinatedEntry-Assessing%20Vulnerability-Risk_0.pdf

34. For example, Postmus, Judy L., Gretchen L. Hoge, Jan Breckenridge, Nicola Sharp-Jeffs, and Donna Chung. 2020. "Economic Abuse as an Invisible Form of Domestic Violence: A Multicountry Review." *Trauma, Violence, & Abuse* 21 (2): 261–83. https://doi.org/10.1177/1524838018764160

35. Shoener, 2016, *The Price of Safety.*

36. Ibid.

37. Miller, Chanel. 2020. *Know My Name: A Memoir.* New York: Penguin Random House, at 69.

38. Ibid., at 70.

39. Showalter, Kathryn. 2016. "Women's Employment and Domestic Violence: A Review of the Literature." *Aggression and Violent Behavior* 31: 37–47. doi:10.1016/j.avb.2016.06.017

40. Swanberg, Jennifer, Caroline Macke, and T. Logan. 2006. "Intimate Partner Violence, Women, and Work: Coping on the Job." *Violence and Victims* 21 (5): 561–78. doi:10.1891/0886-6708.21.5.561

41. Ibid.

42. Ridley, E., John Riox, Kim C. Lim, DesiRae Mason, Kate F. Houghton, Faye Luppi, and Tracey Melody. 2005. *Domestic Violence Survivors at Work: How Perpetrators Impact Employment.* Augusta, ME: Maine Department of Labor and Family Crisis Services. Cited in https://iwpr.org/publications/economic-cost-intimate-partner-violence-sexual-assault-stalking/

43. Roepe, Lisa Rabasca. 2016. "The Hidden Impact of Domestic Violence on the Gender Wage Gap." Fast Company. August 30.

44. Ibid.

45. Ibid.

46. Swanberg et al., 2006, "Intimate Partner Violence, Women, and Work."

47. Ibid., at 571.

48. "Chicago Doctor Called 911 Moments Before Ex-Fiance Killed Her, 2 Others." 2018. https://www.cbsnews.com/news/chicago-hospital-shooting-dr-tamara-oneal-called-911-moments-before-ex-fiance-juan-lopez-killed-her-2-others/

49. de Jonge, Alice. 2018. "Corporate Social Responsibility Through a Feminist Lens: Domestic Violence and the Workplace in the 21st Century." *Journal of Business Ethics* 148 (3): 471–87. doi:10.1007/s10551-015-3010-9

50. Office of the Federal Register, National Archives and Records Administration. 2012. "DCPD-201200281 – Memorandum Establishing Policies for Addressing Domestic Violence in the Federal Workforce." Government. Govinfo.Gov. Office of the Federal Register, National Archives and Records Administration. April 18. https://www.govinfo.gov/app/details/https%3A%2F%2Fwww.govinfo.gov%2Fapp%2Fdetails%2FDCPD-201200281

51. Swanberg et al., 2006, "Intimate Partner Violence, Women, and Work."

52. Kantor, Jodi, and Megan Twohey. 2019. *She Said: Breaking the Sexual Harassment Story That Helped Ignite a Movement.* New York: Penguin Press, at 2.

53. "Harvey Weinstein Lawyer Says She's Never Been Sexually Assaulted 'Because I Would Never Put Myself in that Position." 2020. CNN. https://www.cnn.com/2020/02/07/us/harvey-weinstein-lawyer-donna-rotunno/index.html.

54. Turner, Laura. 2017. "Perspective | The Religious Reasons Mike Pence Won't Eat Alone with Women Don't Add Up." *Washington Post.* https://www.washingtonpost.com/news/acts-of-faith/wp/2017/03/30/the-religious-reasons-mike-pence-wont-eat-alone-with-women-dont-add-up/

55. Keveney, Bill. 2018. "Ashley Judd Discusses Her Lawsuit Against Harvey Weinstein on 'Good Morning America." USA Today. https://www.usatoday.com/story/life/people/2018/04/30/ashley-judd-sues-harvey-weinstein-alleging-acting-career-sabotaged/567243002/

56. "Select Task Force on the Study of Harassment in the Workplace." 2016. Equal Employment Opportunity Commission. https://www.eeoc.gov/select-task-force-study-harassment-workplace

57. Ibid.

58. For example, Robinson, Sandra L., Wei Wang, and Christian Kiewitz. 2014. "Coworkers Behaving Badly: The Impact of Coworker Deviant Behavior upon Individual Employees." *Annual Review of Organizational Psychology and Organizational Behavior* 1 (1): 123–43. https://doi.org/10.1146/annurev-orgpsych-031413-091225

59. "The Facts Behind the #MeToo Movement: A National Study on Sexual Harassment and Assault." 2018. Report from Stop Street Harassment. http://www.stopstreetharassment.org/wp-content/uploads/2018/01/Full-Report-2018-National-Study-on-Sexual-Harassment-and-Assault.pdf

60. "Hands Off Pants On—Sexual Harassment in Chicago's Hospitality Industry." n.d. Accessed June 29, 2021. https://www.handsoffpantson.org/

61. Babcock, Rebecca L., and Anne P. DePrince. 2013. "Factors Contributing to Ongoing Intimate Partner Abuse: Childhood Betrayal Trauma and Dependence on One's Perpetrator." *Journal of Interpersonal Violence* 28 (7): 1385–1402. https://doi.org/10.1177/0886260512468248.

62. Piquero et al., 2021, "Domestic Violence During Covid-19."

63. Agnew, Robert, and Timothy Brezina. 2019. "General Strain Theory." In *Handbook on Crime and Deviance*, edited by M. D. Krohn, 145–60. Dordrecht: Springer Nature.

64. Anderberg, Dan, Helmut Rainer, Jonathan Wadsworth, and Tanya Wilson. 2016. "Unemployment and Domestic Violence: Theory and Evidence." *The Economic Journal* 126 (597): 1947–79. doi:10.1111/ecoj.12246

65. Benson, Michael L., and Greer Litton Fox. 2004. "When Violence Hits Home: How Economics and Neighborhood Play a Role." *National Institute of Justice: Research in Brief.*

66. Ibid.

67. Schneider, Daniel, Kristen Harknett, and Sara McLanahan. 2016. "Intimate Partner Violence in the Great Recession." *Demography* 53 (2): 471–505. https://doi.org/10.1007/s13524-016-0462-1

68. Ibid.

69. Pattavina, April, Kelly M. Socia, and Malgorzata J. Zuber. 2015. "Economic Stress and Domestic Violence: Examining the Impact of Mortgage Foreclosures on Incidents Reported to the Police." *Justice Research and Policy* 16 (2): 147–64. https://doi.org/10.1177/1525107115623938

70. Peterson, Cora, Megan C. Kearns, Wendy Likamwa Mcintosh, Lianne Fuino Estefan, Christina Nicolaidis, Kathryn E. Mccollister, Amy Gordon, and Curtis Florence. 2018. "Lifetime Economic Burden of Intimate Partner Violence among U.S. Adults." *American Journal of Preventive Medicine* 55 (4): 433–44. doi:10.1016/j.amepre.2018.04.049

71. Busch-Armendariz, Noel, Nicole L. Nale, Matt Kammer-Kerwick, Bruce Kellison, Melissa I.M. Torres, Laurie Cook-Heffron, and John Nehme. 2016. *Human Trafficking by the Numbers: Initial Benchmarks of Prevalence & Economic Impact in Texas.* Austin, TX: Institute on Domestic Violence and Sexual Assault, University of Texas at Austin.

72. Greenfield, Jennifer C., Nancy Reichman, Paula M. Cole, and Hannah Galgiani. 2019. "Projected Economic Impacts of Paid Family Leave in Colorado." https://socialwork. du.edu/sites/g/files/lmucqz281/files/2019-02/Paid-Family-Leave-Report.pdf

73. "Overview of Paid Sick Time Laws in the United States." 2021. https://www. abetterbalance.org/paid-sick-time-laws/?export

74. "Creating Sustainable Lives for Refugees." n.d. Accessed June 29, 2021. https://dani els.du.edu/hospitality-management/rah/.

Chapter 6

1. Farrow, Ronan. *Catch and Kill: Lies, Spies, and a Conspiracy to Protect Predators.* 2019. New York: Little, Brown and Company.

2. Deer, Sarah. 2015. *Beginning and End of Rape Confronting Sexual Violence in Native America.* Minneapolis: University of Minnesota Press, at 137.

3. Ibid.; McGuire, Danielle L. 2010. *At the Dark End of the Street: Black Women, Rape, and Resistance: A New History of the Civil Rights Movement, from Rosa Parks to the Rise of Black Power,* 1st ed. New York: Alfred A. Knopf.

4. Deer, Sarah, 2015, *The Beginning and End of Rape.*

5. For example, Dewan, Shaila. 2020. "Here's One Issue That Could Actually Break the Partisan Gridlock." *The New York Times.* November 24, sec. U.S. https://www. nytimes.com/2020/11/24/us/criminal-justice-reform-republicans-democrats.html

6. "Civil Legal System | Legal Information Network of Colorado." n.d. Accessed July 28, 2021. https://www.coloradolinc.org/legal-information/civil

7. "Justice Department Announces $3.4 Billion in Grants to Aid Crime Victims Nationwide." August 9, 2018. https://www.justice.gov/opa/pr/justice-departm ent-announces-34-billion-grants-aid-crime-victims-nationwide; "The Violence Against Women Act (VAWA): Historical Overview, Funding, and Reauthorization" November 19, 2018. https://www.everycrsreport.com/files/20181119_R45410_ 06a20aa20a8b554086269608be3f289ad96fdf85.pdf

8. https://thecrimereport.org/2019/12/18/congress-cutting-aid-to-crime-victim- programs/

9. DePrince, Anne P., Naomi Wright, Kerry L. Gagnon, Tejaswinhi Srinivas, and Jennifer Labus. 2020. "Social Reactions and Women's Decisions to Report Sexual Assault to Law Enforcement." *Violence Against Women* 26 (5): 399–416. https://doi. org/10.1177/1077801219838345

10. O'Neal, Eryn Nicole, and Brittany E. Hayes. 2020. "'A Rape Is a Rape, Regardless of What the Victim Was Doing at the Time': Detective Views on How 'Problematic' Victims Affect Sexual Assault Case Processing." *Criminal Justice Review* 45 (1): 26–44, at 34. https://doi.org/10.1177/0734016819842639

11. See for example US Department of Justice, Federal Bureau of Investigation. 2004. *Uniform Crime Reporting Handbook,* at 79. https://ucr.fbi.gov/additional-ucr- publications/ucr_handbook.pdf

12. Lisak, David, Lori Gardinier, Sarah C. Nicksa, and Ashley M. Cote. 2010. "False Allegations of Sexual Assault: An Analysis of Ten Years of Reported Cases." *Violence Against Women* 16 (12): 1318–34. doi:10.1177/1077801210387747; Spohn, Cassia, Clair White, and Katharine Tellis. 2014. "Unfounding Sexual Assault: Examining the Decision to Unfound and Identifying False Reports." *Law and Society Review* 48 (1): 161–92. doi:10.1111/lasr.12060

13. US Department of Justice, Federal Bureau of Investigation. 2004. *Uniform Crime Reporting Handbook*, at 79. https://ucr.fbi.gov/additional-ucr-publications/ucr_handbook.pdf

14. Ibid., at 80–81.

15. Spohn, Cassia, and Katharine Tellis. 2010. "Justice Denied?: The Exceptional Clearance of Rape Cases in Los Angeles." *Albany Law Review* 74: 1379–1421.

16. Ibid.

17. For discussion, see Pattavina, April, Melissa Morabito, and Linda M. Williams. 2016. "Examining Connections Between the Police and Prosecution in Sexual Assault Case Processing: Does the Use of Exceptional Clearance Facilitate a Downstream Orientation?" *Victims & Offenders* 11 (2): 315–34. doi:10.1080/15564886.2015.1046622

18. Spohn Tellis, 2010, "Justice Denied?". Pattavina et al., 2016, "Examining Connections"; Wentz, Ericka A. 2019. "Funneled Through or Filtered Out: An Examination of Police and Prosecutorial Decision-Making in Adult Sexual Assault Cases." *Violence Against Women* 26 (15–16): 1919–1940. doi:10.1177/1077801219890419

19. Campbell, Rebecca, and Giannina Fehler-Cabral. August 2020. "'Just Bring Us the Real Ones': The Role of Forensic Crime Laboratories in Guarding the Gateway to Justice for Sexual Assault Victims." *Journal of Interpersonal Violence* 0886260520951303. https://doi.org/10.1177/0886260520951303

20. Spohn and Tellis, 2010, "Justice Denied?"; Pattavina et al., 2016, "Examining Connections"; Wentz, 2019, "Funneled Through or Filtered Out."

21. For example, Arnsten, Amy F. T. 2009. "Stress Signalling Pathways That Impair Prefrontal Cortex Structure and Function." *Nature Reviews. Neuroscience* 10 (6): 410–22. https://doi.org/10.1038/nrn2648

22. Kozlowska, Kasia, Peter Walker, Loyola McLean, Pascal Carrive. 2015. "Fear and the Defense Cascade: Clinical Implications and Management." *Harvard Review of Psychiatry, 23*(4), 263–87.

23. Hopper, Jim. 2018. "Sexual Assault and Neuroscience: Alarmist Claims vs. Facts." *Psychology Today.* https://www.psychologytoday.com/us/blog/sexual-assault-and-the-brain/201801/sexual-assault-and-neuroscience-alarmist-claims-vs-facts. See also, for example, Arnsten, Amy F. T. 2015. "Stress Weakens Prefrontal Networks: Molecular Insults to Higher Cognition." *Nature Neuroscience* 18 (10): 1376–85. https://doi.org/10.1038/nn.4087

24. Hopper, Jim. 2015. "Why Many Rape Victims Don't Fight or Yell." *The Washington Post.* https://www.washingtonpost.com/news/grade-point/wp/2015/06/23/why-many-rape-victims-dont-fight-or-yell/

25. Cohen, Noga, Liat Pell, Micah G. Edelson, Aya Ben-Yakov, Alex Pine, and Yadin Dudai. 2015. "Peri-Encoding Predictors of Memory Encoding and Consolidation." *Neuroscience and Biobehavioral Reviews* 50: 128–42. doi:10.1016/j.neubiorev.2014.11.002

26. For example, Schwabe, Lars. 2017. "Memory Under Stress: From Single Systems to Network Changes." *European Journal of Neuroscience* 45 (4): 478–89. doi:10.1111/ejn.13478

27. Antony, James W., Catarina S. Ferreira, Kenneth A. Norman, and Maria Wimber. 2017. "Retrieval as a Fast Route to Memory Consolidation." *Trends in Cognitive Sciences* 21 (8): 573–76. doi:10.1016/j.tics.2017.05.001

28. Franklin, Cortney A., Alondra D. Garza, Amanda Goodson, and Leana Allen Bouffard. 2020. "Police Perceptions of Crime Victim Behaviors: A Trend Analysis Exploring Mandatory Training and Knowledge of Sexual and Domestic Violence Survivors' Trauma Responses." *Crime and Delinquency* 66 (8): 1055–86. https://doi.org/10.1177/0011128719845148

29. Smith, Sherman. 2019. "Five Years of Sexual Abuse: Inmates at Topeka Women's Prison Repeatedly Complained About Dental Lab Instructor." *The Leavenworth Times*, Leavenworth, KS. https://www.leavenworthtimes.com/news/20191207/five-years-of-sexual-abuse-inmates-at-topeka-womens-prison-repeatedly-complained-about-dental-lab-instructor

30. Stark, Cortlynn. 2020. "Jury Acquits Ex-Kansas Prison Dentist of All but One Charge of Unlawful Relations." *Kansas City Star*. https://www.kansascity.com/news/local/crime/article239838068.html

31. "Concerning Rates of Attrition for Sexual Assault Cases: New Report | Wellesley Centers for Women." 2019. https://www.wcwonline.org/2019/concerning-rates-of-attrition-for-sexual-assault-cases-new-study

32. Edwards, Katie M., Megan C. Kearns, Christine A. Gidycz, and Karen S. Calhoun. 2012. "Predictors of Victim-Perpetrator Relationship Stability Following a Sexual Assault: A Brief Report." *Violence and Victims* 27 (1): 25–32. doi:10.1891/0886-6708.27.1.25

33. Miller, Chanel. *Know My Name*.

34. Snyder, Rachel Louise. 2019. *No Visible Bruises: What We Don't Know About Domestic Violence Can Kill Us*. New York: Bloomsbury.

35. Burke, Mary, Heather McCauley, Anne Rackow, Bradley Orsini, Bridget Simunovic, and Elizabeth Miller. 2015. "Implementing a Coordinated Care Model for Sex Trafficked Minors in Smaller Cities." *Journal of Applied Research on Children: Informing Policy for Children at Risk* 6 (1). https://digitalcommons.library.tmc.edu/childrenatrisk/vol6/iss1/7

36. DePrince, Anne P., Joanne Belknap, Jennifer S. Labus, Susan E. Buckingham, and Angela R. Gover. 2012. "The Impact of Victim-Focused Outreach on Criminal Legal System Outcomes Following Police-Reported Intimate Partner Abuse." *Violence Against Women* 18 (8): 861–81. https://doi.org/10.1177/1077801212456 523; DePrince, Anne P., Jennifer Labus, Joanne Belknap, Susan Buckingham, and Angela Gover. 2012. "The Impact of Community-Based Outreach on Psychological

Distress and Victim Safety in Women Exposed to Intimate Partner Abuse." *Journal of Consulting and Clinical Psychology* 80 (2): 211–21. https://doi.org/10.1037/a0027224

37. http://www.coloradolinc.org/need-help/legal-assistance/civil-legal-system

38. Stoever, Jane. 2019. "Access to Safety and Justice: Service of Process in Domestic Violence Cases." *Washington Law Review* 94 (1): 333–400.

39. Ibid.

40. Ibid.

41. "UW Staffer Killed by Stalker." 2007. *Seattle Times.* April 2. https://www.seattletimes.com/seattle-news/uw-staffer-killed-by-stalker/

42. Dowling, Christopher, Anthony Morgan, Shann Hulme, Matthew Manning, and Gabriel Wong. 2018. *Protection Orders for Domestic Violence: A Systematic Review.* Woden: Australian Institute of Criminology.

43. Ibid.

44. Bejinariu, Alexa, Emily Troshynski, and Terance Miethe. 2019. "Civil Protection Orders and Their Courtroom Context: The Impact of Gatekeepers on Legal Decisions." *Journal of Family Violence* 34 (3): 231–43. doi:10.1007/s10896-018-9999-7

45. Hardesty, Jennifer L., and Brian G. Ogolsky. 2020. "A Socioecological Perspective on Intimate Partner Violence Research: A Decade in Review." *Journal of Marriage and Family* 82 (1): 454–77. https://doi.org/10.1111/jomf.12652

46. Work related to the needs assessment has been described in trainings and a technical report. For example, DePrince, A. P., Tejaswinhi Srinivas, T., and Michelle S. Lee. 2014. *Partnering to Access Legal Services (PALS): A Needs Assessment for the Denver Wrap Around Legal Services for Victims of Crime Project.* Submitted to Rocky Mountain Victim Law Center.

47. For example, Babcock Fenerci, Rebecca L., and Anne P. DePrince. 2018. "Shame and Alienation Related to Child Maltreatment: Links to Symptoms Across Generations." *Psychological Trauma: Theory, Research, Practice, and Policy* 10 (4): 419–26. https://doi.org/10.1037/tra0000332; DePrince, Anne P., Ann T. Chu, and Annarheen S. Pineda. 2011. "Links Between Specific Posttrauma Appraisals and Three Forms of Trauma-Related Distress." *Psychological Trauma: Theory, Research, Practice, and Policy* 3 (4): 430–41. https://doi.org/10.1037/a0021576; Srinivas, Tejaswinhi, Anne P. DePrince, and Ann T. Chu. 2015. "Links Between Posttrauma Appraisals and Trauma-Related Distress in Adolescent Females from the Child Welfare System." *Child Abuse & Neglect* 47 (September 1): 14–23. https://doi.org/10.1016/j.chiabu.2015.05.011 Hebenstreit, Claire L., Shira Maguen, Kelly H. Koo, and Anne P. DePrince. 2015. "Latent Profiles of PTSD Symptoms in Women Exposed to Intimate Partner Violence." *Journal of Affective Disorders* 180 (July 15): 122–28. https://doi.org/10.1016/j.jad.2015.03.047

48. Ullman, Sarah E. 2010. *Talking About Sexual Assault: Society's Response to Survivors,* 1st ed. Washington, DC: American Psychological Association.

49. DePrince, Anne P., Julia Dmitrieva, Kerry L. Gagnon, and Tejaswinhi Srinivas. 2021. "Women's Experiences of Social Reactions from Informal and Formal Supports: Using a Modified Administration of the Social Reactions Questionnaire." *Journal of Interpersonal Violence,* 36 (3-4), 1498–1519. doi:10.1177/0886260517742149

50. Dworkin, Emily R., Charlotte D. Brill, and Sarah E. Ullman. 2019. "Social Reactions to Disclosure of Interpersonal Violence and Psychopathology: A Systematic Review and Meta-Analysis." *Clinical Psychology Review* 72. doi:10.1016/j.cpr.2019.101750

51. Wright, Naomi, and Anne P. DePrince. 2018 "Victim Services Start in the Waiting Room." Trauma Research Notes blog. December 10. https://traumaresearchnotes.blog/2018/12/10/victim-services-start-in-the-waiting-room/

Chapter 7

1. brown, adrienne maree. 2017. *Emergent Strategy: Shaping Change, Changing Worlds.* Chico, CA: AK Press.

2. Ibid.

3. Ibid.

4. Hudson, David. 2015. *Building a Movement to End the New Jim Crow: An Organizing Guide.* Published by the Veterans of Hope Project.

5. Ibid.

6. Gordon, Hava Rachel. 2021. *This Is Our School! Race and Community Resistance to School Reform.* New York: New York University Press.

7. brown, 2017, *Emergent Strategy.*

8. For example, "Prevention," Centers for Disease Control and Prevention, accessed August 1, 2021. https://www.cdc.gov/pictureofamerica/pdfs/picture_of_america _prevention.pdf. See also Compton, Michael T., and Ruth S. Shim. 2020. "Mental Illness Prevention and Mental Health Promotion: When, Who, and How." *Psychiatric Services* 71 (9): 981–83. https://doi.org/10.1176/appi.ps.201900374

9. Green, Beth L., Catherine Ayoub, Jessica Dym Bartlett, Carrie Furrer, Rachel Chazan-Cohen, Katherine Buttitta, Adam Von Ende, Andrew Koepp, and Eric Regalbuto. "Pathways to Prevention: Early Head Start Outcomes in the First Three Years Lead to Long-Term Reductions in Child Maltreatment." *Children and Youth Services Review* 118 (November 1, 2020): 105403. https://doi.org/10.1016/j.childyouth.2020.105403

10. https://www.healthaffairs.org/do/10.1377/hpb20190321.382895/full/

11. Greenfield, Jennifer C., Nancy Reichman, Paula M. Cole, and Hannah Galgiani. 2019. "Projected Economic Impacts of Paid Family Leave in Colorado." https://socialwork.du.edu/sites/g/files/lmucqz281/files/2019-02/Paid-Family-Leave-Report.pdf

12. For example, Garcetti, Eric. 2019. "Opinion: If You Want to Be President, You Must Address the Housing Crisis." *Los Angeles Times.* December 20. https://www.latimes.com/opinion/story/2019-12-19/homelessness-housing-crisis-section-8-eric-garcetti-presidential-election

13. Baker, Charlene K., Kris A. Billhardt, Joseph Warren, Chiquita Rollins, and Nancy E. Glass. 2010. "Domestic Violence, Housing Instability, and Homelessness: A Review of Housing Policies and Program Practices for Meeting the Needs of Survivors." *Aggression and Violent Behavior* 15 (6): 430–39. https://doi.org/10.1016/j.avb.2010.07.005

14. World Health Organization. 2009. "Promoting Gender Equality to Prevent Violence Against Women." Series of Briefings on Violence Prevention: The Evidence. https://apps.who.int/iris/bitstream/handle/10665/44098/9789241597883_eng.pdf?sequence=1&isAllowed=y

15. For example, Smith, Carly Parnitzke, and Jennifer J. Freyd. 2013. "Dangerous Safe Havens: Institutional Betrayal Exacerbates Sexual Trauma: Institutional Betrayal Exacerbates Sexual Trauma." *Journal of Traumatic Stress* 26 (1): 119–24. https://doi.org/10.1002/jts.21778; Bartlett, Tom. 2021. "Why Are Colleges So Cowardly?" *Chronicle of Higher Education.* July 23. https://www.chronicle.com/article/why-are-colleges-so-cowardly

16. For example, Smidt, Alec. September 2020. "Addressing the Harm of Workplace Sexual Harassment: Institutional Courage Buffers Against Institutional Betrayal." https://scholarsbank.uoregon.edu/xmlui/handle/1794/25695

17. For steps that workplaces can take, see Manning, Katharine. 2021. *The Empathetic Workplace: 5 Steps to Compassionate, Calm, and Confident Response to Trauma on the Job.* New York: HarperCollins Leadership.

18. Deer, Sarah. 2016. *Beginning and End of Rape Confronting Sexual Violence in Native America.* Minneapolis: University of Minnesota Press.

19. McGuire, Danielle L. 2010. *At the Dark End of the Street: Black Women, Rape, and Resistance: A New History of the Civil Rights Movement, from Rosa Parks to the Rise of Black Power*, 1st ed. New York: Alfred A. Knopf.

20. https://blacklivesmatter.com/what-we-believe/

21. For example, "Push for Stronger Enforcement of Denver's Homeless Camping Ban Would Complicate Already Fraught Law." 2021. *The Denver Post* blog. May 5. https://www.denverpost.com/2021/05/05/denver-homeless-camping-ban-initiative/

22. For example, see Goodmark, Leigh. 2020. "Reimagining VAWA: Why Criminalization Is a Failed Policy and What a Non-Carceral VAWA Could Look Like." *Violence Against Women*, article 107780122094968. https://doi.org/10.1177/1077801220949686

23. "Co-Responder Program." n.d. Mental Health Center of Denver. Accessed August 1, 2021. https://mhcd.org/co-responder-program/

24. "Support Team Assisted Response (STAR) Program." n.d. Accessed August 1, 2021. https://www.denvergov.org/Government/Departments/Public-Health-Environment/Community-Behavioral-Health/Behavioral-Health-Strategies/Support-Team-Assisted-Response-STAR-Program

25. For example, Decker, Michele R., Charvonne N. Holliday, Zaynab Hameeduddin, Roma Shah, Janice Miller, Joyce Dantzler, and Leigh Goodmark. 2019. "'You Do Not Think of Me as a Human Being': Race and Gender Inequities Intersect to Discourage Police Reporting of Violence Against Women." *Journal of Urban Health* 96 (5): 772–83. https://doi.org/10.1007/s11524-019-00359-z; Herman, Judith. 2005. "Justice from the Victim's Perspective." *Violence Against Women* 11(5): 571–602; McGlynn, Clare, and Nicole Westmarland. 2019. "Kaleidoscopic Justice: Sexual Violence and Victim-Survivors' Perceptions of Justice." *Social & Legal Studies* 28 (2): 179–201. https://doi.org/10.1177/0964663918761200

26. For example, see brown, 2017, *Emergent Strategy*; Kim, Mimi E. 2018. "From Carceral Feminism to Transformative Justice: Women-of-Color Feminism and Alternatives to Incarceration." *Journal of Ethnic and Cultural Diversity in Social Work* 27 (3): 219–33. https://doi.org/10.1080/15313204.2018.1474827

27. brown, 2017, *Emergent Strategy*.

Index